50 More *Things You Need to Know:*
The science behind best people practices
for managers & HR professionals
Volume 2

Dave Ulrich
Robert W. Eichinger
John Kulas
Ken De Meuse

www.kornferry.com
www.lominger.com

ISBN 1-933578-08-4

Item number 01076

50 More *Things You Need to Know:*
The science behind best people practices
for managers & HR professionals printings:
version 07.1a 1st—02/07
version 07.1a 2nd—03/11
version 07.1a 3rd—03/12
version 07.1a 4th—10/12
version 07.1a 5th—11/13

INTRODUCTION

We're back!

In 2004, we published *100 Things You Need to Know: Best People Practices for Managers & HR*. We wanted to counter the various fads, fashions, and folderol that passed for management practices at the time. Researchers and practitioners have been investigating and reporting on the science behind best practice management and leadership for the past 100 years. Our goal was to help managers and leaders learn and apply better and more effective people practices.

Thousands of *100 Things* have left the warehouse. We hope we made a small impact on the quality of people management for those who read it. Since then, the world has changed. We have gone from knowing the world is round to believing that it may be flat (Friedman, 2005). We have gone from the glass ceiling (obstacles preventing women from advancing) to the gray ceiling (the *non*-retirement of baby boomers preventing a younger generation from climbing the corporate ladder; Fisher, 2006). We have migrated from classroom learning to e-learning. The world is getting smaller and global and the jobs are getting bigger.

It was time for an update. In this book, there are 50 new scientific "facts" that form the basis for best practices. For instance, we explore such questions as (1) Do virtual teams or traditional teams have more conflict? (2) How effective is e-learning compared to traditional face-to-face learning? (3) What are the two most deadly mistakes of outsourcing? (4) In what type of culture might 360-degree feedback be the least effective? (5) How important is a leader's character? and (6) What is the best way to get employees more engaged? These questions are relevant and timely. As leaders of your organization, these are issues and concerns that you likely have to deal with day in and day out. Our answers were derived from science. We gathered our material from such publications as the *Journal of*

Applied Psychology, Human Resource Management, Science, Personnel Psychology, Journal of Personality, Administrative Science Quarterly, Accounting Review, Psychopharmacology, International Journal of Training and Development, Academy of Management Journal, and the *British Medical Journal,* to name a few. Our answers to the questions are based on science—what we know and don't know at this point in time. As we accumulate more knowledge over the years, we plan on publishing The **Next** *50 Things You Need to Know.*

Who Should Read This Book?

The book was written for:

1. **Current and future leaders.** The research findings presented in this book will assist anyone who wants to become a better orchestrator of people and processes. The chapters address such topics as business strategy, outsourcing, quality improvement processes, and corporate governance issues such as Sarbanes-Oxley compliance.

2. **Managers and supervisors.** The findings will help managers gain insight into the "best practices" related to job performance, motivation, attitudes, teams, and decision making. Learning what's in this book will make the management of people more effective, as well as more rewarding.

3. **HR professionals.** Any individual with HR responsibilities needs to know the research presented here. The answers to the questions form the foundation for "best practices" in human resources. Particular topics of interest include 360-degree feedback, corporate culture, ethics, and the identification and management of counterproductive behaviors in the workplace.

4. **Students of organizations.** Undergraduate and graduate business students and professors who want to increase their knowledge of organizational behavior and human resources will benefit from using this book. The scientific basis will

provide timely references which can be used for in-class and out-of-class assignments.

Contents of Each Chapter

We begin each chapter with a question and five possible answers. Your task is to select the correct alternative. On the following page, we answer the question with the most scientifically supported answer and add how confident we are with the answer at this time. The following scale is used to indicate level of confidence:

HOW SURE ARE WE AT THIS TIME?				
1	2	3	4	5
Hint	Suggestive	Trending	Substantial	Solid

1 – Hint: Indicates the answer is tentative, pending additional research. Either only a few studies have been conducted on this topic or what has been conducted is mixed or inconclusive.

2 – Suggestive: Indicates that some research evidence points to this answer, but other results are either not supportive or do not exist. Further research might point us in a different direction or not enough has been conducted to form a definite view yet.

3 – Trending: Suggests the findings are mixed, with the noted chapter answer being slightly favored over the other possible answers, or there has only been one or two studies to date.

4 – Substantial: Reveals that sufficient research has been performed to feel strongly about the answer, although further research might shade our answer slightly in strength but unlikely in direction.

5 – Solid: Indicates considerable research has been performed and the answer is agreed to by nearly all. The findings will probably not change in our lifetime.

After providing the answer and sharing our confidence level in it, we review the topic in general terms in a section labeled "Discussion." Then, we highlight selected research studies and findings. We conclude with what these results mean for you. That is, how you can apply and benefit from what is known. Our objective is to provide concrete action items to implement. At the end of each chapter, we provide the research references if you care to dig deeper into the topic.

Challenge Yourself and Test Your Knowledge

Before you read each chapter, answer the chapter question. At the end of the book is a fold-out answer sheet. Go to the first page of each chapter, read the question, select an answer, and record it on the answer sheet. See how much (or little) you know about people practices. Based on an article by Sara Rynes and her colleagues (2002), we estimate the following scale to give you feedback on your performance:

- 43 – 50   Very high score; should be an expert.

- 28 – 42   Average score; you would benefit from more study.

- < 15   Low score; we encourage you to re-read this book and the previous *100 Things* book, take notes, then take the test again.

Our hope is that everyone will learn something new, be inspired to examine their work world a little differently, and develop additional insight into human behavior. We also hope that you will have a little fun along the way.

Acknowledgements

This undertaking required a staff of dedicated people to complete it. We wish to thank Guangrong Dai for the many hours spent looking up and verifying references. We also want to thank Kim Ruyle for the insights he provided us. Bonnie Parks has an uncanny ability to find grammatical errors and punctuation problems. Her attention to detail and care given this project made our jobs as authors easier. We are very grateful to Diane Hoffmann, Lesley Kurke, and Eric Ekstrand for the effort on book layout, formatting, and cover design. We also want to thank all the researchers, journal editors, and reviewers who have contributed to our scientific knowledge base. Few of us realize the many, many hours it takes to get an article published in a peer reviewed journal. Human pregnancy lasts nine months. The gestation of an article, in most cases, is longer (and may be equally as painful). Finally, we wish to thank our wives, whose ongoing encouragement enable a group of authors the freedom and family support to pursue their passion.

References

Eichinger, R. W., Lombardo, M. M., & Ulrich, D. (2004). *100 things you need to know: Best people practices for managers & HR.* Minneapolis, MN: Lominger International: A Korn/Ferry Company.

Fisher, A. (2006, August 21). Have you outgrown your job? *Fortune,* pp. 46-56.

Friedman, T. L. (2005). *The world is flat: A brief history of the twenty-first century.* New York: Farrar, Straus & Giroux.

Rynes, S. L., Colbert, A. E., & Brown, K. G. (2002). HR professionals' beliefs about effective human resource practices: Correspondence between research and practice. *Human Resource Management, 41*(2), 149-174.

Author Biographies

Dave Ulrich is a professor of business at the University of Michigan and a partner at the RBL Group, a consulting firm focused on helping organizations and leaders deliver value. He studies how organizations build capabilities of speed, learning, collaboration, accountability, talent, and leadership through leveraging human resources. He has helped generate award-winning databases that assess alignment between strategies, human resource practices, and HR competencies. Dave has published over 100 articles and book chapters and 12 books. He was editor of the *Human Resource Management Journal,* served on the editorial boards of 4 other journals, is on the Board of Directors for Herman Miller, is a Fellow of the National Academy of Human Resources, and cofounder of the Michigan Human Resource Partnership. His honors include being ranked the number one most influential person in HR by *HR Magazine* and being ranked by *BusinessWeek* as the number one management educator and guru. He has consulted and done research with over half of the Fortune 200.

Bob Eichinger is CEO of Lominger International, A Korn/Ferry Company and cofounder of Lominger Limited. He is cocreator of The LEADERSHIP ARCHITECT® Suite of management, executive, and organizational development tools. During his 40+ year career, he has worked inside PepsiCo and Pillsbury, and as a consultant in Fortune 500 companies in the U.S., Europe, Japan, Canada, and Australia. Bob lectures extensively on the topic of executive and management development and has served on the Board of the Human Resource Planning Society. He has worked as a coach with more than 1,000 managers and executives. Bob's books include *The Leadership Machine,* written with Mike Lombardo, and *100 Things You Need to Know: Best People Practices for Managers & HR,* written with Mike Lombardo and Dave Ulrich.

John Kulas is assistant professor of Industrial and Organizational Psychology at Saint Cloud State University. His applied background includes current and past appointments as a test publisher, an internal HR practitioner, and an external organizational consultant (focusing primarily on topics of managerial selection and performance assessment). He has authored over 20 conference and journal presentations, primarily dealing with the issue of measurement in organizational settings. His works appear in the *Journal of Psychology, Organizational Research Methods,* the *Journal of Applied Measurement,* the *Journal of Business and Psychology,* and *Social Justice Research.* He has received research awards from the Society for Industrial and Organizational Psychology and the American Psychological Society.

Ken De Meuse is associate vice president of research at Lominger International. Prior to joining Lominger, he was on the faculties at the University of Wisconsin – Eau Claire, Iowa State University, and the University of Nebraska at Omaha. Ken has published numerous articles on employee attitudes and organizational behavior in several leading professional journals. His most recent book entitled *Resizing the Organization: Managing Layoffs, Divestitures, and Closings* was published by Jossey-Bass in 2003. He has appeared on ABC News, CNN, AP Radio, and National Public Radio and has been featured in national publications such as the *Wall Street Journal, BusinessWeek, Fortune, U.S. News & World Report,* the *New York Times,* and *USA Today* for his expertise on the impact organizational change has on the workforce. More than 100 universities and 150 corporations have contacted him regarding his research work in this area.

Table of Contents

Chapter   **Page**

Table of Contents by Subject

TABLE OF CONTENTS BY SUBJECT

A Subject Matter Index combining *100 Things You Need to Know* and *50 More Things You Need to Know* is provided at the end of the book.

CORPORATE CULTURE

1.

Which of the following is true regarding the impact of organizational citizenship behaviors (OCBs—going beyond your job description and doing something nice for someone else)?

SELECT ONE:

- ☐ A. OCBs produce tangible measurable outcomes for organizations.

- ☐ B. OCBs, while nice, have no direct impact on work outcomes.

- ☐ C. While desirable, OCBs can't be measured in organizations, so the impact is unknown.

- ☐ D. People who do OCBs progress more rapidly, but they don't help the organization perform any better.

- ☐ E. While desirable and even measurable, OCBs don't have a tangible impact on organizational outcomes.

1

1. **Which of the following is true regarding the impact of organizational citizenship behaviors (OCBs)?**

The correct answer is A: OCBs produce tangible measurable outcomes for organizations.

HOW SURE ARE WE AT THIS TIME?				
1	2	3	**4**	5
Hint	Suggestive	Trending	**Substantial**	Solid

Discussion

People who go out of their way or beyond their job requirements and do useful and positive things for others can have an impact on how the total organization functions. Examples of OCBs include:

- Helping others with their work who have been absent

- Helping orient new employees into the department

- Assisting the supervisor with his/her duties

- Coming to work early or staying late

- Standing up to protect the reputation of the company

- Telling outsiders good news about the company

- Making suggestions to improve the operation of the company

- Actively attending company meetings

- Helping colleagues solve work and nonwork-related problems

- Complying with company policies, even though nobody is watching

- Not talking behind others' backs

- Keeping up-to-date in one's field or profession

- Not conducting personal business on company time

- Expressing pride in working for the company

- Being enthusiastic about the company's direction

These examples were taken from a variety of sources, including: Lambert (2000); Farh, Earley, & Lin (1997); Mackenzie, Podsakoff, & Fetter (1993); and Podsakoff, MacKenzie, & Hui (1993).

There are people who do these types of extra things and others who don't. Leaders and organization cultures that cultivate and support OCBs will benefit.

Selected Research

- Organizational citizenship behaviors (OCBs) have been defined as work-related behaviors that are discretionary, not related to the formal organizational reward system and, in the aggregate, promote the effective functioning of the organization (Moorman, 1991). In essence, individuals exhibit OCBs when they go outside of their job description to exert positive influence without reward or recognition from the organization. OCBs have received much attention in recent years, given the need for organizations to be innovative, flexible, and responsive to changing external conditions (Dyne, Graham, & Dienesch, 1994).

- Bolino and Turnley (2003) summarize several empirical studies investigating the impact of OCBs on firm performance. An empirical investigation of sales performance in an insurance company found a positive relationship between employee citizenship and several measures of organizational performance, including the amount of new business generated by agents, the degree to which the agents surpassed previous productivity levels, the average number

3

of policies sold, and the total number of policies sold. In a separate study, employee citizenship was positively related to product quantity and quality in a sample of machine crews in a paper mill. Sales teams in a pharmaceutical firm that engaged in more citizenship behaviors were significantly more likely to reach their sales goals than those exhibiting fewer citizenship behaviors. OCBs were positively related to the amount of new business generated, average number of policies sold, and total policies sold. Higher levels of OCBs resulted in higher levels of revenue, customer satisfaction, and quality of service for several fast-food restaurant chains. Restaurants with higher levels of OCBs were significantly more profitable and had a higher level of profits as a percentage of sales than those units that had lower levels of OCBs. See Podsakoff and MacKenzie (1997) for a more thorough review of the research relating to the tangible benefits of OCBs.

- The relationship between job satisfaction and organizational citizenship has been found to be stronger than that between job satisfaction and productivity (Organ & Ryan, 1995). In other words, while happy workers may not be more productive workers, they do tend to be good organizational citizens.

- It has also been found that employees who work for transformational leaders tend to engage in more citizenship behaviors (Podsakoff, et al. 2000). The research shows that employees engage in more citizenship behaviors to the extent that their managers get to know them and show respect for them.

- Leaders can elicit more citizenship behaviors by providing employees with work that is more interesting and meaningful as opposed to more repetitive and routinized (Diefendorff, et al. 2001).

- Organizational and leadership support is also a strong factor in bringing out citizenship behavior. The more employees believe that the organization values their work and cares about their well-being, the more likely they will be to engage in citizenship behaviors. One study examined the relationship between work-life benefits and employee citizenship. It found that employees were more willing to engage in citizenship behavior when they worked for companies with better work-life balance policies (Lambert, 2000).

- Research by Moorman (1991) showed that high levels of distributive, procedural, and interactional justice within organizations serve to increase the prevalence of citizenship behaviors on the part of their employees. In other words, environments characterized by high levels of trust will tend to foster more OCBs.

So what difference do these findings make?

People exhibit more OCBs in supportive, trusting cultures. In turn, OCBs help the organization achieve many results at a higher level. OCBs can be measured and tracked and encouraged and supported with the following:

Recruitment and Selection

- Seek out candidates who are more likely to exhibit OCBs. For example, look for candidates who participated in extracurricular activities while in college or those who have a history of being involved in volunteer activities. These individuals might also be inclined to go beyond their normal duties as employees (Bolino & Turnley 2003). Past performance is the best predictor of future performance.

1

- Research by Latham and Skarlicki (1995) found that situational interviews are especially useful in identifying good corporate citizens. In a situational interview, candidates are presented with job-related scenarios and asked how they would behave in the situation. One could develop questions that pose organizational citizenship behavior scenarios to the candidate.

Performance Appraisal and Compensation/Benefits

- Another way to increase citizenship behavior in organizations is to support and reward it. It should be noted, however, that offering direct rewards for citizenship behavior could have a downside. Some researchers assert that directly compensating employees for being good organizational citizens may make those individuals pay less attention to their regular job responsibilities (Bolino, Turnley, & Niehoff, 2004).

Management Training

- New supervisors and managers should be oriented to OCBs and the research and techniques to encourage them.

- Training programs can demonstrate OCBs during the program through the ways material is presented, through case studies, and through reflection by participants on their history of these behaviors.

Cultural Assessment

- A measure of OCBs in an organization should provide insights about the health of the unit. These can be measured through cultural audits.

Some Key Sources

1

Bolino, M. C., & Turnley, W. H. (2003). Going the extra mile: Cultivating and managing employee citizenship behavior. *Academy of Management Executive, 17*, 60-71.

Bolino, M. C., Turnley, W. H., & Niehoff, B. P. (2004). The other side of the story: Reexamining prevailing assumptions about organizational citizenship behavior. *Human Resource Management Review, 14*, 229-246.

Diefendorff, J. M., Brown, D. J., Kamim, A. M., & Lord, R. G. (2001). Examining the roles of job involvement and work centrality in predicting organizational citizenship behaviors and job performance. *Journal of Organizational Behavior, 23*(1), 93-108.

Dyne, L. V., Graham, J. W., & Dienesch, R. M. (1994). Organizational citizenship behavior: Construct redefinition, measurement, and validation. *Academy of Management Journal, 37*, 765-802.

Farh, J. L., Earley, P.C., & Lin, S-C (1997). Impetus for action: A cultural analysis of justice and organizational citizenship behavior in Chinese society. *Administrative Science Quarterly, 42*, 421-444.

Lambert, S. J. (2000). Added benefits: The link between work-life benefits and organizational citizenship behavior. *Academy of Management Journal, 43*, 801-815.

Latham, G. P., & Skarlicki, D. P. (1995). Criterion-related validity of the situational and patterned behavior description interviews with organizational citizenship behavior. *Human Performance, 8*, 67-80.

Mackenzie, S. B., Podsakoff, P. M., & Fetter, R. (1993). The impact of organizational citizenship behavior evaluations of salesperson performance. *Journal of Marketing, 57*(1), 70-80.

1

Moorman, R. H. (1991). Relationship between organizational justice and organizational citizenship behaviors: Do fairness perceptions influence employee citizenship? _Journal of Applied Psychology, 76,_ 845-855.

Organ, D. W., & Ryan, K. (1995). A meta-analytic review of attitudinal and dispositional predictors of organizational citizenship behavior. _Personnel Psychology, 48,_ 775-802.

Podsakoff, P. M., & MacKenzie, S. B. (1997). Impact of organizational citizenship behavior on organizational performance: A review and suggestions for future research. _Human Performance, 10,_ 133-151.

Podsakoff, P. M., Mackenzie, S. B., & Hui, C. (1993). Organizational citizenship behaviors as determinants of managerial evaluations of employee performance: A review and suggestions for future research. In K. M. Rowland & G. R. Ferris (Eds.), _Research in Personnel and Human Resource Management_ (pp. 1-42). Greenwich, CT: JAI.

Podsakoff, P. M., MacKenzie, S. B., Paine, J. B., & Bachrach, D. G. (2000). Organizational citizenship behavior: A critical review of the theoretical and empirical literature and suggestions for future research. _Journal of Management, 26,_ 513-563.

2.

What are the two most "deadly" reported mistakes associated with outsourcing efforts?

SELECT ONE:

☐ A. Outsourcing activities not suitable for outsourcing and selecting the wrong vendor.

☐ B. Overlooking the hidden costs of outsourcing and failing to plan a cost-efficient exit strategy.

☐ C. Overlooking internal personnel issues and selecting the wrong vendor.

☐ D. Failing to plan an exit strategy and writing a loose contract.

☐ E. Writing a loose contract and not actively managing or losing control over the outsourced activity.

2

2. What are the two most "deadly" reported mistakes associated with outsourcing efforts?

The correct answer is E: Writing a loose contract and not actively managing or losing control over the outsourced activity.

HOW SURE ARE WE AT THIS TIME?				
1	2	**3**	4	5
Hint	Suggestive	**Trending**	Substantial	Solid

Discussion

Evidence to date suggests that carefully crafted outsourcing increases the overall performance of a firm (Gilley & Rasheed, 2000). Although only a few studies have been done, loose arrangements on the front end (#3 below) and failure to monitor the quality of the process (#5 below) appear most likely to harm outsourcing efforts. Additionally, five other factors should be considered.

Selected Research

- In a study examining 91 outsourcing efforts performed by European and North American firms, Barthelemy (2003) identified a set of seven common mistakes that plagued most of the failed outsourcing efforts. Thirty-three percent (33 of 91) were considered failures. This was determined by asking senior managers how satisfied they were with the results of the outsourcing efforts. These are the seven "deadly sins" and a description of each.

1. *Outsourcing activities that should not be outsourced.* Although there are some exceptions, activities that are intimately tied to a company's core business should generally not be outsourced. An exception might be when a firm experiences seasonal fluctuations in its business and must enlist contract support to deal with the increased workload. Outsourcing core activities makes it more difficult to control and monitor the work. However, outsourcing noncore activities may allow a firm to focus on their competitive-edge activities and can result in reduced operating costs if an external firm can do the outsourced activity more efficiently.

2. *Selecting the wrong vendor.* Firms must perform adequate due diligence in selecting a vendor. Such things as experience and financial strength of the vendor should be considered. In addition, intangible factors such as cultural fit and shared values should be taken into account. One approach to identifying the right vendor is to outsource a few pilot activities to several vendors and monitor their performance. A less costly way is to identify and interview former and/or current clients of the vendor.

3. *Writing a poor contract.* Contracts must be well-thought-out and written with precise language. Be sure to determine if there are extra fees involved, which fees are fixed and which are variable, and make sure there is an option to get out of the contract should the relationship go south. Finally, some companies make the mistake of thinking that a soundly written contract is not as important when the firm-vendor relationship is based on trust and a sense of partnership. This is not a safe assumption. On the contrary, a well-written contract can form the basis of building a strong and lasting relationship between a firm and its vendors.

4. *Overlooking personnel issues.* Outsourcing activities can sometimes lead to costly counterproductive behaviors,

11

2

such as absenteeism, sabotage, and quitting. To the extent that it is crucial for the firm to retain key personnel and maintain performance levels, steps should be taken to actively communicate with the workforce and to identify those employees who may deserve special attention in such uncertain times. Managers and HR should be prepared to offer increased salaries and more training to those who may be crucial to retain but who may have to assume different responsibilities.

5. *Losing control over the outsourced activity.* The loss of control associated with outsourcing an activity should not be overlooked. The work, and the quality of that work, must be managed through a contract rather than through direct control. Managing a contract or a vendor may actually require more effort, and certainly implies a different skill set, than that of managing the activity directly. Firms may even need to hire talent from the outside to manage the vendor relationship, which adds to the cost of the outsourcing. In the end, vendors must be actively managed and contracts vigilantly enforced in order to realize the full benefits of an outsourced activity.

6. *Overlooking the hidden costs of outsourcing.* Hidden costs of outsourcing include those associated with researching and selecting a vendor (see #2 above), writing the contract (see #3 above), and managing the contract and work to be performed (see #5 above). Ironically, while selecting the right vendor, writing a good contract, and adequately overseeing the work are essential elements to any successful outsourcing effort, these elements can also be the undoing of an outsourcing effort should

the costs run rampant, especially the ongoing costs of managing the contract. Perhaps the best way to minimize the ongoing costs of managing a contract is to select the right vendor and to write a good contract. The right vendor will be responsive to your needs and a good contract will allow you to hold them accountable with minimal negotiating. While the benefits of involving legal experts is obvious in any contracting situation, the benefits of utilizing technical experts to establish the performance parameters of the contract are less obvious.

7. *Failing to plan an exit strategy.* It must be considered up front that an outsourced activity may eventually be brought back in-house, or it may be desirable to switch vendors after a period of time for one reason or another. Failing to plan for such possibilities is a mistake and one that can often be mitigated by writing a good contract in the first place. Consider a scenario where there are many qualified vendors for a particular activity; in such a case, it might make sense to include a clause in the contract that allows for an annual review of the relationship and the option of terminating the relationship.

2

- In a summary of the benefits of outsourcing, the Corporate Leadership Council identified the reasons why people approached outsourcing:

OUTSOURCING OUTCOME	PERCENT MARKING IMPORTANT
Provide high-quality HR services to organization	93%
Reduce and control HR operating costs	89%
Gain access to skills and expertise not available inside	88%
Free HR staff from administrative duties	85%
Gain access to technologies not available in-house	84%
Off-load activities that are not contributing to competitiveness	83%
Share risks of investing in technology with external environment	54%

- The Corporate Leadership Council also identified the challenges from outsourcing:

CHALLENGES WITH HR OUTSOURCING	PERCENT MARKING IMPORTANT
Benefits Capture: Maintaining consistent high-quality level of service; ensuring cost savings achieved vs. promised; determining costs associated with outsourcing	69%
Change Management: Managing transition in HR function; educating organization about HR outsourcing; deciding which activities to outsource	59%
Vendor Governance: Having vendor accountability; setting vendor performance standards; ensuring value and goal congruence of vendor; providing direction to vendor; lack of internal skills to manage vendor contract	53%
Vendor Selection: Identifying suitable vendor; comparing vendors' service and price policies; understanding HR outsourcing market	51%

2

So what difference do these findings make?

Until further research is done, follow the seven recommendations from Barthelemy:

2

1. Outsource the right things.

2. Select the best vendor.

3. Write a good contract.

4. Create a plan to retain key internal talent at the initiation of outsourcing.

5. Create and follow a plan to monitor and manage the outsourcing activity and vendor.

6. Anticipate variable costs.

7. Plan ahead for an exit if necessary.

Some Key Sources

Barthelemy, J. (2003). The seven deadly sins of outsourcing. *Academy of Management Executive, 17*(2), 87-98.

Corporate Leadership Council. (2003). *Strategic HR outsourcing*. Washington, DC.

Gilley, K., & Rasheed, A. (2000). Making more by doing less: An analysis of outsourcing and its effects on firm performance. *Journal of Management, 26*, 763-790.

Lawler, E. E., III., Ulrich, D., Fitz-enz, J., & Madden, J. (2004). *Human resources business process outsourcing: Transforming how HR gets its work done*. San Francisco, CA: Jossey-Bass.

CREATIVITY

3.

Which person in an organization is most likely to produce the most creative ideas?

SELECT ONE:

- ☐ A. One with relatively few, but strategically important, social ties.

- ☐ B. One with relatively few, but extremely strong, social ties.

- ☐ C. One with many, but relatively weak, social ties.

- ☐ D. One with an equal mix of weak and strong social ties.

- ☐ E. One with no need for any social ties.

3   **Which person in an organization is most likely to produce the most creative ideas?**

The correct answer is C: One with many, but relatively weak, social ties.

HOW SURE ARE WE AT THIS TIME?				
1	2	3	**4**	5
Hint	Suggestive	Trending	**Substantial**	Solid

3

Discussion

Creative people are often curious loners. They have many, but not very deep, social ties and relationships. The advantage of this is to increase their knowledge from disparate sources and increase the chance of making novel connections. Since they are less interested in fostering and maintaining relationships, they can concentrate on ideas, discussion, and debate. They also do not concentrate their time on a few close colleagues thereby opening up more transactions with a more diverse population.

Selected Research

* Research by Granovetter (1973) looked at the "tie strength" of relationships. He examined: (1) amount of interaction, (2) emotional intensity of the interaction, and (3) reciprocity between the actors. The study found that weak ties are likely to lead to enhanced creativity and strong ties are likely to constrain it. This is largely due to the fact that much of the information and perspectives shared among people with strong ties is redundant and confirming. People with strong ties tend to share similar views and perspectives, which can hinder creativity. We tend to like to build strong ties with people like us, so we are not as innovative.

- Enhancing relevant knowledge can increase the incidence of creativity due to the improved ability to generate and evaluate potential solutions (Campbell, 1960; Mumford & Gustafson, 1988; Simonton, 1999). In a study of marketing professionals, it was found that those with more knowledge of the external environment generated more creative marketing ideas (Andrews & Smith, 1996).

- Depth of knowledge is necessary for creativity but not sufficient. Research has shown that creativity can be enhanced through training (Basadur, Graen, & Green, 1982; Basadur, Wakabayashi, & Graen, 1990). Other research has shown that by simply giving people creativity goals or instructing them to be creative can increase incidents of creativity (Shalley, 1991).

- Whereas strong ties are typically formed between people who are similar (Ibarra, 1992), weak ties likely exist between those who have more diverse perspectives, interests, and outlooks (Granovetter, 1982).

- Individuals with weaker connections tend to interact with a wider range of people and exchange information that is nonredundant (Burt, 1997). Information that travels through networks made up of stronger ties is more apt to be redundant and confirming and follow a circular route. What happens in strong-tie networks is that the same story comes from six different people.

- According to Perry-Smith and Shalley (2003), creativity does not necessarily require strong ties and may be enhanced in those with weaker social ties, given the access they provide to fresh information and diverse organizational members. Access to diverse individuals likely increases the amount of unique knowledge gathered. Further, the exposure to new and unique knowledge can foster previously unexplored thoughts, force one to think about things differently, and can lead to innovative solutions.

- Those with weak ties are likely to be more autonomous and less encumbered by group conformity and are therefore more apt to be creative (Woodman, Sawyer, & Griffin, 1993).

- Work by Kanter (1988) suggests that organizations who want to increase innovation and creativity should take steps to foster interactions across units, departments, etc.

3

So what difference do these findings make?

- Breakthrough thinking can be enhanced through encouraging more diverse relationships: membership in professional associations, pulling together one-time groups to look at a problem, setting up competing teams with diverse memberships, learning from benchmarking tours, exposure to noncompetitive organizations, and university courses, to name a few. Some organizations orchestrate seating assignments during meetings to expose people to fresh thinking.

- It might also suggest that creative people be deployed across diverse units, rather than grouped together. Or it might indicate that normal team-building and morale-boosting intervention designed to form better relationships within the team might be counterproductive to the creative process.

- When hiring creative people, pay particular attention to their networks. The more diverse, the better. Don't look for a social animal. Passable would work.

Some Key Sources

Amabile, T. M. (1996). *Creativity in context*. Boulder, CO: Westview.

Andrews, J., & Smith, D. C. (1996). In search of marketing imagination: Factors affecting creativity of marketing programs for the mature products. *Journal of Marketing Research, 33*, 174-187.

Basadur, M. S., Graen, G. B., & Green, S. G. (1982). Training in creative problem solving: Effects on ideation and problem finding and solving in an industrial research organization. *Organizational Behavior and Human Performance, 30*, 41-70.

Basadur, M. S., Wakabayashi, M., & Graen, G. B. (1990). Attitudes toward divergent thinking before and after training: Focusing upon the effect of individual problem-solving styles. *Creativity Research Journal, 3*, 22-32.

Burt, R. S. (1997). The contingent value of social capital. *Administrative Science Quarterly, 42*, 339-365.

Campbell, D. T. (1960). Blind variation and selective retention in creative thought as in other knowledge processes. *Psychological Review, 67*, 380-400.

Granovetter, M. S. (1973). The strength of weak ties. *American Journal of Sociology, 78*, 1360-1380.

Granovetter, M. S. (1982). The strength of weak ties: A network theory revisited. In P. V. Marsden & N. Lin (Eds.), *Social structure and network analysis* (pp. 105-130). Beverly Hills, CA: Sage.

Ibarra, H. (1992). Homophily and differential returns: Sex differences in network structures and access in an advertising firm. *Administrative Science Quarterly, 37*, 422-447.

Kanter, R. M. (1988). When a thousand flowers bloom: Structural, collective, and social conditions for innovation in organization. *Research in Organizational Behavior, 10*, 169-211.

Mumford, M. D., & Gustafson, S. B. (1988). Creativity syndrome: Integration, application, and innovation. *Psychological Bulletin, 103*, 27-43.

Perry-Smith, J. E., & Shalley, C. E. (2003). The social side of creativity: A static and dynamic social network perspective. *Academy of Management Review, 28*, 89-106.

Shalley, C. E. (1991). Effects of productivity goals, creativity goals, and personal discretion on individual creativity. *Journal of Applied Psychology, 76*, 179-185.

Simonton, D. K. (1999). *Origins of genius*. New York: Oxford University Press.

Woodman, R. W., Sawyer, J. E., & Griffin, R. W. (1993). Toward a theory of organizational creativity. *Academy of Management Review, 18*, 293-321.

3

TEAMS

4.

Do virtual teams or traditional teams have more conflict?

SELECT ONE:

☐ A. Traditional teams experience greater levels of task conflict, but less affective (emotional) conflict than do virtual teams because they don't have to live with each other every day.

☐ B. Traditional teams experience lower levels of task conflict because they are together and can quickly resolve task issues, but higher levels of affective conflict than do virtual teams for the same reason.

☐ C. Virtual teams experience greater levels of task conflict, but less affective conflict than do traditional teams.

☐ D. Virtual teams experience greater levels of both task and affective conflict than do traditional teams.

☐ E. Traditional teams experience more task and affective conflict than virtual teams.

4

4. Do virtual teams or traditional teams have more conflict?

The correct answer is D: Virtual teams experience greater levels of both task and affective conflict than do traditional teams.

HOW SURE ARE WE AT THIS TIME?				
1	2	3	4	**5**
Hint	Suggestive	Trending	Substantial	**Solid**

4

Discussion

Virtual teams are those whose members are not co-located. They do not have day-to-day, face-to-face interaction. Although they may meet periodically, their most likely means of communication will be electronic and paper. Such teams are becoming more common in today's business world as global organizations seek to leverage the expertise that exists across geographic boundaries and time zones. The increase in outsourcing and offshoring has caused a corresponding increase in the number of virtual teams. Virtual teams can be long-term, such as a committee, or short-term, focused on a particular project or task.

Sharing complex information and coming to consensus on even mundane tasks can be difficult for any team, but more so for dispersed teams.

All of the research on high-performing teams points to the importance of trust among its members. It also shows that team processes work better when members of the team know each other well.

In pure virtual teams, the personal and social aspect is missing. Nonverbal cues which have been shown to carry a considerable weight in correctly interpreting messages and communication are also missing.

Unnecessary conflict would probably be higher in virtual teams because of incomplete and misinterpreted communication and many of the tools of conflict resolution are not available. So, a virtual team will have more conflict and find it more difficult to resolve it.

Selected Research

4

- Communicating via an indirect channel, such as email, takes longer (Straus & McGrath, 1994), is subject to delay (Kraut, Fish, & Chalfonte, 1992), and can require more mental effort (Hinds, 1999). As a result, it can be more difficult for virtual teams to resolve conflict in a timely way.

- Research spanning more than 30 years has shown that affective conflict (that caused by anger or hostility) detracts from team performance (Jehn, 1994; Evan, 1965; Amason, 1996; Eisenhardt, Kahwajy, & Bourgeois, 1997). On the contrary, there is solid evidence to support the notion that task conflict (that arising from disagreements on work content) has a positive relationship with performance. This of course assumes that the conflict is dealt with, and dealt with in an effective manner. Conflict that is avoided or not dealt with effectively can hinder team performance.

- Hinds and Bailey (2000) assert that communicating via indirect channels and operating from different contexts causes higher levels of affective and task conflict among group members. As such, it was proposed that virtual teams should experience more affective and task conflict than traditional teams. It was also proposed that unresolved affective and task conflict would be associated with reduced performance in virtual teams.

4

- It was found in Straus and McGrath (1994) that communication media affect group functioning mostly by the degree to which they transmit social context cues. Results from this study demonstrated that computer-mediated groups, such as those that communicate via email, were less productive than face-to-face groups, and responded much more negatively to the medium and to a given task than did face-to-face groups. Computer-mediated groups also reported having more difficulty understanding each other than did face-to-face groups, despite the availability of a record of the discussion.

- In a study examining conflict among groups of MBA students working on class projects, Kraut, Fish, and Chalfonte (1992) reported that the project teams had difficulty coming to consensus and coordinating work among members. The authors attributed these problems to the reliance of the teams on indirect communication channels (primarily email) to express complex ideas.

- In a chapter by Griffin, Mannix, and Neal (2003), it was stated that task conflict among virtual teams actually improves decision quality, allowing team members to drop old patterns of interaction and adopt new perspectives. In fact, the presence of task conflict accompanied by an effective resolution should improve team performance. Trust was found to be a key factor in reducing conflict among virtual team members. So while task conflict has been shown to improve decision quality in virtual teams, this assumes the team is able to effectively and productively resolve the conflict, which can be more difficult in a virtual team setting.

- Armstrong and Cole (1994) observed that conflicts in virtual teams often went unaddressed for longer periods of time than in traditional teams.

- In research focusing on how well people responded to virtual teams and telework (telecommuting), Workman, Kahnweiler, and Bommer (2003) noted that an employee's cognitive style affects his/her commitment to the virtual team and telework environment. Specifically, the ambiguous, isolated, and unstructured nature of these work settings can adversely affect a person's commitment to the team. A major finding was that internal cognitive styles (prefer working alone) had greater commitment to telework than external cognitive styles (prefer working in groups).

So what difference do these findings make?

4

- In global, dynamic, and changing businesses, virtual teams are not optional. Virtual teams are on the rise.

- The distance at which virtual teams operate, combined with the reliance on indirect communication channels, means that virtual teams' interactions are depersonalized. Such depersonalized interactions have a tendency to lead to inappropriate behaviors and make it difficult to share information. In addition, a virtual team setting does not allow for the feedback necessary to identify and deal with miscommunication. The result is more conflict, and a more difficult time dealing with such conflict, which can hinder the performance of virtual teams.

- When implementing a virtual team format, more care than usual will need to be directed at information management, decision making, and power balancing. Rules and structure need to be carefully constructed up front and enforced. Managing virtual teams is more complex and time consuming than managing a traditional team. Managers of virtual teams must be better at managing through remote systems and must focus heavily on establishing trust among the work group. In many ways, managing virtual teams requires better supervisory skills than those needed to manage traditional teams (Cascio, 2000). It

27

is often good counsel for a virtual team to begin with a face-to-face meeting where the team purpose, roles, decision-making processes, and norms are discussed. This face-to-face interaction allows relationships to form that might be managed better virtually after the face-to-face interactions. Periodic face-to-face meetings continue to reinforce the relationship gel that holds teams together.

4

- Special training can be offered for teleworkers and their supervisors. Establish ground rules for communicating, such as using email to share reports and chat rooms to discuss other issues related to the project. Personal relationships among team members go a long way toward helping to address conflict when it does arise, as it inevitably will. Since communication among virtual team members lacks the richness of being face-to-face, perhaps it would help to encourage more frequent communication to make up for the lack of richness.

- Performance management is crucial in managing virtual teams. Managers must take extra care in defining performance expectations for team members. Managers must also be sure to provide the necessary support by removing performance barriers and providing the necessary resources (e.g., up-to-date equipment).

Some Key Sources

Amason, A.C. (1996). Distinguishing the effects of functional and dysfunctional conflict on strategic decision making: Resolving a paradox for top management teams. *Academy of Management Journal, 39,* 123-148.

Armstrong, D. L., & Cole, P. (1995). Managing distance and differences in geographically distributed work groups. In S. Jackson & M. Ruderman (Eds.), *Diversity in work teams: Research paradigms for a changing workplace* (pp. 187-215). Washington, DC: American Psychological Association.

Cascio, W. F. (2000). Managing a virtual workplace. *Academy of Management Executive, 14*(3), 81-90.

4

Eisenhardt, K. M., Kahwajy, J. L., & Bourgeois, L. J. (1997). Conflict and strategic choice: How top management teams disagree. *California Management Review, 39*(2), 42-62.

Evan, W. (1965). Conflict and performance in R&D organizations. *Industrial Management Review, 7,* 37-46.

Griffin, T. L., Mannix, E. A., & Neal, M. A. (2003). Conflict in virtual teams. In C. B. Gibson & S. G. Cohen (Eds.), *Virtual teams that work* (pp. 335-351). San Francisco, CA: Jossey-Bass.

Hinds, P. J. (1999). The cognitive and interpersonal costs of video. *Media Psychology, 1,* 283-311.

Hinds, P. J., & Bailey, D. E. (2000). Virtual teams: Anticipating the impact of virtuality on team process and performance. In S. J. Havlovic (Ed.), *Proceedings of the 2000 Academy of Management Meetings,* Toronto, Canada, OCIS, c1-c6.

Jehn, K. A. (1994). Enhancing effectiveness: An investigation of advantages and disadvantages of value-based intragroup conflict. *International Journal of Conflict Management, 5,* 223-238.

Kraut, R. E., Galegher, J., Fish, R., & Chalfonte, B. (1992). Task requirements and media choice in collaborative writing. *Human Computer Interaction, 7,* 375-407.

Straus, S. G., & McGrath, J. E. (1994). Does the medium matter? The interaction of task type and technology on group performance and member reactions. *Journal of Applied Psychology, 79,* 87-97.

Workman, M., Kahnweiler, W., & Bommer, W. (2003). The effects of cognitive style and media richness on commitment to telework and virtual teams. *Journal of Vocational Behavior, 63,* 199-219.

4

5.

Which area is most vulnerable to legal, professional, and ethical challenges in the current legal/regulatory environment?

SELECT ONE:

☐ A. Compensation.

☐ B. Selection.

☐ C. Performance management.

☐ D. Employee training and development.

☐ E. Benefits.

5

5. Which area is most vulnerable to legal, professional, and ethical challenges in the current legal/regulatory environment?

The correct answer is A: Compensation.

HOW SURE ARE WE AT THIS TIME?				
1	**2**	3	4	5
Hint	**Suggestive**	Trending	Substantial	Solid

Discussion

Recent ethical lapses in corporate governance in the U.S. and other countries and the mounting pressure from special constituency advocacy groups have made the quality and equity of people practices a lightning rod of attention. Simply, people practices need to be fair and accurate. People need to be treated and managed equitably as individuals and as members of various groups. Each people process has its special challenges. Hiring needs to be fair and accurate by hiring people who can do the job and, at the same time, not over- or underrepresenting legitimate candidates from protected groups. Pay needs to be equitable. People who perform work better should be paid more; and those who perform less well should be paid less. People of potential should be promoted without regard to their group classification. People should have equal access to training and development. Simply, people should have access to opportunity.

Going beyond these people practices, the Sarbanes-Oxley Act (the Act) of 2002 sends a message to all employees of publicly held (and private) companies: If they witness corporate fraud or an attempt to cover it up, they can report it to authorities without fear of reprisal. The Act is designed to rid public companies of corporate corruption (for instance, in inappropriate pay practices). The Act requires employers to encourage employees to come forward with information regarding corporate fraud without fear of reprisal, to enact policies to prevent corporate fraud, and to prevent the destruction of certain documents. Compliance with the Act will require modification and/or creation of new policies and training, all in coordination with human resources and employment law counsel. SOX also requires transparency in reporting and discipline in processes. Transparency means that what people are paid must be made public according to a set of rules. Discipline in processes means that audits should be done of how work is done in finance, IT, HR, and other corporate staff areas. SOX analyses are being reported and tracked at the board of director's level, and the hope is to avoid corporate greed and malfeasance. Compensation is a lightning rod when executive salaries have risen faster than employee salaries. With alternative forms of executive compensation (stock options, performance shares, and perks), companies are now expected to be more transparent and therefore accountable in how they pay executives.

5

However, reporting or even just confronting wrongdoing comes with it the risk of retaliation and punishment from employers and other stakeholders. Whereas a corporate culture traditionally provided a means to competitive advantage due to its impact on how employees interacted, communicated, and performed, culture is now perhaps a mechanism to promote compliance with Sarbanes-Oxley and hence avoidance of costly lawsuits. Once again, corporate culture is a key to creating sustained competitive advantage for organizations.

Selected Research

- In a survey of 100 HR professionals (two-thirds of whom were VPs or SVPs) that asked about a range of issues impacting HR, including the vulnerability of HR to professional, legal, and ethical standards, 33% of respondents said that the rewards and compensation area is most vulnerable, followed by selection (30%), performance management (29%), and finally employee development (23%) (Beatty, Ewing, Tharp, 2003).

- In the same study, it was found that 79% of respondents said they would "blow the whistle" on an illegal act within their organization, while 83% would report an ethical violation. Further, the respondents expected more legal compliance by fellow senior HR professionals (85%) than by their CEO (74%). Note that this data was collected prior to the passing of the Sarbanes-Oxley Act. An interesting comparison would be between these data and that of a similar study conducted after the passing of the Act. We know of no such study at the time of this writing.

- In order to resolve some of the ethical dilemmas facing organizations today, some have called for the human resource function to be reminded that the interests of customers and investors come before those of senior management (Cooper & Madigan, 2002).

- The degree to which employees feel comfortable being open about potential wrongdoings they witness goes "to the heart of an organization's culture" (Beatty et al., 2003).

- Whistle-blowing is one avenue for maintaining integrity by reporting wrongdoings in organizational settings. In a study conducted by Benisa (2004), seven factors were suggested for an organization to enhance standards and controls for effective corporate governance through "whistle-blowing." Factors that lead to whistle-blowing behavior include vigilance, engagement, credibility, accountability,

5

empowerment, courage, and options. By influencing the development of an organizational culture that facilitates employee communication, questioning, and reporting of corporate misconduct through whistle-blowing, an ethical work environment can be established.

- In order to promote effective ethical standards in organizations, Pots and Matuszewski (2004) advised companies to go beyond legislative and regulatory requirements to build effective ethical programs. Companies that follow sound ethical practices can recruit and retain the best workforces and foster positive, long-term relationships with vendors, customers, investors, and stockholders. Due to increased economic power wielded by corporations today, it is important that today's global corporations put strong values-based ethics standards in place to ensure the "responsible management" of this power.

5

So what difference do these findings make?
- Corporate malfeasance is not a new concern. Unfortunately, power corrupts and absolute power corrupts absolutely. Where large sources of money and status are in play, leaders without sound values may abuse their power and opportunity. Organizations have been struggling with these issues for some time. Most everyone has the same goal—best practice people processes that are fair and equitable that do not put any identified special group at a disadvantage.

- Pay equity is the cause de jure at the moment. While everyone advocates pay for performance, it is difficult to justify huge gaps between the pay of some executives and average employees. That's probably why HR identifies it as the number one driver at the moment. That could easily change.

- The path is well known. All best practice people processes include fair and equitable treatment under the law and under common sense. If an organization moves to best practices, they will also move to fair and equitable treatment. They will have compensation systems that everyone understands, that allow employees at all levels to share in company gains and to be at risk for company losses, and that are transparent and open to public scrutiny.

- Managers should model appropriate behavior by being open and candid about potential wrongdoings. Frequent reinforcement of the importance of being open and candid is crucial. Reward openness and punish behavior that violates trust. Managers must be willing to go beyond merely declaring their disdain for illegal and unethical acts. Managers must also be willing to take swift and appropriate action when such behavior occurs.

- Setting up systems and processes that encourage openness is a must. Establish executive compensation systems in such a way that reported earnings for the firm cannot be misrepresented. Also, ensure the lure of rewards does not override the desire to adhere to ethical and legal standards. Consider a sales manager who must offer premium commission to those who sell the most. For some, the prospect of such financial rewards can cause one's judgment to tip into the realm of illegal or unethical.

- Organizations can select those who are most likely to adhere to legal and ethical standards. Inquiring about past behavior in the face of legal or ethical dilemmas is one way to identify those most likely to comply. There are also commercial tests that measure integrity.

- Several firms are now offering auditing services to measure the degree to which an organization is in compliance with legal/ethical standards. Investment in such a service can help organizations to "nip problems in the bud" and would likely be looked upon favorably should a legal violation be uncovered by the authorities.

Some Key Sources

Beatty, R. W., Ewing, J. R., & Tharp, C. G. (Fall 2003). HR's role in corporate governance: Present and prospective. *Human Resource Management, 42*, 257-269.

Benisa, B. (2004). Organization culture: A framework and strategies for facilitating employee whistle-blowing. *Employee Responsibilities and Rights Journal, 16*, 1-11.

Cooper, J. C., & Madigan, K. (2002, July 22). Corporate crime isn't fazing consumers yet. *BusinessWeek,* p. 23.

Potts, S. D., & Matuszewski, L. (2004). Ethics and corporate governance. *Corporate Governance: An International Review, 12*, 177-179.

5

6.

How much do investors consider non-financials (intangibles) when making investment decisions?

SELECT ONE:

☐ A. 10% or less; current and past and future financial performance is almost the only thing that matters.

☐ B. 25%.

☐ C. About one-third.

☐ D. 50%.

☐ E. As much as 70% of the decision is based on non-financial performance.

6

6. How much do investors consider non-financials (intangibles) when making investment decisions?

The correct answer is D: 50%.

HOW SURE ARE WE AT THIS TIME?				
1	2	3	**4**	5
Hint	Suggestive	Trending	**Substantial**	Solid

Discussion

In times past, it was the numbers, just the numbers. Investments were made on the strength of past performance, current trends, and future financial projections (based mostly upon the past). We are seeing a trend in investing. Professional investors and maybe some portion of individual investors are looking more to the intangibles. Many times there will be significant shifts in stock price when there are announcements of key people leaving or significant people joining. Investors are beginning to sense that the quality of leadership makes a financial difference. More remotely, they understand that the preparation of future leaders (succession planning and talent development) makes a future difference. Most of the intangibles center on talent and what talent does.

Selected Research

- Only 14% of analysts and 12% of investors surveyed believe that annual reports from retail and consumer goods companies adequately convey the value of an organization. As a result, analysts and investors must examine external sources of information because management has less control over the quality or accuracy of the data. Most look for data on such non-financial indicators as corporate strategy, quality of management, brand reputation, customer retention, systems and processes, intellectual capital, research and development, innovation, and social and environmental policies (Financial Management Advisor retrieved online at http://advisor.com/doc/08127).

- In research conducted in 1999-2000 by Ernst & Young, 35% (and much more in some cases) of fund managers' investment decisions were attributed to non-financial performance. Further, the greater the uncertainty in the market, the greater the proportion. The report asserts, "Tangible assets and forecasted cash flows are no longer the primary sources of value. It's intangibles that differentiate companies, especially in highly competitive industries." Ernst & Young examined 39 non-financial indicators and found the top 10 that have a significant influence on investors' evaluations to be: execution of corporate strategy, quality of corporate strategy, market position, management credibility, ability to innovate, management experience, research leadership, quality of major business processes, global capability, and the ability to attract and retain talented people. It seems in today's business world, the advantage goes to those who can innovate, execute rapidly, and make quick managerial decisions. With regard to management, "Demonstrating a breadth and depth of management experience across the business creates investor confidence in the firm's ability to execute."

- In a survey of more than 100 large U.S. companies, researchers at Hewitt Associates found that only 55% consistently use a formal approach to *identify* future leaders and only 30% consistently use a formal approach to *develop* leaders. However, of those companies that perform in the top 75% of total shareholder return, 100% consistently use a formal approach to identify high-potential leaders. The study concludes that while managing talent takes time and resources, there is clearly a link between investing in talent and delivering results to shareholders.

- A Watson Wyatt study of more than 750 companies in the United States, Canada, and Europe over the five-year period from 1996–2001 found that the better an organization is doing in managing its human capital, the better its shareholder returns. The participating companies were assigned a value of low, medium, or high with respect to their effectiveness in managing human capital, based on their score on Watson Wyatt's Human Capital Index (HCI), a measure quantifying exactly which HR practices and policies have the greatest correlation to shareholder value. Those in the low category had an average five-year return of 21%, medium 39%, and high 64%. Those with the most effective human capital management had three times more return on shareholder investment than did those with the least effective human capital management practices.

- Dess and Pickens (1999) assert that in today's knowledge economy, organizations must "go beyond productivity" to develop new approaches and techniques that successfully leverage the knowledge and human capital of their employees. The authors say that the more effective management of human capital will also likely improve the utilization of tangible assets, which in turn will boost overall firm performance.

- Baruch Lev (2001) found that the correlation of corporate earnings to market value has declined from about 85% to about 50% in the last 30 years. The remaining 50% is due to intangibles.

- Robert Kaplan and David Norton (2004) argue in the balanced scorecard work that intangibles make up close to 85% of a firm's market value in some industries.

6

So what difference do these findings make?

- Two firms in the same industry with the same earnings may have different market value. The intangibles demonstrate the perceived value that investors have in a firm's culture and management and confidence in future earnings.

- The so-called intangibles can become like tangible assets. Investors seem to be looking for more evidence of stability of financial performance and growth. They are looking for evidence that there is sufficient talent on board to create and execute differentiating strategies. Companies that implement and publicize best practice succession planning and talent management should be rewarded by more predictable financial performance and higher stock price evaluations. Companies that craft productive and attractive cultures should win.

- We have summarized the work on intangibles into an architecture for intangibles that suggests four levels of intangible value:

  - Keeping promises. Executives need to manage expectations and make sure that they can deliver what they promise.

  - Having a clear strategy for growth. Executives need to have a story and strategy about how they will grow in the future. They cannot be all things to all people.

  - Developing core competencies. Core competencies are the functional requirements for a firm to succeed: supplier management, IT, manufacturing, marketing, distribution, financial discipline, etc. A firm must align these core competencies to a company's strategies.

6

    – Ensuring organization capabilities. Organization capabilities are the identity of the firm. Ulrich & Smallwood (2003) propose seven capabilities that leaders use to build intangible value. These include: Shared Mind-set/Culture, Talent, Speed, Learning, Accountability, Collaboration, and Quality of Leadership. They assert that intangibles can become tangible when they are understood and managed properly.

Some Key Sources

Dess, G. G., & Pickens, J. C. (1999). *Beyond productivity: How leading companies achieve superior performance by leveraging their human capital.* New York: AMACOM.

Kaplan, R. & Norton, D. (2004). Measuring the strategic readiness of intangible assets [Special issue on developing leaders]. *Harvard Business Review,* 52-63.

Lev, B. (2001). *Intangibles: Management, measurement, and reporting.* Washington, DC: Brookings Institution Press.

Micucci, J., & Laffey, J. (2003, April). Shareholders benefit from organizations that focus on building great leaders [Press Release]. Hewitt Associates, Lincolnshire, IL.

Slywotzky, A. J. (1986). *Value migration: How to think several moves ahead of the competition.* Boston: Harvard Business School Press.

Ulrich, D., & Smallwood, N. (2003). *How to build value through people and organization: Why the bottom line isn't.* Hoboken, NJ: Wiley & Sons.

Watson Wyatt Worldwide. (2001). *Human Capital Index*®*: Human capital as a lead indicator of shareholder value.* Washington, DC.

6

WORKFORCE STABILITY

7.

Organizational downsizing today is:

SELECT ONE:

☐ A. Much more common in U.S. companies than other companies around the world.

☐ B. Much more common in non–U.S. companies.

☐ C. Much more common in U.S. companies; whereas, organizational *upsizing* is more common around the world.

☐ D. Much more common outside the U.S.; whereas, organizational *upsizing* is much more common in U.S. companies.

☐ E. Common to companies around the world, as is organizational upsizing.

7

7. Organizational downsizing today is:

The correct answer is E. Common to companies around the world, as is organizational upsizing.

HOW SURE ARE WE AT THIS TIME?				
1	2	3	**4**	5
Hint	Suggestive	Trending	**Substantial**	Solid

Discussion

Corporate layoffs, divestitures, and plant closings have become commonplace in American business and industry today. What once were infrequent and, in some instances, unheard-of occurrences in most organizations now have become regularly occurring actions. As the global economy changed during the late1980s and early 1990s, the dynamics in the workplace likewise changed. Companies in the U.S. were at the forefront of shedding, what was perceived as, excess labor. Throughout the 1990s decade, U.S. corporations downsized approximately half a million jobs per year. This figure increased to over two million jobs per year from 2001–2004 (Bureau of Labor Statistics 2006).

It is easy to forget that not too long ago U.S. companies espoused the virtues of stability, security, lifetime employment, and long-range planning. In 1956, William H. Whyte coined the term, "organization man," to describe a phenomenon in corporate America in which a (male) employee invested himself completely into his company. He would work 50- to 60-hour weeks, relocate on a minute's notice, and demonstrate blind loyalty to the organization. In return, he received a good job with good pay, was offered plenty of advancement opportunities, and received generous employee benefits (e.g., family health care coverage, company pensions).

7

It was a period of "a fair day's work for a fair day's pay"—a womb-to-tomb mentality (De Meuse & Tornow, 1990; Rousseau, 1995). It was a time of stability and security for the employee and employer alike. Nowadays, it appears that organizational agility, employee flexibility, and strategic nimbleness are valued. Companies are constantly in a state of flux, remaking and reengineering themselves, continuingly bending and flexing to meet the needs of an ever-changing global marketplace (Friedman, 2005; Mische, 2001; O'Toole & Lawler, 2006).

The question is (1) whether workforce upheaval is really as prevalent as it may appear, and if it is, (2) are other countries around the world also experiencing this state of labor dynamics? In other words, are companies around the globe continually upsizing and downsizing their workforce?

Selected Research

- Workforce reduction in the U.S. has been studied in a stream of research conducted by Ken De Meuse and his colleagues. Initially, they focused on downsizing among the Fortune 100 companies from 1988–1991. They report that 65% of those companies which had downsized in 1988 downsized again in 1989, and 82% downsized yet again in 1990 (De Meuse, Vanderheiden, & Bergmann, 1994). In a subsequent study, they investigated the Fortune 100 over a 12-year period (1988–2000) and found that these companies continued to downsize (De Meuse, Bergmann, Vanderheiden, & Roraff, 2004). In fact, they reported that some companies implemented layoffs every year during this period (e.g., General Motors). On the other hand, it should be pointed out the same U.S. companies that were laying off employees were hiring new ones, presumably with the types of skills needed to implement new strategies. The American Management Association found that 72% of the companies which eliminated jobs in the previous year also reported that they had created new ones (Koretz, 2000).

7

47

- Wayne Cascio and Clifford Young (2003) examined both downsizing and upsizing in U.S. companies during an 18-year period. Specifically, they tracked employment (as well as asset) changes in the Standard & Poor's (S&P) 500 from 1982 to 2000. To control for employment changes due to mergers, acquisitions, or divestitures, they eliminated those companies from their analysis. They found 10.2% of the companies had *reduced* their employment by more than 5% during this time; whereas, 6.4% had *increased* employment by more than 5%.

- Historically, Japanese companies dealt with declining market conditions through wage adjustment, reduction of overtime hours, and the dismissal of contract laborers. Oriental cultures traditionally have supported lifelong relationships between employees and employers (Ahmadjian & Robinson, 2001; Ouchi, 1981). In China, for example, mores were so powerful at one time that organizational downsizing was referred to as "taking away someone's rice bowl," because the company would be removing an individual's ability to provide income for himself and his family. However, as the stock market burst and the economy stagnated during the 1990s, highly visible companies such as Toyota, Mitsubishi, and Sony began to lay off employees. Other lesser-known firms soon followed suit. As the economy bounced back, these companies then rehired and retooled the workforce.

- Downsizing and upsizing trends in Japanese companies also were investigated by De Meuse and his fellow researchers. They followed employment levels in the 71 largest public companies in Japan over a 14-year period (1991–2004). Their data revealed that only three of those 71 companies did not implement a downsizing during this time (Honda, Toyota, and Nippon Dentsu). Companies such as Asahi Mutual Life Insurance, East Japan Railroad, Mazda, Mitsubishi Heavy Industry, Nippon Steel, and Nissan conducted downsizings several times during this period. They found that Nippon

7

Steel, for example, implemented a reduction-in-force 12 of the 14 years.

- Likewise, De Meuse et al. (2006) observed that these same 71 Japanese companies upsized their workforce on several occasions. For example, Bridgestone, Canon, Matsushita Electronic, Sony, and Toyota added employees 10 or more years during this 14-year period. What became very apparent is a continuous recalibration of the labor force in Japan. For instance, whereas Sanyo Electronic downsized four times, they also upsized six times. Zaun (2005) also noted that many Japanese companies have been replacing full-time employees with part-timers and contract workers.

- Although strong labor unions and governmental laws have hampered efforts of European companies to downsize, numerous labor adjustments have occurred throughout England, France, Germany, the Netherlands, Belgium, Turkey, and the like. Multinational corporations, such as Ford, General Electric, and General Motors, have implemented several waves of job cuts throughout Europe in order to avoid plant closings. Moreover, European companies themselves (including British Airways, Vivendi, Alcatel, and Volvo) have experienced layoffs, divestitures, and closings in recent years. French companies have even offered monetary incentives to entice employees to leave their payrolls in order to start their own entrepreneurial ventures. Likewise, as the European economy grew and markets expanded, employees were hired (Norris, 2006).

7

- The Maquiladora program in Mexico prospered throughout the 1990s but substantially subsided during the past five years. Maquiladoras are manufacturing factories located in Mexico which are owned by foreign companies. Companies headquartered in Korea, Japan, Germany, the U.S., and elsewhere ship raw materials and parts for assembly. The processed goods are returned to the home country (with little or no tax) to be sold. In 2001, there were approximately

50,000 Maquiladora plants located in every region of Mexico, employing more than 1.3 million Mexicans. Since 2001, however, tens of thousands of jobs have been lost due to the appreciation of the peso, changes in the way the processed goods are taxed, and modifications in Mexico's trade policy (Sargent & Matthews, 2003).

- Unemployment and employment rates are another indication that workforce stability is changing. Traditionally, Europe had high unemployment, brought on by rigid labor laws that made it difficult to fire workers and, therefore, discouraged companies from hiring them. In contrast, the U.S. had low unemployment due to its robust and flexible economy. During the past several years, unemployment in the U.S. has increased, hovering around the 5% to 7% range (Rosen, 2005). This rate remains lower than in Europe, but compares very closely with Japan and Australia in recent times ("Australia: Rise in," 2006; Zaun, 2005). In addition, one can also contrast employment rate. A decade ago (in 1995), the employment rate in the U.S. for men aged 25 to 54 was 87.6%; whereas, in Europe, the rate was 85.3%—a difference of 2.3 percentage points. By 2005, the U.S. rate had decreased and the Europe figure had increased, leaving a difference of just 0.3 percentage point (Norris, 2006).

So what difference do these findings make?

- The next time someone asks, "What do GM, GE, AT&T, and Lucent Technologies have in common with Nissan, Hitachi, Alcatel, British Airways, and Sony?" now, you can have an answer. At least, one thing they have in common is corporate restructuring. Both sets of companies have continuously recalibrated their workforces to meet the changing needs of the marketplace and the changing level of the competition and the economy. And, it is not just downsizing the workforce, but revamping it (sometimes downsizing, sometimes acquiring talent).

- Cultural mores in the Orient and governmental laws and labor unions in Europe continue to make hiring and firing employees more difficult there than in the U.S. However, permanent employment in Japanese and European companies likewise is being questioned today. Executives in those countries appear to be reacting in large measure the same as U.S. executives when faced with increased global competition, declining levels of growth, and reduced sales. Workforce stability is giving way (albeit at a slower pace) to organizational agility and strategic flexibility. Large, global companies tend to act similarly to each other to compete with other large, global companies.

- The bottom line is that we truly are becoming a global economy. As Thomas Friedman asserted, "The world is flat." Organizational leaders must constantly readjust their workforce to remain competitive, no matter what country of the planet the company calls home. With everyone "going global," continuous downsizing and upsizing is becoming the norm.

Some Key Sources

Ahmadjian, C., & Robinson, P. (2001). Safety in numbers: Downsizing and the deinstitutionalization of permanent employment in Japan. *Administrative Science Quarterly, 46,* 622-654.

Australia: Rise in Q2 headline inflation to 4% and labour market data make another 25-basis point rate rise almost certain in August. (2006, July 28). *Hilfe Daily Briefing,* pp. 1, 3.

Bureau of Labor Statistics. (2006). *Mass layoff statistics.* Washington, DC: The United States Department of Labor. Retrieved January 19, 2007, from htpp://www.bls.gov/mls/

7

Cascio, W. F., & Young, C. E. (2003). Financial consequences of employment-change decisions in major U.S. corporations, 1982-2000. In K. P. De Meuse & M. L. Marks (Eds.), *Resizing the organization: Managing layoffs, divestitures, and closings* (pp. 131-156). San Francisco: Jossey-Bass.

De Meuse, K. P., Bergmann, T. J., Vanderheiden, P. A., & Roraff, C. E. (2004). New evidence regarding organizational downsizing and a firm's financial performance: A long-term analysis. *Journal of Managerial Issues, 16,* 155-177.

De Meuse, K. P., Lester, S. W., Oh, S. H., & Kickul, J. (2006, August). *Downsizing and upsizing in Japan: Its frequency, magnitude, and effects on corporate performance.* Paper presented at the Academy of Management Meeting, Atlanta.

De Meuse, K. P., & Tornow, W. W. (1990). The tie that binds has become very, very frayed! *Human Resource Planning, 13,* 203-213.

De Meuse, K. P., Vanderheiden, P. A., & Bergmann, T. J. (1994). Announced layoffs: Their effect on corporate financial performance. *Human Resource Management Journal, 33,* 509-530.

Eisenstodt, G. (1995, July 31). Job Shokku. *Forbes, 156*(3), 42-43.

Friedman, T. L. (2005). *The world is flat: A brief history of the twenty-first century.* New York: Farrar, Straus & Giroux.

Kivimaki, M., Vahtera, J., Pentti, J., & Ferrie, J. E. (2000). Factors underlying the effect of organizational downsizing on health of employees: Longitudinal cohort study. *British Medical Journal, 320,* 971-975.

Koretz, G. (2000, March 13). Hire math: Fire 3, add 5. *BusinessWeek,* p. 28.

Mische, M. A. (2001). *Strategic renewal: Becoming a high-performance organization.* Upper Saddle River, NJ: Prentice Hall.

Norris, F. (2006, September 30). A statistic that shortens the distance to Europe. *The New York Times,* p. C 3.

7

O'Toole, J., & Lawler, E. E., III. (2006). *The new American workplace.* New York: Palgrave Macmillan.

Ouchi, W. G. (1981). *Theory Z: How American business can meet the challenge of Japanese management.* Reading, MA: Addison-Wesley.

Rosen, H. S. (2005, May 18). Data bait. *The Wall Street Journal*, p. A 14.

Rousseau, D. M. (1995). *Psychological contracts in organizations: Understanding written and unwritten agreements.* Thousand Oaks, CA: Sage.

Sargent, J., & Matthews, L. (2003, March-April). Boom and bust: Is it the end of Mexico's Maquiladoras? *Business Horizons, 46*(2), 57-64.

Whyte, W. H., Jr. (1956). *The organization man.* New York: Simon & Schuster.

Zaun, T. (2005, June 1). Japan's unemployment rate fell to 6-year low in April. *The New York Times*, p. C 7.

7

8.

Who is most likely to change as a result of receiving 360-degree feedback?

SELECT ONE:

☐ A. Those who overrate themselves compared to how others rate them.

☐ B. Those who underrate themselves.

☐ C. Those whose ratings are the same as other raters.

☐ D. Everyone improves equally, but not much, regardless of the accuracy of self-ratings.

☐ E. There is no clear relationship between accuracy of self-ratings and who changes based upon feedback.

8

8.   Who is most likely to change as a result of receiving 360-degree feedback?

The correct answer is A: Those who overrate themselves compared to how others rate them.

HOW SURE ARE WE AT THIS TIME?				
1	2	3	**4**	5
Hint	Suggestive	Trending	**Substantial**	Solid

Discussion

There is substantial evidence indicating that how you rate yourself compared to how others rate you predicts a lot. In general, "overraters" have the most to learn from others' feedback and typically are the most surprised. In contrast, people who score themselves just like others score them have no surprises and few gaps; whereas, people who "underrate" themselves are pleasantly surprised. The overraters, on the other hand, have the most distance to go. Research reveals that those employees whose views are most out of whack with others around them have the greatest opportunity to change, shifting their self-views and possibly improving their performance.

Selected Research

8

- Smither, London, Vasilopoulos, Reilly, Millsap, and Salvemini (1995) showed overraters improve, regardless of whether or not they received individual feedback. So, simply learning about what the other raters see and value with regard to the behavior of managers was enough to prompt performance improvements.

- Walker and Smither (1995) found that managers who initially received low or moderate ratings from their subordinates showed more improvement over time than managers who initially received higher ratings. Such a finding suggests that 360-degree feedback is beneficial, especially for those who initially receive poor or moderate ratings.

- Atwater, Rouse, and Fischthal (1995) report that when self- and other ratings are in agreement and also high, effectiveness is high. Effectiveness decreases as self- and other ratings agree and become lower. In addition, performance tends to be lower when self-ratings are greater than other ratings. Effectiveness was higher when self-ratings were lower than other ratings as well. So, underraters performed better than overraters.

- In a study of over 1,800 managers examining the effects of upward feedback, Johnson and Ferstl (1999) found that managers who overrated themselves relative to how others rated them showed more improvement from one year to the next than did those who underrated themselves. In fact, the performance of underraters tended to decline from one year to the next.

- In terms of actual promotion (as well as performance), the higher the self-rating compared with those of other groups, the more likely a person is to be later terminated (Lombardo & Eichinger, 2003). Those who are terminated rate themselves higher. Those who are not promoted rate more similarly to their rater groups. And those who are promoted rate themselves lower than do any rater group. The same trend holds for career stallers. Those terminated rate themselves lower (more favorable) on career stalling behaviors; those promoted rate themselves higher (less favorable) on career-stalling behaviors.

8

So what difference do these findings make?

- **To the person getting feedback:** If you have received feedback and learned that you tend to overrate your skills compared to how others see you, take caution. You may not have an accurate view of yourself. You may have flaws that others see that you don't. You may be headed down the path of derailment. Check your calibration. Why did you rate yourself higher? Are there any particular skills where you rated yourself much higher? What would be true about you and your career if you are the person your raters are describing? Do you have enough to do what you want to do in your career? Do you need to get better in some things? Look back at past feedback you have in your files. Did the same thing happen before? This is a caution sign. Get more data. Get a friend or coach to help. Self-awareness is one key to success. Be cautious about your bold decisions because they may be wrong. Find some friends who can give you candid feedback and who will help you figure out how you really behave.

- **To the person giving feedback:** For those of you giving feedback to an overrater, it is in the best interest of the person to know that he or she may be heading for trouble. Make them aware of the implications. Show them this research. Ask them what they think it means for them? Ask them if this is a pattern in other settings outside this data feedback? Help them craft new, better-calibrated self-views. Talk about the career of the person the raters are describing. Not alerting them to their potential fate is not doing them any favors.

- **To the organization:** Overraters need more calibrating feedback and assistance. They also might be the ones to benefit most from the process. See if there is a pattern of over- or underraters in the company.

8

Some Key Sources

Atwater, L., Roush, P., & Fischthal, A. (1995). The influence of upward feedback on self- and follower ratings of leadership. *Personnel Psychology, 48*, 35-59.

Johnson, J. W., & Ferstl, K. L. (1999). The effects of interrater and self-other agreement on performance improvement following upward feedback. *Personnel Psychology, 52*, 271-303.

Lombardo, M., & Eichinger, R. (2003). *The LEADERSHIP ARCHITECT® norms and validity report*. Minneapolis: Lominger International: A Korn/Ferry Company.

Smither, J. W., London, M., Vasilopoulos, N. L., Reilly, R. R., Millsap, R. E., & Salvemini, N. (1995). An examination of the effects of an upward feedback program over time. *Personnel Psychology, 48*, 1-34.

Walker, A. G., & Smither, J. W. (1999). A five-year study of upward feedback: What managers do with their results matters. *Personnel Psychology, 52*, 393-423.

8

BUSINESS STRATEGY

9.

The use of a CRM (customer relationship management) strategy and system:

SELECT ONE:

☐ A. Significantly improves organization performance.

☐ B. Actually alienates a large portion of customers because of knowing too much about them.

☐ C. Helps in some industries, is neutral in some, and is negative in others.

☐ D. Helps strategically, although the software is not quite there yet, leading to mixed results (depending upon which software vendor you select).

☐ E. Helps if the strategy, support system, and the technology work well together.

9

9. The use of a CRM (customer relationship management) strategy and system:

The correct answer is E: Helps if the strategy, support system, and the technology work well together.

HOW SURE ARE WE AT THIS TIME?				
1	2	**3**	4	5
Hint	Suggestive	**Trending**	Substantial	Solid

Discussion

With technological and data management advances, organizations are increasingly capable of tracking consumers more closely in terms of things like preferences and profitability, customizing communications, and tailoring their marketing and delivery efforts in a more customer-by-customer approach. A primary source of customer information is knowing simply how big (or small) a player any customer is. Sometimes customers are small players but spend a lot with one organization; other times they are large players but spend a little (or a lot) with one organization. Customer Relationship Management (CRM) helps determine the priority or important customers.

Customer relationship management programs are technology-driven systems designed to enable organizations to fulfill consumer needs more profitably. They begin by segmenting customers along dimensions like their volume, profitability, and potential. The central feature of CRM approaches is mutual beneficiality for organizations and consumers (Boulding, Staelin, Ehret, & Johnston, 2005). Customers get better served and the organization benefits through improved performance. Also, central to the concept is the belief that consumers are involved and concerned with the entire buying experience, not just the purchase of a product or service. Customer relationships through

9

this perspective are treated like other valued organizational assets—carefully cultivated and managed. The CRM approach is contrasted with the traditional "4P" approach to marketing (product, price, promotion, and placement) that focuses solely on the point of transaction. Building relationships with targeted customers means that the company will create a customer centric experience more than just a transaction.

The adoption of CRM assumes a view of customer relations as a strategic organizational investment, resulting in more loyal, consistent, and predictable consumer behavior. Especially in industries that do not have a great deal of differentiation in products, the quality of customer service can make an organization stand out. A premise of CRM is that firms seek more customer share than market share. Customer share means that a firm wants a targeted customer (one who buys a lot of what the firm sells) for life. Amazon wants to gain customer share of those who buy books; Marriott's Rewards® program attracts guests who stay hundreds of nights a year in hotels. Customer share requires that the organization understand who their target customers are now and in the future, and then build ways to bond or connect with them in the short- and long-term. Harley-Davidson® has done a masterful job of bringing their motorcycle owners—the HOGs (Harley Owners Group®)—into a community where they can share their common interests in motorcycles and build the Harley brand.

Although some research fails to show a positive relationship between the use of CRM and desired outcomes (such as increased customer retention rates), this ineffectiveness is likely attributable to mismanaged or uncoordinated programs. Knowing what to do with customers does not mean that it always happens. The preponderance of the evidence seems to support the contention that "well-run CRM activities are associated with better organizational performance (cf., Jayachandran et al., 2005; Ryals, 2005). It is important that the CRM strategy is the focus and that supporting technology

9

serves a support function, rather than vice versa (i.e., do not find a technology and develop the CRM program around that).

Selected Research

- Implementing business-to-consumer CRM activities resulted in a 270% profit increase (above target) for one bank department (Ryals, 2005). The CRM strategy in use for this loan-issuing department largely centered around focusing on profitable consumers and "screening out" projected nonprofitable customers. This research suggests that for both business-to-business and business-to-consumer applications, profitable CRM applications need to consider the relative value of the targeted consumer.

- The IT systems of CRM increase an organization's knowledge of its consumers which, in turn, increase customer satisfaction (Mithas, Krishnan, & Fornell, 2005). Additionally, the gain in knowledge of customers is further increased if an organization shares information with supply chain partners.

- Hong-kit Yim, Anderson, and Swaminathan (2004) assert that successful CRM implementation is dependent on the following four things: (1) key customer focus, (2) using CRM as an organizing framework, (3) knowledge management, and (4) developing and/or utilizing appropriate technology. The authors contend that the mutual consideration of the first three of these domains leads to greater customer satisfaction, retention, and sales growth. It should be noted that their study failed to demonstrate a direct relationship between specific types of technology and customer satisfaction, retention, or growth.

- With stronger ties to organizations, customers become more knowledgeable of the company's products and services. Although these consumers develop longer-term relationships, the quality of service remains extremely important—as important as it is to new customers. The

9

moral of this study is to *not* take long-term customers for granted, assuming they will remain loyal. It is important to remember that the quality of service provided is equally important for retention of current customers as it is for the attraction of new customers (Bell, Auh, & Smalley, 2005).

- Jayachandran, Sharma, Kaufman, and Raman (2005) documented a complex relationship between using CRM technology and improving customer retention and satisfaction. Engaging in "relational information processes" that provide feedback to complaints, communicate quickly and effectively, and generally view customer relationships as a valuable asset increases the effectiveness of CRM programs. CRM in this light facilitates a relationship-oriented customer orientation. Without this strategic orientation, CRM could feasibly *hurt* retention and satisfaction.

So what difference do these findings make?

- Evidence shows that a CRM strategy and software improves organizational performance. Some customers are more valuable to the organization than others. The old 80/20 rule is probably more real than not. Eighty percent of the organization's performance probably comes from 20% of its customers. CRM helps classify customers in terms of value and worth to the organization. This is not just a data play, but rather using data to make intelligent decisions that will connect targeted customers to the firm. These actions might include involving customers in people decisions such as staffing, training, performance management, and communication. It likewise could include customer input in strategy decisions such as product design, features, distribution, and allocation of resources. Technology provides the data, but leaders need to provide the insight and wisdom of connecting with target customers.

9

- CRM strategy and systems help serve each individual customer better because it helps focus the entire organization on the needs of one customer at a time, matching its products and services and delivery to the needs of each customer. Mass customization means that each customer may feel treated in a unique and special way.

- CRM implementation should be need-driven (as opposed to technology-driven). That is, a firm should not find a CRM platform and work within its limitations. In contrast, organizations should select a consumer orientation and pursue a CRM platform that supports this strategy.

- CRM success does not seem dependent on industry, it is rather a function of coordination and implementation. Systems must all be interconnected to effectively manage consumer needs. Suppliers and front-line employees, in particular, need to be aligned with the CRM goals in order to deliver high-quality customer service.

9

Some Key Sources

Bell, S. J., Auh, S., & Smalley, K. (2005). Customer relationship dynamics: Service quality and customer loyalty in the context of varying levels of customer expertise and switching costs. *Journal of the Academy of Marketing Science, 33,* 169-183.

Boulding, W., Staelin, R., Ehret, M., & Johnston, W. J. (2005). A customer relationship management roadmap: What is known, potential pitfalls, and where to go. *Journal of Marketing, 69,* 155-166.

Hong-kit Yim, F., Anderson, R. E., & Swaminathan, S. (2004). Customer relationship management: Its dimensions and effect on customer outcomes. *Journal of Personal Selling and Sales Management, 24,* 263-278.

Payne, A., & Frow, P. (2005). A strategic framework for customer relationship management. *Journal of Marketing, 69,* 167-176.

Jayachandran, S., Sharma, S., Kaufman, P., & Raman, P. (2005). The role of relational information processes and technology use in customer relationship management. *Journal of Marketing, 69,* 177-192.

Mithas, S., Krishnan, M. S., & Fornell, C. (2005). Why do customer relationship management applications affect customer satisfaction? *Journal of Marketing, 69,* 201-209.

Ryals, L. (2005). Making customer relationship management work: The measurement and profitable management of customer relationships. *Journal of Marketing, 69,* 252-261.

9

10.

What effect do strong subcultures have on an organization's overall culture?

SELECT ONE:

☐ A. They undermine the overall culture, making it less effective.

☐ B. They create silos within the organization, making communication and work across boundaries more difficult.

☐ C. They allow outlets for individual expression at the local level, and therefore make for a happier, more satisfied workforce.

☐ D. They allow strong central culture organizations to be more agile without losing their overall strength.

☐ E. They create inflexibility due to their divisive nature of multiple cultures within organizations.

10

10. What effect do strong subcultures have on an organization's overall culture?

The correct answer is D: They allow strong central culture organizations to be more agile without losing their overall strength.

HOW SURE ARE WE AT THIS TIME?				
1	2	**3**	4	5
Hint	Suggestive	**Trending**	Substantial	Solid

Discussion

Culture matters as long as the culture inside is aligned with customer expectations outside. Having values and a common mind-set everyone can identify with is a powerful tool for effectiveness, made more powerful when the mind-set aligns with customer expectations. Strong cultures guide decision making, resource allocation, and priority setting. Customer centric cultures guide actions to meet customer expectations. An organization's culture brand can be an additional tool to attract and hire people who fit the needs of the firm as defined by customers. On the other hand, in any large organization, there will be functional, geographic, and SBU cultures that differ somewhat from the central culture. Instead of making all subunits comply, it seems best to let the subcultures flourish. What then happens, is when the central culture needs to shift to meet marketplace conditions and pressures, the subcultures hold things together while the central culture shifts. In large and complex firms with many subcultures, the shared culture generally focuses on the process of how work is done more than the content of the work. For example, General Electric is a complex conglomerate of 15 or so diverse businesses. The shared culture in the '90s was speed, simplicity, and self–confidence, and in the next decade, invention, innovation,

10

and customer focus. Both of these cultures are the processes by which work is done, which may vary depending on the business. Speed in building power plants is quite different from speed in financial services. Innovation for appliances might be very different than innovation for medical devices. The shared culture is the process that will be adapted to each business. In another way, a subculture may need to dramatically shift to meet some special circumstance locally, but will be surrounded by stable other subcultures and the central culture while it readjusts.

Selected Research

- Boisnier and Chatman (2003) review the literature on subcultures and offer a theory of why subcultures can be beneficial to organizations. Specifically, the authors reason that subcultures can respond to and address change without taxing the values and norms of the larger organization. In this way, subcultures can act as mechanisms for responding to volatility in the environment, while maintaining the more beneficial stable characteristics of the larger culture. The authors go on to assert that strong cultures can foster creativity and innovation by stimulating subcultures that value creativity.

- Martin and Siehl (1983) put forth a typology of subcultures consisting of three distinct types. *Enhancing* subcultures consist of members who are more radical and intense than others in their support of the overall culture. These members are ultra-committed to the organization's values. *Countercultures* are at odds with the core values of the dominant culture and adhere to values that conflict with organizational values. Such countercultures threaten the strength of the dominant culture. Finally, *orthogonal* subcultures consist of those who embrace the values of the overall culture, but who also have their own set of values that are distinct, but not at odds, with the overall culture. Where there are differences among values between orthogonal

10

subcultures and the overall culture, those differences tend to be in areas that are not central to the organization's basic mission. In other words, the differences are more in the periphery values. It is the orthogonal subcultures that can be beneficial to the organization when it needs to adapt to changing conditions.

- Galunic and Eisenhardt (2001) report on an organization where subcultures are beneficial to the company's overall success. In this company, different divisions, while governed by a very strong centralized value system, are encouraged and even rewarded for competing with each other for market share. Such competition ensures that the company fields the best lineup of divisions against external competitors. At the same time, employees embrace cooperative values that prevent competitive behavior from deteriorating into chaos and antagonism.

- Successful innovation requires the generation of novel ideas as well as following through with implementation. Kanter (1988) suggests subcultures can provide a place for creativity to grow and a way to coordinate with members of the dominant culture to achieve successful implementation.

So what difference do these findings make?

- A strong but flexible and adaptable central culture connected to customers tends to aid consistent performance. On the other hand, the organization should be supportive and tolerant of cultural deviations for distinct locations, functions, and product lines. These differences often occur because customers of these different organization units have differing expectations of those units. The advantages of subcultures are many. Forcing compliance with too heavy a hand doesn't seem to be as good a strategy as strong central guidance with flexibility and tolerance for aligned and justifiable differences across different units.

10

Some Key Sources

Boisnier, A., & Chatman, J. (2003). The role of subcultures in agile organizations. In R. Peterson & E. Mannix (Eds.), *Leading and managing people in the dynamic organization* (pp. 87-112). Mahwah, NJ: Lawrence Earlbaum Associates.

Galunic, D. C., & Eisenhardt, K. M. (2001). Architectural innovation and modular corporate forms. *Academy of Management Journal, 44*, 1229-1249.

Kanter, R. M. (1988). When a thousand flowers bloom: Structural, collective, and social conditions for innovation and organization. In L. Cummings & B. Staw (Eds.), *Research in Organizational Behavior* (pp. 169-211). Stamford, CT: JAI Press.

Martin, J., & Siehl, C. (1983). Organizational culture and counterculture: An uneasy symbiosis. *Organizational Dynamics, 12*(2), 52-65.

10

11.

What will the training and development of the baby boomer generation (age 45+) look like going forward?

SELECT ONE:

☐ A. Access barriers to training need to be removed for older workers.

☐ B. The aging workforce provides mostly valuable experience and a sense of history—less development/training is needed toward the end of their careers.

☐ C. Motivation to learn is more important than age in predicting outcomes, but motivation to learn new things decreases with age, therefore less training is needed.

☐ D. The aging part of the workforce is not as computer literate, so technology adjustments need to be made (i.e., large-print materials, audio-enhancement, paper-based materials made available).

☐ E. The unfortunate fact is that older people learn more slowly and are less motivated to learn new things, so training and development should be tapered off slowly.

11

11. **What will the training and development of the baby boomer generation (age 45+) look like going forward?**

The correct answer is A: Access barriers to training need to be removed for older workers.

HOW SURE ARE WE AT THIS TIME?				
1	2	3	**4**	5
Hint	Suggestive	Trending	**Substantial**	Solid

Discussion

It is not uncommon for the average worker in early twenty-first century organizations in North America and Europe to exceed 40 years of age. The increased numbers of midlife and older people in the U.S. workforce is a result of several factors, including the aging of the baby boomer generation, lower birthrates during the last third of the twentieth century, and economic conditions that discourage early retirement.

Although the workforce in North America and Europe is aging, it is important to realize that "older workers are as flexible, trainable, and cost-effective as younger employees" (Sterns & Miklos, 1995, p. 249).

Traditional career models assumed a linear and stair-step character to career development. Employees progress along a predictable linear path. At the end of that path is a stage at which employee skills stabilize and the worker leaves the organization at retirement age. One of the problems with this model is that it associates age with career stages. The traditional career trajectory—entry, stability, retirement—is no longer the norm (see Chapter 36).

Training and development challenges and solutions apply, regardless of the age of the workforce. Advancement and development barriers have been well documented for older workers, but these are not typically capability-based age-related barriers (cf., Armstrong-Stassen & Templer, 2005; Taylor & Urwin, 2001). Rather, the barriers to training and development opportunities for older workers are organizational. Older workers tend to be offered training less than their younger counterparts. They also are more likely to be viewed by coworkers as not needing or wanting training. Older workers, who are called *traditionalists,* (Dychtwald, Erickson, & Morison 2006) tend to learn by experience and reading more than younger workers, who learn through technology.

Part of the stereotype and myth of aged (or highly tenured) workers not "wanting" training is due to a perception that these workers are less likely to obtain the benefits from training/skills development. This is probably erroneous thinking—older (and highly tenured) workers are likely to desire training and development opportunities because they assist in the maintenance of professional competence (the extent to which an employee functions well on essential tasks within a given profession; Sterns, Barrett, Czaja, & Barr, 1994). Training programs that are aimed at an aging workforce, therefore, should focus on (1) trainee motivation (i.e., to maintain one's professional competence), (2) the identification and removal of training barriers (i.e., perceptions of older workers as not needing training), as well as (3) training design (i.e., extended sessions may be needed to accommodate an aged workforce's learning style), and (4) learning techniques that draw on participants' experiences.

11

TRAINING			
EMPLOYEE CHARACTERISTIC	YOUNGER	MIDDLE AGE	OLDER
Preferred setting	Self-directed	Classroom	Small group
Role of technology	Integrated, visual	Solve problems	Gather information
Attention span	Short segments	Scan	Read
Interaction	Role play, experiment, question	Peer-to-peer discussion	Teach and learn
Short-term goal	Have fun	Good grades	Satisfaction
Long-term goal	Be marketable	Succeed at work	Remain viable
Insists upon	Relevance	Relevance	Relevance
Myth	Not motivated	Know enough	Slow learners

Adapted from Dychtwald, Erickson, & Morison (2006).

Selected Research

- The Bureau of Labor Statistics (2002) estimates that by 2010, almost half of the U.S. workforce will be made up of individuals aged 45 years or older. The report estimates similar workforce age trends in non-U.S. developed countries.

- According to the Institute of Management Administration's Safety Director's Report (2001), the category of workers aged 25–54 will grow 5.5% between 1998 and 2008; the category of workers 55 and over will increase almost 48% during that same time.

- Job performance generally does not suffer as workers age (Sterns & Miklos, 1995).

- Older workers are less likely to participate in training than are their younger counterparts. They are also less likely to be offered the opportunity to attend training. This leads researchers to conclude that the lower incidence of training is primarily attributable to organizations stereotyping older workers, rather than the willingness of the worker (Armstrong-Stassen & Templer, 2005; Taylor & Urwin, 2001).

- Research by Simpson, Greller, and Stroh (2002) found that it's the motivational variables (not chronological age or cognitive abilities) that account for barriers to employee development and successful work outcomes for middle-aged and older workers.

- A study conducted in Australia examined the connection between workers' attitudes on the concepts of work and learning at work and found that these concepts, not necessarily chronological age, accounted for successful integration into the workforce. The study further evaluated, by age group, the elements that constituted learning for younger and older workers and found that older workers believed that learning consisted of formal coursework and younger workers believed learning consisted of "on-site observing and experiencing."

- Research by Maurer and Rafuse (2001) argues that ADEA laws in the U.S. (which state that it is unlawful to discriminate against older workers in terms, conditions, or privileges of employment) may soon be expanded to include learning and development opportunities for older workers. Citing numerous age discrimination lawsuits, the researchers note an increase in litigation stemming from reduced training opportunities for older workers that, in turn, reduces their value to organizations.

So what difference do these findings make?
- Almost everyone will be managing an older workforce.

- Due primarily to stereotypes and myths, the older a group of workers gets, less training and development is offered and less is taken.

- Career tracks are not as linear as they were before. People move laterally and even down, and some start over later in life.

- The need to keep one's skills current does not decrease with age. The need to learn new skills is lifelong.

- Many of the barriers faced by older workers are due to unsupportable biases, myths, and stereotypes. The specific appointment of older worker advocates has been suggested but not yet empirically evaluated (Lefkovich, 1992). Furthermore, age awareness training (for managers of an older workforce) may help break down age-related training and development barriers.

- Older workers should be specifically targeted for training and development opportunities. This cohort will comprise a major percentage of early twenty-first century organizations; ensuring that this group is sufficiently trained/skilled is imperative. Additionally, training opportunities are important for retention (Armstrong-Stassen & Templer, 2005).

- It's also likely, as we forge headlong into virtual teams and e-learning applications, that you may have to slow down and backwards adapt training methods and distribution platforms to match the older workers' preferred learning styles and skills.

Some Key Sources

11

Armstrong-Stassen, M., & Templer, A. (2005). Adapting training for older employees: The Canadian response to an aging workforce. *Journal of Management Development, 24,* 57-67.

Bureau of Labor Statistics. (2002). *Occupational outlook handbook* (2002-2003 ed.). Washington, DC: U.S. Department of Labor.

Dychtwald, K., Erickson, T., & Morison, R. (2006). *Workforce crisis.* Boston, MA: Harvard Business School Press.

Griffiths, A. (1997). Ageing, health and productivity: A challenge for the new millennium. *Work & Stress, 11,* 197-214.

Institute of Management Administration. (2001, April). How to prepare for the coming older workforce. *IOMA's Safety Director's Report, 1*(4), 12-13.

Lefkovich, J. L. (1992). Older workers: Why and how to capitalize on their powers. *Employment Relations Today, 19,* 63-79.

Maurer, T. J., & Rafuse, N. E. (2001). Learning, *not litigating: Managing employee development and avoiding claims of age discrimination. Academy of Management Executive, 15*(4), *110-122.*

Pillay, H., Boulton-Lewis, G., Wilss, L., & Rhodes, S. (2003). Older *and younger workers' conceptions of work and learning at work: A challenge to emerging work practices. Journal of Education & Work, 16, 427-445.*

Simpson, P. A., Greller, M. M., & Stroh, L. K. (2002). Variations in human capital investment activity by age. Journal of Vocational Behavior, 61, 109-138.

Sterns, H. L., Barrett, G. V., Czaja, S. J., & Barr, J. K. (1994). Issues in work and aging. Journal of Applied Gerontology, 13, 7-19.

11

Sterns, H. L., & Miklos, S. M. (1995). The aging worker in a changing environment: Organizational and individual issues. Journal of Vocational Behavior, 47, 248-268.

Taylor, P., & Urwin, P. (2001). Age and participation in vocational education and training. *Work, Employment & Society*, 15, 763-779.

ADVANCEMENT OPPORTUNITIES

12.

What advancement (including a move) obstacles are especially difficult for dual-career families?

SELECT ONE:

☐ A. Differential status between the two career opportunities.

☐ B. Two careerists wanting a stable environment for children.

☐ C. Difficulty for the trailing partner to consider moving, including finding suitable work.

☐ D. The secondary earning partner getting the offer.

☐ E. The offer is seldom enough to counter the costs of the move.

12

12. What advancement (including a move) obstacles are especially difficult for dual-career families?

The correct answer is C: Difficulty for the trailing partner to consider moving, including finding suitable work.

HOW SURE ARE WE AT THIS TIME?				
1	2	3	**4**	5
Hint	Suggestive	Trending	**Substantial**	Solid

Discussion

At the turn of the twenty-first century, 64% of traditional families (husband, wife, and kids) were dual-income households. The past model of having one primary male earner represented only 19% of families (Bureau of Labor Statistics, 2000). Increasingly, organizations are developing programs and policies aimed at accommodating employees who are in dual-career families. Programs may include counseling, flextime, job-sharing, and/or day-care facilities. Policies can involve the allowance of partners to work within the same organization (or even department)— the relaxation of so-called "anti-nepotism" policies.

Although organizations are becoming more flexible with on-site "family friendly" policies and programs, employees who are offered opportunities for advancement that include transfer or relocation often raise concerns regarding partner employment (Eby et al., 2002). In fact, one of the few consistent predictors of "why employees turn down offers to relocate" is the negative attitudes of their spouse/partner (cf., Challiol & Mignonac, 2005; Eby & Russell, 2000).

Relocation is fairly common—16% of the American population relocates annually, and more than half of these individuals do so for work-related considerations. These numbers do not reflect voluntary versus involuntary relocation, however. Relocation is an important tool for flexible and growing organizations.

Selected Research

- The Department of Labor reports that dual careers describe more than 80% of marriages (Kruger, 1998). Dual-career households are more likely to give each career equal weight, rather than having one career take precedence over another.

- Although turn of the current century couples both work, this situation may be trending backwards. A Cornell University study (2000) reported that some working couples are reverting to a 1950's type of arrangement (a breadwinner and a housewife). These families cite a growing realization that "two careers do not allow an adequate quality of life."

- Ricklin (1991) noted a dramatic increase in employee refusals to relocate from 1986 (36% refusal rate) to 1989 (70% refusal rate). Part of this increase is due to a realization that relocation, even with a raise and promotion, will result in a loss of net income for the family. Employment assistance during relocation should therefore be focused on the spouse (as well as the relocating employee and the organization).

- Roughly 65% of employees who turn down a transfer offer do so for family reasons (Flynn, 1996). Forty-two percent of dual-income couples report a decrease in their standard of living after relocation (as opposed to 23% of single-income relocated employees). The majority of relocated spouses report lower salaries and benefits after relocation.

- Spouse/partner attitudes toward moving *greatly* impact an employee's willingness to relocate (Eby & Russell, 2000). Employees with children are also less likely to accept a relocation offer than are employees without children. A

12

relocation package that is attractive to both partners (or at least considerate of the partner's career needs) is more likely to be accepted.

- Willingness to relocate for dual-career families is unrelated to the relocating employee's gender or quality of marriage (Challiol & Mignonac, 2005). Willingness *is* related to spouse's willingness and the relative priority the family places on the spouse's career and quality of family life. In order for an employee to relocate, both partners have to find a solution that satisfies these priorities.

So what difference do these findings make?

- The relocating partner's attitude greatly influences whether a relocation offer will be accepted or rejected. Organizations that wish to increase the likelihood that a transfer will be accepted therefore need to make the relocation conditions attractive to both the relocating employee and his/her partner. In addition, the dependent children need to be considered in the relocation decisions. Assistance with the spouse's job search is increasingly crucial. This may include pursuing cooperative agreements with other (local) organizations to provide partner employment opportunities or engaging a search firm to help the spouse find satisfying employment.

- Although probably fraught with all kinds of other issues, employment of both partners might be worth pursuing.

- Involvement of nonemployed partners in organization activities and vision and strategy communications might lead to more willingness to support the employed partner.

- Asking current employees' family members to socialize and orient potential employees and their families helps prepare them and induct them to the new job.

- Attention needs to be paid to singles who work enormously hard in the new job, but often find discouragement after a period of time because they left behind their social community and do not take time to create a new one.

12

Some Key Sources

Bureau of Labor Statistics. (2000). *Employment characteristics of families summary*. Retrieved January 18, 2007, from http://www.bls.gov/news.release/famee.nr0.htm

Challiol, H., & Mignonac, K. (2005). Relocation decision-making and couple relationships: A quantitative and qualitative study of dual-earner couples. *Journal of Organizational Behavior, 26,* 247-274.

Eby, L. T., (2001). The boundaryless career experiences of mobile spouses in dual-earner marriages. *Group & Organization Management, 26,* 343-368.

Eby, L. T., DeMatteo, J. S., & Russell, J. E. A. (1997). Employment assistance needs of accompanying spouses following relocation. *Journal of Vocational Behavior, 50,* 291-307.

Eby, L. T., Douthitt, S. S., Noble, C., Atchley, K. P., & Ladd, R. T. (2002). Managerial support for dual-career relocation dilemmas. *Journal of Vocational Behavior, 60,* 354-373.

Eby, L. T., & Russell, J. E. A. (2000). Predictors of employee willingness to relocate for the firm. *Journal of Vocational Behavior, 57,* 42-61.

Flynn, G. (1996). Heck no – We won't go! *Personnel Journal, 75*(3), 37-42.

Kruger, P. (1998). The good news about working couples. *Parenting, 12*(2), 69.

Lawson, M. B., & Angle, H. L. (1994). When organizational relocation means family relocation: An emerging issue for strategic human resource management. *Human Resource Management, 33,* 33-54.

Ricklin, H. (1991). Spouse career relocation assistance is becoming an important part of corporate benefits package. *Employee Benefits Journal, 16*(1), 33-38.

12

13.

Is a happier worker a better worker?

SELECT ONE:

13

☐ A. Yes.

☐ B. Yes, but it depends upon the definition of "happiness."

☐ C. Only under conditions of low stress in the workplace.

☐ D. Might be, but it has never been documented in real-life research.

☐ E. There is actually a negative relationship with productivity; a positive relationship with satisfaction; happy people do not work as hard.

13. Is a happier worker a better worker?

The correct answer is B: Yes, but it depends upon the definition of "happiness."

13

HOW SURE ARE WE AT THIS TIME?				
1	2	3	**4**	5
Hint	Suggestive	Trending	**Substantial**	Solid

Discussion

The debate about happy workers being more productive has gone on for a long time. It is a constant subject of exploration and comment, but different researchers come to different conclusions. This probably started formally with the famous Hawthorne studies, where the "happy worker is a productive worker" hypothesis was first supported, then later questioned.

Really it depends on what is meant by the term "happy worker." The most consistent findings are that people with more *positive affect,* or who in other words have more positive *psychological well-being,* are in fact better workers. There is a distinction made between the concepts and the research on job satisfaction and productivity (in general not much relationship) and psychological well-being (there is a relationship). Both might result in increases in loyalty and increases in retention, but well-being has the stronger relationship to productivity.

Part of the difficulty in assessing the happier worker-better worker relationship is attributable to the complex relationship between positive affect, negative affect, and psychological well-being. Positive affect involves the experience of more positive feelings (i.e., joy, enthusiasm). Someone lower in positive affect does not experience as many positive emotions and may experience more boredom—getting excited about less and motivated by less. Negative affect involves the experience of more negative feelings (i.e., general anxiety, restlessness).

90

Someone low in negative affect experiences less of these feelings (i.e., these individuals might report contentment and/ or lack of negative feelings about things). Psychological well-being consists of a balance of both positive and negative affect (Charles, Reynolds, & Gatz, 2001). It is sometimes conceptualized as a balance between positive and negative affect, such that someone may experience greater well-being by either increasing positive affect or decreasing negative affect.

13

Generally, well-being in this sense can be conceptualized as "happiness" or the tendency to experience more positive and less negative emotional states—this is free of context and is not specific to any particular situation (i.e., it is different than the commonly cited "job satisfaction").

Taking all of this into consideration, the best answer to the happy worker question is: A worker who is satisfied at work is not necessarily a more productive employee, but a happy person is. Both states are good, but are different.

In old survey questions, people would ask, "Do you like your boss, pay, working conditions, and so forth?" These questions about satisfaction with work setting did not correlate much with productivity or performance. Now, questions are asked about engagement or commitment: To what extent does your boss give you the training or knowledge to do your job well? To what extent are you paid for doing the right work? These questions about engagement or commitment do relate to productivity. And, the questions about self-esteem and emotional maturity show that people with emotional well-being have the resilience to work hard.

Selected Research
- Cropanzano and Wright (2001) argue that historical findings are inconsistent (some confirm/some deny an effect) because of the many different definitions of "happiness" (job

satisfaction, lack of negative emotions). Their conclusion, after dismissing the measurement of "happiness" in a large number of studies, is that a happier (a deep presence of positive emotional states and feelings and less negative feelings) worker truly is a more productive worker.

13

- Trying again to explain some of the contradictory findings of previous researchers, Wright and Cropanzano (2000) explored the relative effects of (1) psychological well-being and (2) job satisfaction on performance. With two studies, they documented the well-being/performance relationships, but not the satisfaction/performance relationships.

- A comprehensive review of happiness-performance linkages across multiple life domains (relationships, health, work) found that happiness generally facilitates success, regardless of domain. The key element of "happiness" that is related to success is "positive affect," which is the essential element of well-being (Lyubomirsky, King, & Diener, 2005).

- High levels of well-being are associated with high performance up to a year after assessment (of well-being), but this association deteriorates as time between assessment increases. At a point of 4.5 to 5 years between assessments, there is no association between initial levels of "general happiness" and current (five years later) performance (Cropanzano & Wright, 1999).

- One precursor to well-being is the worker *belief* that progress is being made toward a goal (Wiese & Freund, 2005). Workers who are pursuing more difficult goals tend to have stronger associations between attainment of those goals and psychological well-being. Difficult goal-setting and careful assistance toward the attainment of those goals can positively impact employees' well-being.

- Although, maybe more people are generally happy rather than depressed (Diener & Diener, 1996). But we are constantly reminded of the pervasiveness of being "unhappy" (television and magazines are filled with information on depression and depression drugs, etc.). The establishment of Employee Assistance Programs (EAPs) for depressed employees is one way organizations can encourage unhappy workers to seek resources for betterment.

So what difference do these findings make?

13

- Organizations may be able to improve productivity through increasing the psychological well-being of their workforce. The two primary options would seem to be (1) in the selection process, select people who in the past and presently are more positive than negative in general, that is, they have and do currently demonstrate higher levels of psychological well-being, and/or (2) engage in management practices that enhance well-being.

- Managing well-being at work involves familiar best practice management tactics: Provide subordinates with challenging but attainable tasks, allow them a manageable degree of autonomy, and provide access to Employee Assistance Programs (EAPs). Informing, listening, and communicating also help.

- There is a subtle difference between job and organization satisfaction and psychological well-being. There are programmatic differences between helping people be more satisfied with their jobs and the organization and helping them with their psychological well-being. Paying people more, for example, might increase satisfaction more than well-being. Paying people more might increase retention but may not impact productivity as much. Setting tougher (stretch) goals might help increase well-being but may have the opposite impact on satisfaction.

- In the end, management has to think of well-being and satisfaction as two end-measurements. They lead to different outcomes and are caused by different programming. Both are positive but for different reasons.

13

Some Key Sources

Charles, S. T., Reynolds, C. A., & Gatz, M. (2001). Age-related differences and change in positive and negative affect over 23 years. *Journal of Personality and Social Psychology, 80,* 136-151.

Cropanzano, R., & Wright, T. A. (1999). A 5-year study of change in the relationship between well-being and job performance. *Consulting Psychology Journal: Practice and Research, 51,* 252-265.

Cropanzano, R., & Wright, T. A. (2001). When a "happy" worker is really a "productive" worker: A review and further refinement of the happy-productive worker thesis. *Consulting Psychology Journal: Practice and Research, 53,* 182-199.

Diener, E., & Diener, C. (1996). Most people are happy. *Psychological Science, 7,* 181-185.

Lyubomirsky, S., King, L., & Diener, E. (2005). The benefits of frequent positive affect: Does happiness lead to success? *Psychological Bulletin, 131,* 803-855.

Wiese, B. S., & Freund, A. M. (2005). Goal progress makes one happy, or does it? Longitudinal findings from the work domain. *Journal of Occupational and Organizational Psychology, 78,* 287-304.

Wright, T. A., & Cropanzano, R. (2000). Psychological well-being and job satisfaction as predictors of job performance. *Journal of Occupational Health Psychology, 5,* 84-94.

Wright, T. A., Cropanzano, R., & Meyer, D. G. (2004). State and trait correlates of job performance: A tale of two perspectives. *Journal of Business and Psychology, 18,* 365-383.

Wright, T. A., & Staw, B. M. (1999). Affect and favorable work outcomes: Two longitudinal tests of the happy-productive worker thesis. *Journal of Organizational Behavior, 20,* 1-23.

13

14.

Who make better leaders, men or women?

SELECT ONE:

☐ A. Women, because they are better with people than men.

☐ B. Men, because they are better at business than women.

14

☐ C. Women, because the majority of the people they manage are now women.

☐ D. It's a toss-up, although men and women have a general tendency to use different leadership styles.

☐ E. Men, because they have been leaders longer and have more experience.

14. Who make better leaders, men or women?

The correct answer is D: It's a toss-up, although men and women have a general tendency to use different leadership styles.

HOW SURE ARE WE AT THIS TIME?				
1	2	3	**4**	5
Hint	Suggestive	Trending	**Substantial**	Solid

14

Discussion

It's getting to be quite common in the popular and business press to announce that a recent survey declared women make better managers. Sometimes when women get higher scores on evaluations or 360-degree assessments, the conclusion drawn is that they are "better" somethings—usually leaders or managers. But alas, although that would be an exciting finding, it isn't (yet) true. There are many reasons (bias, avoidance of conflict, pioneer class—the few women who make it to the top of male organizations might be better, etc.) women as a class might score higher. Among them isn't that they are better managers.

Although there is generally still a "male" bias with regard to good management, popular media outlets, theoretical textbooks, and trade magazine articles frequently cite a female advantage in leadership (cf., Eagly & Carli, 2003a). The research findings have not generally supported either claim (cf., Butterfield & Grinnell, 1999; Vecchio, 2003).

Women are continuing to make advances in holding senior executive positions. While women occupied only 21% of managerial positions in the U.S. in 1976, this percentage rose to 35% in 1984 and 46% by 1999 (although executive positions remain largely male-occupied).

Although advances have been made, stereotypes of "good" managers still tend to reflect a masculine, rather than feminine, bias (Powell, Butterfield, & Parent, 2002). There are two stereotypes that have to be dealt with here: gender stereotypes (men are assertive, women are collegial) and managerial stereotypes (a good manager is aggressive, a bad manager is passive). The stereotype of the less assertive woman is consistent with the bad manager stereotype; the assertive man better "fits" in the good manager category.

Obviously, there are a number of problems in conceptualizing management or gender differences in this general manner. The basic problem is that the stereotypes do not seem to be true.

14

Female leaders tend to have a *preference* to focus on interdependence and collectivity more than autonomy and competition. However, a given manager in a given situation may choose to take an interdependent approach or not—additionally, the use of this approach may or may not be effective, depending on the situation. A good manager (male or female) knows his/her personal tendencies and also knows when to suppress those tendencies and when to utilize those tendencies.

Often, women begin to demonstrate more traditionally male characteristics in order to be recognized and promoted into senior management positions.

Selected Research
- Contrived laboratory experiments tend to confirm the relative preference of female leaders to use interpersonally oriented and participative leadership styles (as opposed to males' task oriented and controlling styles). These findings are not found as consistently in organizational settings, however, where the interpersonal versus task-orientation preference may disappear (Eagly & Carli, 2003b).

- Looking across multiple studies, Eagly, Johannesen-Schmidt, and van Engen (2003) found that women tend to be more transformational in their leadership styles than do men. Male leaders are also more likely than women to engage in laissez-faire behaviors and to use a management-by-exception approach (standard setting, rule enforcement, and a focus on mistakes). These tendencies, although consistent, are quite *small*.

- McColl-Kennedy and Anderson (2005) looked at the gender composition of manager-subordinate dyads, finding that the effective use of different management styles depended on the constituency of the dyad. For example, female leaders who had female subordinates were most likely to increase subordinate commitment and self-esteem if they engaged in a transformational leadership style. Regardless of subordinate gender, female managers elicited more subordinate optimism and organizational commitment than did their male counterparts.

- Powell, Butterfield, and Parent (2002) found that although women are occupying more managerial positions than they have in the past, the stereotypical "good manager" is still defined by predominantly masculine traits. This stereotype is held by men and women of varying ages, educational backgrounds, and tenure.

- Men and women's leadership skills tend to be quite similar, with women being slightly more interpersonally skilled than men, and men being slightly more skilled at business problem solving (Lombardo & Eichinger, 2005). With such moderate *group* differences, it is important to understand that any individual woman may out-problem-solve a man, while any individual man may excel beyond a female counterpart at interpersonal relationships. Overall, even taking into account the leadership style differences, men and women were rated equal in terms of effectiveness.

So what difference do these findings make?

- Science will ultimately (or should) trump the popular press. It isn't exciting to declare there is no difference between the effectiveness of male and female managers and leaders. But science will not stop the presses. For a long time into the future, these marginal conclusions will continue. There are significant constituencies who dearly wish for it to be true that women make better managers.

- This popular untruth will have some impact on management cultures. A sort of "battle of the genders" will be waged. Males who declare the proposition to be unsupported will be seen as biased and old-fashioned. Females who declare the myth in defense of something or to push a cause will be seen as uninformed partisans. All in all, a waste of time on the part of both sides.

14

- It is unlikely that there is a consistent leadership advantage for one gender versus the other across a wide variety of leadership positions. It is possible for one gender to have an advantage over another within any given position, depending on the needs of that position. What this means is there seems to be a small gender-difference in preferred leadership style, but this difference does not necessarily translate into differences in leadership *effectiveness.*

- For the long-term, simply, females have an EQ (people and interpersonal skills) advantage and males have a business and assertiveness advantage. Whether this slight group difference continues or not is anybody's guess. From a development standpoint, in general, males should receive earlier and more EQ training and development and females more business development.

- One of the problems of generalizing gender differences is that there is a large range of behaviors among both women and men. Looking at the average does not give a full description of the behaviors demonstrated by each group.

Some Key Sources

Becker, J., Ayman, R., & Korabik, K. (2002). Discrepancies in self/subordinates' perceptions of leadership behavior: Leader's gender, organizational context and leader's self-monitoring. *Group & Organization Management, 27,* 226-244.

Butterfield, D. A., & Grinnell, J. P. (1999). "Re-viewing" gender, leadership and managerial behavior: Do three decades of research tell us anything? In G. N. Powell (Ed.), *Handbook of gender and work* (pp. 223-238). Thousand Oaks, CA: Sage.

Eagly, A. H., & Carli, L. L. (2003a). The female leadership advantage: An evaluation of the evidence. *Leadership Quarterly, 14,* 807-834.

Eagly, A. H., & Carli, L. L. (2003b). Finding gender advantage and disadvantage: Systematic research integration is the solution. *Leadership Quarterly, 14,* 851-859.

Eagly, A. H., Johannesen-Schmidt, M. C., & van Engen, M. L. (2003). Transformational, transactional, and laissez-faire leadership styles: A meta-analysis comparing women and men. *Psychological Bulletin, 129,* 569-591.

Eagly, A. H., & Karau, S. J. (2002). Role congruity theory of prejudice toward female leaders. *Psychological Review, 109,* 573-598.

Lombardo, M. M., & Eichinger, R. W. (2005). *The leadership machine* (3rd ed.). Minneapolis: Lominger International: A Korn/Ferry Company.

McColl-Kennedy, J. R., & Anderson, R. D. (2005). Subordinate-manager gender combination and perceived leadership style influence on emotions, self-esteem and organizational commitment. *Journal of Business Research, 58,* 115-125.

Neubert, M. J., & Taggar, S. (2004). Pathways to informal leadership: The moderating role of gender on the relationship of individual differences and team member network centrality to informal leadership emergence. *Leadership Quarterly, 15,* 175-194.

14

Powell, G. N., Butterfield, D. A., & Parent, J. D. (2002). Gender and managerial stereotypes: Have the times changed? *Journal of Management, 28,* 177-193.

van Engen, M. L., & Willemsen, T. M. (2004). Sex and leadership styles: A meta-analysis of research published in the 1990s. *Psychological Reports, 94,* 3-18.

Vecchio, R. P. (2002). Leadership and gender advantage. *Leadership Quarterly, 13,* 643-671.

Vecchio, R. P. (2003). In search of gender advantage. *Leadership Quarterly, 14,* 835-850.

14

COUNTERPRODUCTIVE BEHAVIOR

15.

What group of individuals is most likely to initiate serious acts of workplace violence?

SELECT ONE:

☐ A. Postal workers.

☐ B. Non-employees.

☐ C. Employees who have been wronged and treated unfairly.

☐ D. Employees who have been involuntarily terminated.

☐ E. Employees with a history of trouble with the criminal justice system.

15

15. What group of individuals is most likely to initiate serious acts of workplace violence?

The correct answer is B: Non-employees.

HOW SURE ARE WE AT THIS TIME?				
1	2	3	4	**5**
Hint	Suggestive	Trending	Substantial	**Solid**

15

Discussion

Although media coverage of violent coworker assaults makes these events seem commonplace, the vast majority of workplace violence is attributable to people who are not employees (LeBlanc & Barling, 2004). Examples of violent activities ranging from assaults to homicides have outsider perpetrator estimates ranging from 85% to 90% (i.e., only 10% to 15% of these violent acts are carried out by employees or past employees of the target organization). In the U.S. alone, it is estimated that two million employees per year experience workplace violence, and half of all U.S. workplaces report at least one threat or actual occurrence of violence in a four-year period (Letizia & Casagrande, 2005).

Having face-to-face contact with the public, working at night, handling money, traveling often, and working at multiple sites all increase the likelihood that an employee will experience violence at work. In addition to physical injury, victims of workplace violence may experience psychological effects, including fatigue (Hogh, Borg, & Mikkelsen, 2003), increased feelings of vulnerability (Macdonald & Sirotich, 2005), decreased levels of morale (Uzun, 2003), or even symptoms of post-traumatic stress disorder (Hogh & Viitasara, 2005). Because non-employees cause most workplace violence, many companies focus on security measures to protect employees, including cameras, check-in procedures, cash boxes, guards, and other security measures.

Although all industries are susceptible to outsider-initiated workplace violence, the health-care sector seems to be especially vulnerable. In 2000, approximately half of all U.S. non-fatal workplace assaults occurred in social services or health-care facilities (Letizia & Casagrande, 2004). This is not a U.S.-only problem, as similar estimates have been calculated in, for example, Turkey (Ayranci, Yenilmez, Balci, & Kaptanoglu, 2006), Canada (Macdonald & Sirotich, 2005), and Sweden (Lawoko, Soares, & Nolan, 2004). Nurses, for instance, are typically convenient targets for patients' aggression. Doctors are authorities who make decisions and diagnoses—if services are not delivered adequately or correctly, they, too, can become victims of patient assault (verbal or physical). Specifically in the context of mental health professions, doctors and nurses may be dealing with unstable individuals already prone to aggression.

Aside from indirect negative effects, there are direct financial ramifications associated with workplace violence—the victim may pursue litigation against the organization for a lack of preventative measures. Furthermore, employees who are *physically* injured at work are typically entitled to workers' compensation.

Selected Research

- Fatalities resulting from assaults and violent acts (i.e., not including accidental injuries) in U.S. workplaces have declined steadily from 1994 to 2004 ([excluding the September 11, 2001 terrorist attacks] 1,080 total aggression-related deaths in 1994, 551 deaths in 2004; U.S. Bureau of Labor Statistics, 2004).

- Fatalities occurring during the act of a crime (such as burglary) account for most employee homicides—organizational members who control the exchange of money (e.g., tellers, cashiers, taxi drivers) are the most common victims of this category of crime (LeBlanc & Barling, 2004).

- Hogh, Borg, and Mikkelsen (2003) found that workers who were exposed to workplace threats or violence in 1990 were more likely to report fatigue five years later in 1995. The negative effects of exposure to violence, then, may last for a long time after the event.

- Of workplace violence incidents reported to police, 32% were motivated by a perceived injustice (i.e., being wrongfully treated as a customer) and 21% involved a domestic violence "spillover" to the workplace (i.e., domestic violence at home following the employee to work; Scalora, Washington, Casady, & Newell, 2003).

- Close to 20% of surveyed psychologists claim to have been stalked for two weeks or more by current or former clients (Purcell, Powell, & Mullen, 2005). The psychologists largely believe that the stalking was instigated by resentment or infatuation. Thirty percent of these stalked individuals considered giving up their profession—the majority changed the way in which they conduct business.

- Mental health professionals who have physical contact with patients (i.e., lifting or holding) are especially vulnerable to workplace violence (Lawoko, Soares, & Nolan, 2004). Other physical environment characteristics such as overcrowding, dim lighting, and/or poor ventilation are also associated with increased risks of violence.

15

So what difference do these findings make?

- Because cases of worker-on-worker serious violence are rare compared to public-on-worker violence, organizations should focus the majority of their employee safety efforts on the interface between their organization and the public. This is especially true for especially vulnerable positions—ones that are responsible for the exchange of money between the public and the organization and complaint intake.

- Organizations that want to target outsider-initiated violence can invest in security systems, institute cash-handling policies, and provide training to employees. This general approach is known as Crime Prevention Through Environmental Design (CPTED), and operates on the premise that crime and violence can be reduced through altering the business environment. Training in these programs involves helping employees recognize when a customer may become violent and teaching them how to intervene before the violence occurs.

15

- Federal and (some) state legislation requires that employers provide safe working conditions and take preventative action to protect employees—failing to set up adequate security or otherwise minimize employee risk can leave an organization at risk for negligence (cf., *Hart v. National Mortgage & Land Co.,* 1987; *Issacs v. Huntington Memorial Hospital,* 1985; *Yunker v. Honeywell, Inc.,* 1993).

- Company policies regarding appropriate workplace behavior need to extend to customers, clients, and patients—especially in the health-care sector. Policies should include the mandatory reporting of violent behavior to criminal authorities and specified grounds for discontinuation of services to clients/patients.

Some Key Sources

Ayranci, U., Yenilmez, C., Balci, Y., & Kaptanoglu, C. (2006). Identification of violence in Turkish health care settings. *Journal of Interpersonal Violence, 21,* 276-296.

Beech, B., & Leather, P. (2006). Workplace violence in the health care sector: A review of staff training and integration of training evaluation models. *Aggression and Violent Behavior, 11,* 27-43.

Fox, S., & Spector, P. E. (1999). A model of work frustration-aggression. *Journal of Organizational Behavior, 20,* 915-931.

Hogh, A., Borg, V., & Mikkelsen, K. L. (2003). Work-related violence as a predictor of fatigue: A 5-year follow-up of the Danish work environment cohort study. *Work & Stress, 17,* 182-194.

Hogh, A., & Viitasara, E. (2005). A systematic review of longitudinal studies of nonfatal workplace violence. *European Journal of Work and Organizational Psychology, 14,* 291-313.

Lawoko, S., Soares, J. J. F., & Nolan, P. (2004). Violence towards psychiatric staff: A comparison of gender, job and environmental characteristics in England and Sweden. *Work & Stress, 18,* 39-55.

LeBlanc, M. M., & Barling, J. (2004). Workplace aggression. *Current Directions in Psychological Science, 13,* 9-12.

Letizia, J. M., & Casagrande, K. (2005). Workplace violence: A continued threat to home care employers and employees. *Home Health Care Management & Practice, 17,* 327-329.

Lin, Y., & Liu, H. (2005). The impact of workplace violence on nurses in South Taiwan. *International Journal of Nursing Studies, 42,* 773-778.

Macdonald, G., & Sirotich, F. (2005). Violence in the social work workplace: The Canadian experience. *International Social Work, 48,* 772-781.

15

Peek-Asa, C., Casteel, C., Mineschian, L., Erickson, R. J., & Kraus, J. F. (2004). Compliance to a workplace violence prevention program in small businesses. *American Journal of Preventive Medicine, 26,* 276-283.

Peek-Asa, C., & Howard, J. (1999). Workplace-violence investigations by the California Division of Occupational Safety and Health, 1993-1996. *Journal of Occupational and Environmental Medicine, 41,* 647-653.

Purcell, R., Powell, M. B., & Mullen, P. E. (2005). Clients who stalk Psychologists: Prevalence, methods, and motives. *Professional Psychology: Research and Practice, 36,* 537-543.

Rai, S. (2002). Preventing workplace aggression and violence—A role for occupational therapy. *Work: Journal of Prevention, Assessment, & Rehabilitation, 18,* 15-22.

Scalora, M. J., Washington, D. O., Casady, T., & Newell, S. P. (2003). Nonfatal workplace violence risk factors: Data from a police contact sample. *Journal of Interpersonal Violence, 18,* 310-327.

Sprouse, M. (1992). *Sabotage in the American workplace: Anecdotes of dissatisfaction, revenge, and mischief.* San Francisco, CA: Pressure Drop Press.

U.S. Bureau of Labor Statistics (2004). *National census of fatal occupational injuries, 2004* (USDL). Washington, DC: Department of Labor.

Uzun, O. (2003). Perceptions and experiences of nurses in Turkey about verbal abuse in clinical settings. *Journal of Nursing Scholarship, 35,* 81-85.

15

STRATEGIC
DECISION MAKING

16.

Making big (or strategic) decisions faster:

SELECT ONE:

☐ A. Increases the number of errors that are made.

☐ B. If anything, helps organizations be more competitive and successful.

☐ C. Is only an advantage if most of the information is available and known.

☐ D. Decreases quality.

☐ E. Has no effect on quality of decision making or success.

16

16. Making big (or strategic) decisions faster:

The correct answer is B: If anything, helps organizations be more competitive and successful.

HOW SURE ARE WE AT THIS TIME?				
1	2	**3**	4	5
Hint	Suggestive	**Trending**	Substantial	Solid

Discussion

To think that an organization makes decisions is wrong—it is really the *people* in the context of the organization (structure, culture, operating system, etc.) who make the decisions. Organizations don't think, behave, or make decisions. People think, behave, and make decisions. Organizations *can,* and do facilitate or inhibit effective decision making. It's possible that speedy decision makers find themselves in slow-moving organizations. Likewise it's possible for paced and reflective, low-risk decision makers to find themselves in fast-paced organizations. Either form of mismatch is bad for workers (who may become frustrated) as well as organizations (that lose efficiency). Misaligned cultures and wrong decision-maker fit decrease the decision-making effectiveness of organizations. For peak organizational effectiveness, the design of the organization should be appropriate for its marketplace, as well as populated with decision makers of matching speed.

Decision-making speed is important for high-performing organizations that reside within *rapidly changing industries* and marketplace conditions. Fast *strategic* decisions are made within two to three months; slow decisions (dealing with similar issues) may take one to two years (Eisenhardt, 1989). These decisions may involve the adoption of a new technology, the introduction of a new product or service, or the decision to engage in a

114

merger or acquisition. These considerations can directly impact the strategic direction of the organization. *Speedy* strategic decision making provides a competitive advantage. Generally, firms are too slow rather than too fast in decision making, thus the importance of speed. And, organizations that move quickly often have built-in learning cycles where they can adjust and learn from both good and bad decisions.

Decision-making speed is a combination of many things—intellectual horsepower, experience and perspective, thinking and problem-solving skills and habits, making decisions under conditions of uncertainty, risk-taking capacity, and track capacity. Track capacity is the ability to bypass linear or sequential thinking—one thing at a time—and, instead, use simultaneous paths of thinking and problem solving. The concept of and work on cognitive complexity has shown that people differ on the number of concurrent flows of information they can process at once. This ability does not appear to be much related to IQ (Buckhalt & Oates, 2002).

Solid, strategic decision makers make good decisions when given complete and accurate information with a comfortable amount of time. Excellent strategists make good decisions in more volatile and turbulent conditions—contexts that do not always provide sequential, complete, or even accurate information. These conditions require faster decision making. Waiting for more information can result in a failure to act within a competitive or profitable window of opportunity. Strategic decision makers should not be afraid to rely on their intuition (see Chapter 50) if the alternative is a failure to capitalize on emerging markets, promising technology, or the need for organizational change.

16

Selected Research

- There is a relationship between speed of decision making and organizational performance for firms in volatile and changing environments (Bourgeois & Eisenhardt, 1988). Decision quality and speed need to be met simultaneously in fast-paced and changing situations. Successful organizations solve these decision-making paradoxes, whereas unsuccessful organizations do not.

- Investigating how speedy decisions are made, Eisenhardt (1989) noted that speedy decision makers actually use more information and identify more alternative solutions than do slow-paced (more reflective) decision makers. He reported that faster decision making in several microcomputer companies was associated with better organizational performance.

- Speedy decision makers tend to be smart, intuitive, tolerate risk, and are action oriented (Wally & Baum, 1994). The structure of the organization can further affect decision-making speed. Decisions are made in less time in centralized organizations where all of the decision makers are within easy reach of each other and there are less overlapping responsibilities.

- According to Judge and Miller (1991), in order to make quick decisions, complex and multitracked information must be considered simultaneously instead of sequentially. Additionally, research suggests that decision-making speed seems related to organizational performance in some industries (e.g., biotechnology) but maybe not others.

- Indecision can reside in organizations (as part of the culture or structure) as well as executives. Whatever the source, failing to implement decisions can cripple an organization (Charan, 2006). For a culture of indecision to be broken, communication within the organization must be open (no

16

predetermined outcome), candid, informal, and have closure (people should know what actions they should take).

So what difference do these findings make?

- Speedy decision making in many cases leads to better organizational performance, especially in changing and volatile environments. On the other hand, faster decision making may not necessarily be more effective in stable environments, where decisions are best made after collecting all relevant information and making a more rational, rather than intuitive, decision.

- To speed up decision making, a decision protocol may be developed. This protocol builds on the following questions:

  - What is the decision to be made? Getting clarity about the decision and its options focuses attention on what has to be decided and what the boundaries are for the decisions. One leader, when confronted by issues in a one-on-one relationship or in staff meetings, would often ask, "What is the decision that needs to be made here?" And without clarity, would go so far as to end a meeting or stop a person presenting in a meeting because the meeting was unfocused or the person unprepared.

  - Who is going to make the decision? Accountability means that a person (or team) knows what the decision is and who will make it. When someone has clear and public stewardship for getting something done, it is more likely to be done quickly.

  - When will the decision be made? Decisions generally take as long as they are given. In college, we learned that term papers due the fourteenth week of the semester often were drafted the night before they were due. Attempt to announce public deadlines for getting

16

decisions made, and then hold people accountable to those deadlines.

- What is the process for making the decision? Some decisions are so important that they require extensive time and resources (e.g., disposing of nuclear waste). Those decisions require a different process than other decisions which may be made faster (e.g., setting a corporate policy on travel), because they can be revisited over time. Figuring out how accurate the decision needs to be, who will be involved in making the decision, what information will be required, and how the decision will be made will help clarify a decision process.

- How will we follow up and monitor the quality of the decision? Lessons can and should be learned from both good and bad decision processes. Debrief, review, analyze, critique, and adapt based on what worked or did not work around a particular decision.

16

• There are individual and organizational elements of making decisions faster. First, there is organizational alignment. What speed is required to compete and win? There are many organizational design tools to aid speedy decision making. Those tools include both structural and process elements. Individuals differ on the skills and comfort of making speedy decisions under conditions of uncertainty. Organizations, designed for whatever the appropriate speed of decision making needs to be, should be staffed by employees who are good at and comfortable with making decisions at that speed.

Some Key Sources

Baum, J. R., & Wally, S. (2003). Strategic decision speed and firm performance. *Strategic Management Journal, 24,* 1107-1129.

Bourgeois, L. J., III, & Eisenhardt, K. M. (1988). Strategic decision processes in high velocity environments: Four cases in the microcomputer industry. *Management Science, 34,* 816-835.

Buckhalt, J. A., & Oates, D. F. (2002). Sensation seeking and performance on divided attention tasks varying in cognitive complexity. *Personality and Individual Differences, 32,* 67-78.

Charan, R. (2006). Conquering a culture of indecision. *Harvard Business Review, 84*(1), 108-117.

Eisenhardt, K. M. (1989). Making fast strategic decisions in high-velocity environments. *Academy of Management Journal, 32,* 543-576.

Joyce, P., & Woods, A. (2003). Managing for growth: Decision making, planning, and making changes. *Journal of Small Business and Enterprise Development, 10,* 144-151.

Judge, W. Q., & Miller, A. (1991). Antecedents and outcomes of decision speed in different environmental contexts. *Academy of Management Journal, 34,* 449-463.

Stepanovich, P. L., & Uhrig, J. D. (1999). Decision making in high-velocity environments: Implications for healthcare. *Journal of Healthcare Management, 44,* 197-205.

Wally, S., & Baum, J. R. (1994). Personal and structural determinants of the pace of strategic decision making. *Academy of Management Journal, 37,* 932-956.

16

PROCESS IMPROVEMENT

17.

Can Six Sigma principles and techniques be applied to staff areas like Human Resource Management?

SELECT ONE:

☐ A. No. Six Sigma is useful mainly in manufacturing applications.

☐ B. No. Staff functions like HR do not have processes Six Sigma techniques would apply to.

☐ C. It depends. I can use Six Sigma if the staff function is in manufacturing-oriented organizations.

☐ D. It depends. I can use Six Sigma only if the staff processes I'm trying to improve do not involve external factors (i.e., customers).

☐ E. Yes. Six Sigma concepts can be applied to any measurable, managed process, including those in staff functions.

17. **Can Six Sigma principles and techniques be applied to staff areas like Human Resource Management?**

   The correct answer is E: Yes. Six Sigma concepts can be applied to any measurable, managed process, including those in staff functions.

HOW SURE ARE WE AT THIS TIME?				
1	2	**3**	4	5
Hint	Suggestive	**Trending**	Substantial	Solid

Discussion

Six Sigma is a process improvement strategy that was created (or at least named and popularized) at Motorola in the 1980s. Its use has been pervasive, being implemented most prominently in manufacturing applications, but also in purchasing, human resources, and facilities management arenas (Holtz & Campbell, 2004). The primary goal of any Six Sigma program is to reduce costs and errors.

17

"Sigma" is the shorthand statistical notation for "standard deviation"—the purpose of any Six Sigma effort is to minimize variability (identified by the statistical notion of the standard deviation) in organizational processes. The theory is that if processes (such as manufacturing) are less variable, these processes should result in fewer defects/errors and therefore be more cost-effective. The general Six Sigma approach does seem to work—some estimates of financial savings attributable to Six Sigma programs run into the billions of dollars (Antony & Banuelas, 2002; Holtz & Campbell, 2004).

The general goal of Six Sigma is to reduce cost, error, or defects (such as customer complaints or flawed products) for all of an organization's processes. The *specific* goal in Six Sigma applications is to achieve a defect rate of less than 3.4 defects per million products or services. The Six Sigma intervention moves through five steps: (1) define (identify what the issue is), (2) measure (identify what constitutes a "defect" and obtain an estimate of current rates of defect), (3) analyze (determine the cause of defects), (4) improve (reduce the rate of defects), and (5) control (maintain the improved process). This general five-step process may be cycled through multiple times before the desired level of defects is realized.

Although Six Sigma programs have been most closely associated with *manufacturing* processes, they have also been successfully applied to customer service domains, targeting and improving customer satisfaction levels (Chen, Chen, & Hsia, 2005). Theoretically, the general approach could be applied to any organizational process.

Grant (2005) has suggested this general Six Sigma approach could be effectively used in *performance management* applications. Grant's suggestion is to use the general five-step process to (1) identify performance goals for employees, (2) measure performance components, (3) communicate with the employees (determine obstacles or impediments), (4) provide targeted developmental interventions, and (5) reward good performance to sustain it over time.

Selected Research
- Six Sigma is particularly useful for (1) identifying specific processes that need to be improved, (2) discovering the underlying reasons for non-optimal performance/production, and (3) developing targeted interventions to optimize performance/productivity (Ehie & Sheu, 2005).

- Six Sigma applications may not be equally well-received in all industries. The health-care industry, for example, has been cited as particularly difficult for Six Sigma practitioners to reach desired outcomes (Caldwell, Brexler, & Gillem, 2005).

- The Six Sigma approach can be applied to the organization as a whole. This macro-orientation has been referred to as "design for Six Sigma" and entails the minimization of errors throughout the whole organization. Six Sigma applied in this manner is essentially an organization development intervention—changing the culture, structure, and processes of the organization (Antony, 2002).

- Elements leading to the successful use of Six Sigma include (1) support from upper management, (2) sufficient organizational structure, (3) employee training, (4) statistical knowledge, and (5) people practices linkages (tying employee rewards or enticements to Six Sigma adherence; Henderson & Evans, 2000).

- Antony and Banuelas (2002) further ranked successful Six Sigma considerations in descending order of importance (ranging from most to least important). According to these researchers, the three most important elements in a successful Six Sigma program are (1) support and involvement from upper management, (2) understanding of the Six Sigma method, and (3) a linkage between the general business strategy and the Six Sigma program.

17

So what difference do these findings make?

- Six Sigma, when properly and knowledgeably applied, works.

- The technology can be applied to any process that converts inputs into outputs.

- All organizations and all functions, line and staff, use processes to get things done.

- In one sense, the "messier" the process, the more Six Sigma might help. Staff functions probably have more variable and messy processes than manufacturing.

- Theoretically, the "process" that is the subject of improvement could be any organizational procedure that transforms input into measurable output. A team meeting, for example, is a process that generally transforms knowledge and ideas into actions. If meetings too often result in "defective" ideas or actions, the general process improvement approach could be applied to identify problematic elements of the meeting process and, ultimately, decrease the number of flawed actions that result from meetings.

- Using Grant's (2005) approach, the Six Sigma framework could be applied to performance management tasks—simply using the (1) define, (2) measure, (3) analyze, (4) improve, and (5) control step progression gives managers a methodology for measuring and improving subordinate performance.

- There *are* certification programs for Six Sigma practitioners. Although this general framework has been advocated for use in (for instance) performance management domains, the manager who effectively uses the Six Sigma principles would ideally be certified as a Six Sigma green-, black-, or master black-belt (note that "knowledge of the Six Sigma method" is the second-most important factor in implementing a successful Six Sigma program; Antony & Banuelas, 2002).

- Six Sigma, like Total Quality Management and Process Reengineering before it, is a general tool for improving process. It applies to all processes. It costs money to implement and use, so a general cost-benefit analysis would be useful before deciding to use it, especially in staff areas.

17

Some Key Sources

Antony, J. (2002). Design for six sigma: A breakthrough business improvement strategy for achieving competitive advantage. *Work Study, 51,* 6-8.

Antony, J., & Banuelas, R. (2002). Key ingredients for the effective implementation of six sigma program. *Measuring Business Excellence, 6*(4), 20-27.

Bhuiyan, N., & Baghel, A. (2005). An overview of continuous improvement: From the past to the present. *Management Decision, 43,* 761-771.

Black belts save Motorola a billion. (2002). *Strategic Direction, 18,* 8-9.

Caldwell, C., Brexler, J., & Gillem, T. (2005). Engaging physicians in lean six sigma. *Quality Progress, 38*(11), 42-46.

Chen, S. C., Chen, K. S., & Hsia, T. C. (2005). Promoting customer satisfactions by applying six sigma: An example from the automobile industry. *Quality Management Journal, 12*(4), 21-33.

De Feo, J. A., & Bar-El, Z. (2002). Creating strategic change more efficiently with a new design for six sigma process. *Journal of Change Management, 3,* 60-80.

Ehie, I., & Sheu, C. (2005). Integrating six sigma and theory of constraints for continuous improvement: A case study. *Journal of Manufacturing Technology, 16,* 542-553.

Grant, M. M. (2005). Use six sigma to manage staff performance. *People Management, 11*(17), 56.

Henderson, K. M., & Evans, J. R. (2000). Successful implementation of six sigma: Benchmarking General Electric Company. *Benchmarking: An International Journal, 7,* 260-281.

Holtz, R., & Campbell, P. (2004). Six sigma: Its implementation in Ford's facility management and maintenance functions. *Journal of Facilities Management, 2,* 320-329.

17

Jeffery, A. B. (2005). Integrating organization development and six sigma: Six sigma as a process improvement intervention in action research. *Organization Development Journal, 23*(4), 20-31.

Snee, R. D. (2005). When worlds collide: Lean and six sigma. *Quality Progress, 38*(9), 63-65.

17

TRAINING & DEVELOPMENT

18.

What is the impact of executive coaching?

SELECT ONE:

☐ A. Unfortunately, as widespread as executive coaching is, there is, as of now, no hard evidence of a return on investment.

☐ B. Increased retention, because the organization shows an interest in an employee's development, but no documented change in behavior.

☐ C. Some evidence of gain, but balanced out with other evidence of either no gain or even negative results.

☐ D. Hard evidence of increases in self-awareness, skills, and performance.

☐ E. A lot of positive anecdotal stories of mostly positive results, but very hard to quantify.

18

18. What is the impact of executive coaching?

The correct answer is D: Hard evidence of increases in self-awareness, skills, and performance.

HOW SURE ARE WE AT THIS TIME?				
1	2	**3**	4	5
Hint	Suggestive	**Trending**	Substantial	Solid

Discussion

The use of executive coaching as a developmental tool has become increasingly common. Managers participate in this type of engagement with a coach in an attempt to enhance skills, performance, or general personal development. Some large organizations are beginning to include coaching as an option within their broader executive development programs (Elder & Skinner, 2002).

One of the aspects of coaching is that it can "cross the border" between personal and professional lives. Some coaching interventions are aimed at quite personal issues which might include off-work behavior, while others target more traditional areas of development (i.e., goal setting, feedback delivery, public speaking).

Coaching is a discipline or profession without much regulation—there is currently no governing body to ensure that someone who labels himself/herself an "executive coach" truly possesses high-level skills in the coaching domain. A list of backgrounds of individuals who engage in executive coaching includes former athletes, lawyers, and academics (cf., Berglas, 2002). Berglas believes that, although these individuals can help in certain domains, they often do more "harm than good" in

18

personal areas and that executive coaches should come from a psychology-related background.

Unfortunately, an agreed-upon professional body of knowledge of the effectiveness of executive coaching is lacking. Most writings on the topic present *suggestions for coaching* or *psychological orientations* to be used with coaching, but do not add evidence of success or effectiveness. It is obvious that many executive coaches are confident with their approaches; it is not empirically apparent which of these approaches results in the most desirable outcomes.

One area of research that has generally supported the effectiveness of coaching is in 360-degree feedback applications. When delivering feedback to managers regarding their rated competencies, focus can be placed on discrepancies between self- and other ratings. Through identifying and determining the reasons for these discrepancies, coaches can help managers become more aware of their relative areas of strength and weakness, and, perhaps more importantly, where their "blind spots" are (where others view them differently from how they view themselves).

Executive coaching is differentiated from traditional therapy by the *focus* of the engagement. Therapy (psychological) focuses on the repair or cure of dysfunctional behavior and its underlying cause; this often takes a retrospective approach—unraveling things that happened in the past that are chilling to useful behavior today. Coaching tends to be more future and "wellness" oriented (Wright, 2005).

18

Citing several case studies, Berglas (2002) concludes that coaches who lack formal psychological training may be more detrimental than beneficial. If the executive coach does not possess psychological training, it is recommended that the client first complete a psychological examination to make sure the target behavior is not deeper in nature or cause.

Selected Research

- Smither et al. (2003) found that managers who had sessions with an executive coach were more likely to seek improvement ideas from their supervisors and to set specific goals for themselves (compared to managers who did not engage in executive coaching sessions). These coached managers also recorded greater 360-rated performance improvements (than did uncoached managers) over a one-year period.

- Olivero, Bane, and Kopelman (1997) recorded performance improvements of 88% for managers who received coaching along with training, while those who received training only had performance improvements of 22% (over previous performance levels). These coaching interventions were skill oriented more than personal issue oriented.

- Because the use of 360-degree assessments usually includes someone (a coach) to deliver the feedback in a constructive and helpful manner, some results have been identified. A coach who focuses on gaps between self- and other ratings while delivering feedback can lessen the gaps in future 360-degree ratings (Luthans & Peterson, 2003). Through focusing on these differences, executive coaches can help managers become more "self-aware."

- In terms of increased leadership effectiveness, the most important element of coaching is subsequent interaction and follow-up with coworkers (Goldsmith & Morgan, 2005). Leaders who show the most improvement share their personal developmental goals and solicit additional feedback from coworkers regarding progress they've made. This suggests that the manager himself/herself must take a proactive role for coaching interventions to be optimally effective.

- Additionally, external mental health professionals should be used to evaluate the coaching outcomes.

18

So what difference do these findings make?

- Individual coaching is beginning to show results. Results probably will ultimately depend upon the nature (simple to complex, surface versus deep, nature versus nurture in origin) of the target behavior and the background and skills of the coach.

- The major results to expect are, first, a decrease in the number and severity of blind spots or gaps between self-ratings and the ratings of others, and second, actual gains in the performance of the target behavior. Through focusing on "blind spots," coaches can help managers become more self-aware regarding their relative areas of strength and developmental need. Increased self-awareness could ultimately lead to improved attitudes and performance.

- Coaching can be an effective tool to enhance trained material (management skills such as goal setting, employee supervision, and communication) and to maximize the likelihood that the trained material will be applied.

- Using coaching in combination with 360-degree feedback may increase the effectiveness of 360-degree applications.

Some Key Sources

Arnaud, G. (2003). A coach or a couch? A Lacanian perspective on executive coaching and consulting. *Human Relations, 56,* 1131-1154.

Berglas, S. (2002). The very real dangers of executive coaching. *Harvard Business Review, 80,* 86-93.

Elder, E., & Skinner, M. (2002). Managing executive coaching behaviors in learning organizations. *Journal of Management Development, 18,* 752-771.

Feldman, D. C., & Lankau, M. J. (2005). Executive coaching: A review and agenda for future research. *Journal of Management, 31,* 829-848.

18

Goldberg, R. A. (2005). Resistance to coaching. *Organization Development Journal, 23,* 9-16.

Goldsmith, M., & Morgan, H. (2005). Leadership as a contact sport. *Leadership Excellence, 22*(8), 6-7.

Goldsmith, M., & Underhill, B. O. (2001). Multisource feedback for executive development. In D. W. Bracken, C. W. Timmreck, & A. H. Church (Eds.), *The handbook of multisource feedback: The comprehensive resource for designing and implementing MSF processes* (pp. 275-288). San Francisco: Jossey-Bass.

Hall, D. T., Otazo, K. L., & Hollenbeck, G. P. (1999). Behind closed doors: What really happens in executive coaching. *Organizational Dynamics, 27*(3), 39-52.

Jay, M. (2003). Understanding how to leverage executive coaching. *Organization Development Journal, 21,* 6-19.

Kampa, S., & White, R. P. (2002). The effectiveness of executive coaching: What we know and what we still need to know. In R. L. Lowman (Ed.), *The California School of Organizational Studies: Handbook of organizational consulting psychology* (pp. 139-158). San Francisco: Jossey-Bass.

Kilburg, R. R. (2000). Introduction to executive coaching. In R. R. Kilburg (Ed.), *Executive coaching: Developing managerial wisdom in a world of chaos* (pp. 3-19). Washington, DC: American Psychological Association.

Luthans, F., & Peterson, S. J. (2003). 360-degree feedback with systematic coaching: Empirical analysis suggests a winning combination. *Human Resource Management, 42,* 243-256.

Olivero, G., Bane, K. D., & Kopelman, R. E. (1997). Executive coaching as a transfer of training tool: Effects on productivity in a public agency. *Public Personnel Management, 26,* 461-469.

Orenstein, R. L. (2002). Executive coaching: It's not just about the executive. *The Journal of Applied Behavioral Science, 38,* 355-374.

18

Smither, J. W., London, M., Flautt, R., Vargas, Y., & Kucine, I. (2003). Can working with an executive coach improve multisource feedback ratings over time? A quasi-experimental field study. *Personnel Psychology, 56,* 23-44.

Story, M. A. (2003). Bringing head and heart to coaching. *Organization Development Journal, 21,* 77-81.

Wasylyshyn, K. M. (2003). Executive coaching: An outcome study. *Consulting Psychology Journal: Practice and Research, 55,* 94-106.

Wright, J. (2005). Workplace coaching: What's it all about? *Work, 24,* 325-328.

18

19.

Expatriation (leaving for an overseas assignment) is a valued experience for both organizations and employees. Repatriation (returning from an assignment) usually results in:

SELECT ONE:

☐ A. The workgroup resenting the returning employee and resisting the application of his/her unique international skills back home.

☐ B. The returning employee experiencing an increase in status due to the special new perspectives he/she has gained.

☐ C. The returning employee experiencing an increase in organizational support and career enhancement due to the value-adding skills he/she obtained in the international assignment.

☐ D. The returning employee being able to successfully contribute an international perspective to his/her workgroup.

19

☐ E. The returning employee struggling with personal, interpersonal, and work-related issues.

19. **Expatriation (leaving for an overseas assignment) is a valued experience for both organizations and employees. Repatriation (returning from an assignment) usually results in:**

The correct answer is E: The returning employee struggling with personal, interpersonal, and work-related issues.

HOW SURE ARE WE AT THIS TIME?				
1	2	3	**4**	5
Hint	Suggestive	Trending	**Substantial**	Solid

Discussion

Multinational organizations need globally competent managers. In order to achieve this goal, many organizations include expatriate assignments as a building block of their leadership development programs. It is without a doubt that competent international managers are hard to build and find. In the long-term, competent managers with one or more international assignments will be of great value to global organizations.

There are multiple adjustments that need to be made when an employee is given his or her first international assignment, but returning "home" after an international appointment also brings its own unique challenges.

"Repatriation" is the term given to the process of getting reassimilated into a home organization after returning from foreign assignments.

Repatriation can be a shock for returning expatriates, as the "home" they return to is not necessarily the same place that they remember. In coping with the stress of international appointments, expatriates may idealize their memories of back

19

home—accentuating the positive attributes and repressing or forgetting the negative (Andreason & Kinneer, 2004). Upon returning home, these false constructions are exposed and disappointment can occur. The same general coping technique may be used during repatriation if the home experience is less than ideal—the repatriate glamorizes the memory of the past overseas assignment and experience, once again accentuating the negative aspects of "home." For some individuals, repatriation may be a more difficult adjustment than the initial adjustment made for the foreign assignment.

In many circumstances, the returning employee encounters status differences between roles in the foreign country and roles in the home environment. Many expatriates become accustomed to the enhanced perks, benefits, or social and cultural opportunities in their foreign assignments. Once home in a domestic position, they are not always able to maintain the lifestyle of the foreign assignment. In some cases, they were provided living quarters, drivers, more generous expense accounts, tax equalization, etc. All that ends back home.

Work-related disappointment can be just as problematic as personal- or family-oriented sources of disappointment. The expectation with an overseas appointment is that it will benefit the employee's career. While away, however, expatriates may remain "out-of-sight and out-of-mind" at the home organization. Returning to an organization that has forgotten who the expatriate is, does not know what he/she did (domestically or overseas), or does not know how to leverage newly gained international skills, can be terribly disappointing. Under these circumstances, repatriates may view their careers as having been put in a "holding pattern" instead of on an accelerated track. Some look at it as "falling behind their class." The people they started with back home who did not have international assignments have advanced more than they.

19

Many times expatriates enjoy more freedom. They are thousands of miles from headquarters. They make more decisions on their own. They are visited infrequently by back-home top management. They can make policy exceptions to operate in a foreign environment. They are on their own for longer periods than their back-home counterparts. They probably have a job or role that is of higher status internationally. Many times they return to what they see as a lower status position. So returning home is usually a step down in their eyes. In fact, many times they are put in a makeshift job or role because the organization doesn't know what to do with them. Sort of a holding job.

One actual fact is that they have missed not being in the "management network." They have not been at all of the headquarters meetings. They have not done lunches with key gatekeepers. They have not been to the off-sites. They have not met the new players. They are out of touch with the home strategies and tactics. They might have missed getting updated on industry knowledge and competitor intelligence. They were not in the normal data flow and social network while on international assignment. They have not marketed themselves for career enhancement in the home environment. They are "behind" those that stayed behind. Although they have gained incremental and unique international perspective, that may not matter back in a domestic role.

Repatriate turnover is therefore a problem. Unmet expectations can lead to lowered levels of commitment or loyalty to the organization and an increased intention to quit. The Society for Human Resource Management estimates that roughly 50% of employees do not remain employed (are either terminated or choose to leave) within two years of returning from a foreign assignment (Poe, 2000). You have to wonder why an organization would invest in the international experience, knowledge, and skill development of its employees, only to lose the workers to competitors within two years.

19

Selected Research

- Although it has been estimated that unassisted readjustment upon organizational reentry may take as long as one year (Linehan & Scullion, 2002), formal repatriation assistance programs are rare. The majority (one estimate is 77%) of returning expatriates do not receive career counseling or reentry orientation. Only 17% of organizations include repatriation expectations as a component of the preparation training for overseas assignments (Poe, 2000).

- Commonly, reentry positions do not provide the same degree of control, autonomy, or status as do expatriate positions. A severe "mismatch" between expatriate and domestic positions can result in the employee feeling dissatisfied, overqualified for the reentry assignment, or undervalued by the organization (Andreason & Kinneer, 2004).

- Employees who have their reentry expectations met or exceeded are more committed to the organization than are those whose expectations are not met (Stroh, Gregersen, & Black, 2000). Managing expectations before expatriation and during repatriation leads to a perception of organizational support that is associated with lowered intentions to leave the organization (Lazarova & Caligiuri, 2001).

- Jassawalla, Connolly, and Slojkowski (2004) interviewed repatriating managers and determined that "retrofit" repatriation programs (ones that are created after the individual has returned to the domestic assignment) are not very effective. One manager, commenting on his perception of a lack of support, noted, "They did not do anything to ease the anxiety of coming back. They assume you are a big boy and you can do it on your own" (p. 39).

19

So what difference do these findings make?

- Expatriation and repatriation should be viewed as two separate events and processes. They are both well-known processes with decades of consistent research findings. Many organizations are preparing people better for out of home country assignments. Fewer are preparing returning expatriates.

- International experience is mission critical to global organizations. It is very expensive. The population of competent global managers is less than the need. Having enough is and will be a competitive advantage in the increasingly global world.

- **From the viewpoint of the organization:** Few organizations have formal transition programs for repatriates. If a formal repatriation program exists, sponsorship should be an included component. Someone of authority within the home organization should be selected as a sponsor or representative who can represent the expatriate's interests while the person is on assignment and help the person adjust upon repatriation.

- **From the viewpoint of the organization:** Managing reentry expectations of repatriating employees is particularly crucial. Organizations should convey realistic expectations regarding the difficulty of cultural reintegration, the likelihood of reentry job prospects, and status differentials between overseas and domestic positions. Acts such as pre-departure awareness training, career counseling, the creation of a pre-departure contract (describing the repatriation position options), and formal reorientation upon return are all viewed as "supportive acts" by repatriates.

- **From the viewpoint of the organization:** Consider returning the repatriates to jobs and roles in the international units and divisions where their skills are better known and

19

appreciated. Create a repatriates group that periodically meets and shares the good news and bad news of returning to home port. Urge top management to meet with the group periodically to solicit their views on current and upcoming global concerns and issues. Arrange social events celebrating their return and integration back into the social network. Use the repatriates to orient and train first-time expatriates. Put the repatriates on task forces and study groups. Assign them a top management orienteer. Make sure they are justly considered for promotions compared to people who stayed behind and are better known to decision makers. Assign an HR reentry assistance person who can run interference and open doors in the organization. Provide special financial and family coaching if needed. In general, work on extreme inclusion in the social and management network. For example, try to put them into a position of presenting up in the organization at meetings so management learns more about them.

- **From the viewpoint of the organization:** Treat repatriates as a special group in the succession planning process. Pay special attention to their expectations of career progress. When promotions are discussed, have someone in the decision-making room who can present their case.

- **From the viewpoint of the individual:** Repatriates can try to be proactive themselves in building social networks (to assist with coping for reentry), staying up-to-date with cultural events (through reading online home-country newspapers), and updating the home organization with accomplishments and learned skill/knowledge sets. Although others tend to take social initiative when expatriates experience a new culture, the repatriate must take initiative to reimmerse himself/herself in the culture of the home country.

19

Some Key Sources

Andreason, A. W., & Kinneer, K. D. (2004). Bringing them home again. *Industrial Management, 46*(6), 13-19.

Caligiuri, P., & Di Santo, V. (2001). Global competence: What is it, and can it be developed through global assignments? *Human Resource Planning, 24*(3), 27-35.

Jassawalla, A., Connolly, T., & Slojkowski, L. (2004). Issues of effective repatriation: A model and managerial implications. *S.A.M. Advanced Management Journal, 69*(2), 38-46.

Lazarova, M., & Caligiuri, P. (2001). Retaining repatriates: The role of organizational support practices. *Journal of World Business, 36*, 389-401.

Linehan, M., & Scullion, H. (2002). Repatriation of European female corporate executives: An empirical study. *International Journal of Human Resource Management, 13*, 254-267.

Poe, A. (2000). Welcome back. *HR Magazine, 45*(3), 94-105.

Stroh, L. K., Gregersen, H. B., & Black, J. S. (2000). Triumphs and tragedies: Expectations and commitments upon repatriation. *International Journal of Human Resource Management, 11*, 681-697.

19

20.

The best way to get employees more engaged is to:

SELECT ONE:

☐ A. Pay them more than the market dictates.

☐ B. Express more care for them.

☐ C. Offer more personalized perks.

☐ D. Increase the value of the benefits packages.

☐ E. Enhance their titles.

20

20. The best way to get employees more engaged is to?

The correct answer is B: Express more care for them.

HOW SURE ARE WE AT THIS TIME?				
1	2	3	4	**5**
Hint	Suggestive	Trending	Substantial	**Solid**

Discussion

An employee who is engaged at work is someone who is motivated to contribute fully with meaning and impact. Engagement requires a personal connection between the employee and the organization and results in the worker going "above and beyond" their formal job requirements. If the employee also possesses the requisite skills, the engaged worker is the ideal worker for organizations—these engaged and skilled individuals are functioning at high productivity.

Unfortunately, for the most part, surveys report that workers are not engaged at work, and the overall levels of engagement are at low and unacceptable numbers. One estimate by Hewitt Associates has over half of all worldwide workers disengaged from work (Gandossy & Kao, 2004). Bates (2004) estimates that in the typical U.S. organization, only 25% of employees are truly enthusiastic about work, half work hard enough to "get by," and another quarter are disengaged.

This lack of employee engagement hurts results—engagement is consistently identified as a key element of performance (see research below). Bates (2004) suggests that the U.S. economy is only running at 30% of its peak efficiency because of the lack of engagement. Additionally, once the job market improves (likely to soon occur either because of economic recovery or

20

the retirement of baby boomers) and more job opportunities open, it is predicted that many disengaged employees will take the opportunity to leave their current organizations. This is all unnecessary and unfortunate because the majority of workers want to be actively involved in making their company. What this means is there is a great deal of untapped potential in the workforce.

Engagement is not a function of how much an employee is paid or how satisfied he/she is at work—it has more to do with the way an employee views his/her work experience and how that employee feels he/she has been treated. Engagement is important for both performance and retention. The more employees *feel* cared for or treated fairly, the more likely they are to be contributing their full capabilities to work.

Selected Research

- According to multiple Gallup surveys, the majority (60%) of British workers are not engaged at work and roughly 20% are "actively disengaged" (possess negative attitudes toward their work). Gallup estimates that the actively disengaged employees cost the British economy between $64 billion and $66 billion per year (U.S. dollars; Flade, 2003). These estimates are projected based on the relationship of disengagement with turnover, absenteeism, and productivity. The lack of engagement is not an American or British phenomenon—of 11 surveyed countries, no average engagement level exceeded 27%.

- Harter, Schmidt, and Hayes (2002) found that highly engaged business units outperformed less engaged units across multiple industries and jobs. The most engaged units had, on average, roughly $100,000 more revenue or sales per month. Highly engaged business units were also shown to have lower levels of employee turnover, greater customer satisfaction, and fewer safety violations.

20

- Both full disengagement and a simple *lack* of engagement hurt individual sales performance. One sales division noted 28% revenue drops for disengaged account executives, and account executives who did "just enough to get by" had 23% revenue drops (compared to the engaged account executives; Bates, 2004).

- May, Gilson, and Harter (2004) studied potential causes of engagement and found that meaningfulness and safety were most highly related to engagement. A supportive and caring supervisor contributes to a "psychologically safe" environment. Job enrichment and perceived "fit" with the work-role contribute to perceptions of meaningfulness.

- The *factors leading to engagement* do not differ based on employee age, tenure, or management status. Engagement itself is directly related to revenue (as noted above), and documentation of this relationship helps obtain management buy-in for engagement initiatives (Harley, Lee, & Robinson, 2005).

- It might be that certain individuals are more likely to be engaged at work than others (Gubman 2004). These select individuals have a greater capability to be "passionate" about their work. Therefore, if these individuals are placed in the proper jobs and roles for the skills they possess, they will be "hyper-engaged." Initial evidence points toward "passionate" employees as having the following characteristics: extraverted, goal oriented, interpersonally diverse, tolerant of change and ambiguity, and variety-seeking.

20

So what difference do these findings make?

- Engagement equals results. It's a simple but powerful finding. Those managers and those organizations providing enhanced engagement will reap enhanced results. Engagement should be a strategic tool for producing better results.

- Engagement is a known technology. There is little left for speculation and the imagination.

- The major source of engagement power is the relationship between the employee and his or her direct boss. All of these points of engagement power then add up to overall engagement of the organization.

- The most important person to communicate engagement is each employee's immediate supervisor. It is crucial that organizations that wish to improve overall levels of employee engagement provide engagement training for managers.

- Managers who want a more engaged workforce should demonstrate more care and concern for their employees, provide more challenging work, treat everyone equitably and fairly, recognize good performance, and provide development opportunities. Managers should listen more. Disengaged employees often do not know what expectations their supervisors have for them, feel as though their managers do not have any concern for them, feel as though their talents are not being utilized, or believe they have no "voice" at work.

- Organizations should periodically measure levels of engagement. This is commonly done through asking (using morale or engagement surveys) how employees feel about their work and about their work culture. If an engagement survey is administered, expect to hear criticisms—these instruments are not designed to collect positive feedback.

20

Obviously, not every organizational decision can involve a participative or democratic process, but if interventions or accommodations are made based on survey feedback, communicate that the changes are a result of employee-stated concerns/requests.

- It should be understood by all that engagement is the responsibility of both the organization and the employees—employers need to construct a workplace that is meaningful and caring, while employees should feel a responsibility to reciprocate by contributing fully to their work.

- Top management must be committed to engagement and they must model engagement behaviors for all of this to work.

Some Key Sources

Bates, S. (2004). Getting engaged. *HR Magazine, 49*(2), 44-51.

Flade, P. (2003). Great Britain's workforce lacks inspiration. *Gallup Management Journal, December 11.* Retrieved January 4, 2007, from http://gmj.gallup.com/content/9847/Great-Britains-Workforce-lacks-Inspiration.aspx

Frank, F. D., Finnegan, R. P., & Taylor, C. R. (2004). The race for talent: Retaining and engaging workers in the 21st century. *Human Resource Planning, 27*(3), 12-25.

Gandossy, R., & Kao, T. (2004). Talent wars: Out of mind, out of practice. *Human Resource Planning, 27*(4), 15-19.

Garvey, C. (2004). Connecting the organizational pulse to the bottom line. *HR Magazine, 49*(6), 70-75.

Gubman, E. (2004). From engagement to passion for work: The search for the missing person. *Human Resource Planning, 27*(3), 42-46.

Harley, A., Lee, D., & Robinson, D. (2005). How O2 built the business case for engagement. *Strategic HR Review, 4*(6), 24-27.

20

20

Harter, J. K., Schmidt, F. L., & Hayes, T. L. (2002). Business-unit-level relationship between employee satisfaction, employee engagement, and business outcomes: A meta-analysis. _Journal of Applied Psychology, 87,_ 268-279.

Hoover, G. (2005). Maintaining employee engagement when communicating difficult issues. _Communication World, 22_(6), 25-27.

Jamrog, J. (2004). The perfect storm: The future of retention and engagement. _Human Resource Planning, 27_(3), 26-33.

May, D. R., Gilson, R. L., & Harter, L. M. (2004). The psychological conditions of meaningfulness, safety and availability and the engagement of the human spirit at work. _Journal of Occupational and Organizational Psychology, 77,_ 11-37.

Shaffer, J. (2004). Measurable payoff: How employee engagement can boost performance and profits. _Communication World, 21_(4), 22-27.

21

MENTORSHIP

21.

What is the main element driving the success and effectiveness of mentoring?

SELECT ONE:

☐ A. Informal mentorship outperforms formal.

☐ B. Same-gender and same-race mentoring.

☐ C. Quality of the relationship.

☐ D. Cross-level mentors add more value than peer mentors.

☐ E. Trained mentors outperform untrained mentors.

21. What is the main element driving the success and effectiveness of mentoring?

21

The correct answer is C: Quality of the relationship (if the protégés are satisfied with the mentorship event).

HOW SURE ARE WE AT THIS TIME?				
1	**2**	3	4	5
Hint	**Suggestive**	Trending	Substantial	Solid

Discussion

There seem to be three primary purposes mentors serve: role modeling effective behaviors and attitudes, career facilitation (help in career progression), and networking or social functioning assistance. Role modeling shows the person how to act more appropriately in order to reach career goals. Career facilitation prepares the person for enhanced job advancement, while social facilitation enhances the person's self-image and ability to constructively network.

In the past, mentorship has mostly taken the form of a senior manager taking a junior manager "under his or her wing." For the most part, these mentoring relationships were informal and driven by mutual self-selection. Downsizing and flattening strategies have reduced the number of senior managers available to mentor. Experienced peers are increasingly serving as mentors for less tenured, same-level, coworkers. Organizations are increasingly creating formal (assigned or arranged matches) mentorship programs, where mentors and protégés are matched. Informal mentoring relationships tend to last longer than formal relationships and have been shown in the past to be of greater value. There is a general tendency for protégés to report more favorable outcomes from informal mentoring relationships (although mentors do not report any differences in formal versus informal relationships).

From the perspective of the organization, mentorship is valued because protégés tend to (1) be more ready for promotion, (2) have more positive work attitudes, and (3) show more commitment to their organization (compared to employees who do not have a mentor; cf., Dreher & Cox, 1996). Although these positive outcomes are generally true across mentoring relationships, they are most likely to occur when the person is satisfied with the mentoring relationship (Ragins, Cotton, & Miller, 2000).

Regarding the bottom-line impact of mentorship, Wilson and Elman (1990) argue that mentorship provides a framework for strengthening organizational culture and contributes to the health of the overall organization's social system. Because of the interpersonal nature of mentor-protégé relationships, mentors can additionally serve the organization through fulfilling "early knower" roles. Through this function, mentors can pick up on early signs of negative workforce mood or attitude before the issues become solidified or problematic. This is most likely to occur when the mentor and protégé are at different levels (and different vertical associations) within the organizational. Although these cultural and deep-sensing functions of mentorship maybe increase organization effectiveness, the specific impact of mentoring on an organization's bottom line has not been directly assessed.

Selected Research

- Organizational commitment and job satisfaction increase if the person is satisfied with the mentoring relationship—this is true whether the mentoring relationship is formal or informal. Similarly, dysfunctional or bad mentoring can be worse than no mentoring (can lead to increased negative work attitudes; Ragins, Cotton, & Miller, 2000). In this study, the quality of the mentoring relationship far outweighed any other factor in determining outcomes.

- Scandura and Williams (2001) found that protégés believe they receive more mentoring within informal rather than formal mentoring relationships. Although protégés claim a difference, mentors do not. Reports from *mentors* in both formal and informal mentorships note no difference in the amount (but not quality) of mentoring provided (Allen & Eby, 2004).

- Not all protégé-mentor relationships are equally valuable. Similarly, not all mentorship events will be positive. Research by Eby, McManus, Simon, and Russell (2000) found that over half of their survey respondents had been involved in at least one "dysfunctional" protégé-mentor relationship throughout their careers. Differences in values, work styles, or personalities were most often cited as the cause of negative experiences.

- Looking at peer mentoring (protégé-mentor relationships that do not cross hierarchical levels), Bryant (2005) found that peers can help extend the knowledge resources of a firm. Increased or enhanced knowledge provides a competitive advantage for organizations. Peer mentors in this study were able to transfer knowledge and provide effective support to their protégés after only one day of training on peer-mentoring skills.

- Tourigny and Pulich (2005) studied the effects of formal and informal mentoring among nurses and found perceived and real advantages and disadvantages to both types of programs.

Formal Mentoring Programs
- Disadvantages to formal (assigned or assisted matching) mentoring programs include the relatively short duration of the mentoring relationship, the focus on organizational

goals over the needs of the protégé, and the greater potential for assignment to a "marginal" mentor.

– Advantages to a formal mentoring program include access to hierarchical career support, consistency between the mentoring program goals and that of the organization, and (usually) a greater time commitment on the part of the mentors.

Informal Mentoring Programs
– Disadvantages of informal mentoring programs include a perception of favoritism, lack of career support, potential role conflict (referring to peer mentor suggestions that might conflict with management guidelines), and the lack of recognition for mentoring efforts.

– Advantages of informal mentoring programs include a better mentor/protégé fit (because of mutual selection), a more favorable perception of protégés by the organization for their efforts initiating the relationship, and a greater likelihood that protégés will be open to feedback and take greater personal responsibility in career planning and the development of tacit knowledge.

• According to de Janasz, Sullivan, and Whiting (2003), aspiring managers need multiple and diverse mentor relationships to succeed in today's ever-changing workplace. Having multiple mentors can help protégés develop mission-critical competencies, achieve personal success within their current position, and create effective relationships and networks to use in future career actions. The most effective mentoring relationships include both informal and formal mentors who are diverse in race, educational background, industry represented, and gender.

• The mentoring process proceeds through multiple phases, and every mentoring relationship will eventually see separation between the mentor and protégé (Kram, 1983).

As the protégé develops more independence and autonomy, mentors and protégés reevaluate their need for each other and the mentoring relationship becomes less important. This can be a time of turmoil and anxiety for both protégés and mentors. With well-adjusted relationships, the mentorship at this point is transformed into friendship.

- Peer relationships can serve similar developmental and supportive functions as traditional cross-level mentoring relationships (Kram & Isabella, 1985). This is important, because workers typically have access to a greater number of coworkers than they do supervisors or mentors. These supportive peer relationships tend to allow for two-way channels of communication and equal amounts of influence upon each person. Supportive peer relationships are particularly important for individuals who do not have or want a mentor.

So what difference do these findings make?

- Although the ROI gained has not generally been quantified, the "investment" itself is not altogether steep. Organizations can improve important individual employee outcomes such as satisfaction, commitment, and performance through encouraging or establishing programs to facilitate mentoring relationships. If a formal program is established, mentors should receive training on how to be an effective mentor.

- The "early knower" role can be achieved better if (1) the mentor and protégé occupy different levels within the organizational hierarchy (ideally two or three levels apart), and (2) the mentor and protégé are not in the same chain of command. The "early sensing" function serves as an informal channel of communication, but the information is not necessarily always negative: through early sensing, mentors may be able to identify other potential protégés or high potentials.

- Both informal and formal systems work and both cross-level and peer mentoring can add value. The driving element seems to be the mentored person's value assessment. Therefore, early measurement of mentoring satisfaction can probably add to the ROI of mentoring. Dysfunctional relationships can be terminated more quickly. Understanding of the nature of satisfaction and dissatisfaction will help in the matching process. Since maybe up to 50% of mentoring events are not seen as helpful, there is much room for improvement.

Some Key Sources

Allen, T. D., & Eby, L. T. (2004). Factors related to mentor reports of mentoring functions provided: Gender and relational characteristics. *Sex Roles, 50,* 129-139.

Bryant, S. E. (2005). The impact of peer mentoring on organizational knowledge creation and sharing: An empirical study in a software firm. *Group & Organization Management, 30,* 319-338.

de Janasz, S. C., Sullivan, S. E., & Whiting, V. (2003). Mentor networks and career success: Lessons for turbulent times. *Academy of Management Executive, 17,* 78-91.

Dreher, G. E., & Cox, T. H. (1996). Race, gender, and opportunity: A study of compensation attainment and the establishment of mentoring relationships. *Journal of Applied Psychology, 81,* 297-308.

Eby, L. T., McManus, S. E., Simon, S. A., & Russell, J. E. A. (2000). The protégé's perspective regarding negative mentoring experiences: The development of a taxonomy. *Journal of Vocational Behavior, 57,* 1-21.

Kram, K. E. (1983). Phases of the mentor relationship. *Academy of Management Journal, 26,* 608-625.

Kram, K. E., & Isabella, L. A. (1985). Mentoring alternatives: The role of peer relationships in career development. *Academy of Management Journal, 28,* 110-132.

O'Reilly, D. (2001). The mentoring of employees: Is your organization taking advantage of this professional development tool? *OHIO CPA Journal, 60*(3), 51-55.

Ragins, B. R., Cotton, J. L., & Miller, J. S. (2000). Marginal mentoring: The effects of type of mentor, quality of relationship, and program design on work and career attitudes. *Academy of Management Journal, 43,* 1177-1194.

Scandura, T. A., & Williams, E. A. (2001). An investigation of the moderating effects of gender on the relationships between mentorship initiation and protégé perceptions of mentoring functions. *Journal of Vocational Behavior, 59,* 342–363.

Tourigny, L., & Pulich, M. (2005). A critical examination of formal and informal mentoring among nurses. *The Health Care Manager, 24,* 68-76.

Wilson, J. A., & Elman, N. S. (1990). Organizational benefits of mentoring. *Academy of Management Executive, 4,* 88-94.

22

COUNTERPRODUCTIVE
BEHAVIOR

22

22.

The percentage of time employees surf (i.e., play) while on the Internet at work?

SELECT ONE:

☐ A. 5%.

☐ B. 10%.

☐ C. 15%.

☐ D. 20%.

☐ E. 30%.

22. The percentage of time employees surf (i.e., play) while on the Internet at work?

The correct answer is E: 30%.

22

HOW SURE ARE WE AT THIS TIME?				
1	2	**3**	4	5
Hint	Suggestive	**Trending**	Substantial	Solid

Discussion

The Internet is an extremely useful tool for creating interconnectedness among business units, customers, and employees. Email, file transfer capabilities, and World Wide Web research are all positive elements of having Internet access. Obviously, all these capabilities can lead to increased employee productivity. Unfortunately, unrestricted access to the Internet also can result in undesired employee activities. One conservative estimate has roughly 30% of Internet use at work being done for nonwork purposes (Greenfield, 1999).

Organizations probably expect that employees will occasionally use the Internet for personal use. It is really no different from the tradition of allowing personal telephone calls when necessary. The issue becomes problematic when the personal use exceeds a reasonable amount. Evidence suggests that this technology seems to lend itself to easy abuse (more than telephone use). There are legal and financial ramifications to employee Internet misuse. One Computer Economics estimate had recreational Internet use resulting in a $5.3 billion cost to companies in 1999 in *lost productivity* alone (Stewart, 2000). The vice president of research for this company estimated that shopping, trading stocks, or even visiting pornographic Web sites was a daily ritual for one-quarter of American employees who had Internet access at work.

22

It probably is unwise to severely restrict the Internet at work, which would likely limit its positive, performance-enhancing capabilities as well. Organizations may be hesitant to engage in "babysitting" activities such as the monitoring of Internet use for fear of introducing a "big brother" element into the corporate culture (Stewart, 2000). However, it should be noted that the development of an acceptable Internet use policy does not mean that the organization has the technology to enforce it. Further, it does not mean that managers have the willingness or knowledge to enforce the policy. An effective Internet use policy includes clear and continual communication of policy, capable but unobtrusive monitoring systems, and appropriate consequences for policy violation (i.e., warnings for minor violations, more severe action for more egregious violations).

Selected Research

- The majority (70%) of U.S. organizations provide Internet access to employees. Over 60% of surveyed companies have disciplined employees for Internet misuse. More than 30% have fired employees for inappropriate surfing (Greenfield & Davis, 2002).

- Cooper, Safir, and Rosenmann (2006) found that almost 20% of individuals who engage in online sexual activities (while not at work) also do so while at work. These behaviors can result in decreased productivity, increased likelihood of sexual harassment in the workplace, and a general decline in worker well-being. Workplace policies can limit the extent to which employees engage in this form of counterproductivity, but a minority of these employees will not conform to policy.

- Internet misuse can (1) decrease employee productivity (one estimate reports a $470 million loss to American companies from misuse related to the Clinton-Lewinsky scandal alone), (2) drain computer resources (clogging bandwidth and degrading network performance), and/or (3) lead to legal trouble through exposing coworkers to explicit material—thereby creating a "hostile work environment" (cf., Stewart, 2000).

- Employees who believe that they are not being treated fairly appear to rationalize their "cyberloafing" behaviors (Lim, 2002). This rationalization allows employees to not feel guilty about their off-task behaviors (i.e., the organization is not treating me fairly, therefore my Internet misuse is justified). This behavior allows disgruntled employees the opportunity to make an "unjust" situation more acceptable by engaging in off-task behaviors.

22

So what difference do these findings make?

- As with almost all other positive things, there is a dark side to Internet access. Before the Internet, there probably was as much personal telephone use, writing personal letters, taking care of personal business, and wasting time around the water cooler. The Internet just makes personal and recreational use at work easier and accessible to all.

- The Internet also enables employees to work away from work. For example, how many of you send emails at night after work or in the morning before work? Consequently, the Internet extends the boundaries of work. Some employees take pride in responding to emails very early in the morning or late at night as a symbol of their commitment to work.

- It does not take much misuse for a "norm" of negative behavior to be developed. Ideally, an Internet use policy would not be used to "catch" people. Rather, it would be used to establish limits and boundaries and to inform well-meaning employees of what is and is not permissible while at work. We would suggest that some form of monitoring needs to accompany the policy if it is to be effectively enforced. Zero use probably pushes the bounds of reasonableness as would a zero use of telephones for personal needs. Most

22

employees need an occasional diversion or break at work during the day to be fully productive.

- There are many vendors that provide electronic monitoring technology. The monitoring system should be able to track different categories of sites. Policies then can be created that specify different consequences for different forms of misuse (i.e., checking personal email versus visiting pornographic sites).

- Making Internet use expectations clearly known at the beginning of the employment contract is important. Employees should be informed of the policy during initial company orientation. Subsequently, reinforcement of the policy can take place at reboot. Technologically, it is possible to have a policy screen appear every time the Internet is accessed or the computer is turned on.

- There is preliminary evidence that Internet addiction is a clinical disorder. If recognized as such, there is the potential for employees to claim their misuse is disability-related as part of the Americans with Disabilities Act. The organizational consequences of such a claim likely would be minor (i.e., the organization would not be asked to provide off-task opportunities as a reasonable accommodation).

Some Key Sources

Anandarajan, M. (2002). Internet abuse in the workplace. *Communications of the ACM, 45,* 53-54.

Beard, K. W. (2002). Internet addiction: Current status and implications for employees. *Journal of Employment Counseling, 39,* 2-11.

Case, C. J., & Young, K. S. (2002). Employee Internet management: Current business practices and outcomes. *CyberPsychology & Behavior, 5,* 355-361.

Cooper, A., Safir, M. P., & Rosenmann, A. (2006). Workplace worries: A preliminary look at online sexual activities at the office—emerging issues for clinicians and employers. *CyberPsychology & Behavior, 9,* 22-29.

Greenfield, D. N. (1999). Psychological characteristics of compulsive Internet use: A preliminary analysis. *CyberPsychology and Behavior, 2,* 403-412.

Greenfield, D. N., & Davis, R. A. (2002). Lost in cyberspace: The Web @ work. *CyberPsychology & Behavior, 5,* 347-353.

Lim, V. K. G. (2002). The IT way of loafing on the job: Cyberloafing, neutralizing and organizational justice. *Journal of Organizational Behavior, 23,* 675-694.

Stanton, J. M., & Weiss, E. M. (2000). Electronic monitoring in their own words: An exploratory study of employee's experiences with new types of surveillance. *Computers in Human Behavior, 16,* 423-440.

Stewart, F. (2000). Internet acceptable use policies: Navigating the management, legal, and technical issues. *Information Systems Security, 9,* 46-53.

Vorobyov, G. D. (2005). Computer and Internet use in the work place: A common sense approach. *Psychologist-Manager Journal, 8,* 177-187.

23

CAREER DEVELOPMENT

23.

23

What best describes the typical managerial career path today?

SELECT ONE:

☐ A. Self-initiated, consisting of both lateral and vertical movement and career interruptions.

☐ B. Organization determined, receiving linear and logical advancement for hard work, achievement, and loyalty.

☐ C. Family-based, dual-career couples are promoted more slowly because of family considerations.

☐ D. Passion-based, those who show the most passion for the work tend to get promoted.

☐ E. Credential-based, those who have the right amount and quality of formal education get promoted most.

23. What best describes the typical managerial career path today?

The correct answer is A: Self-initiated, consisting of lateral and vertical movement and career interruptions.

HOW SURE ARE WE AT THIS TIME?				
1	2	**3**	4	5
Hint	Suggestive	**Trending**	Substantial	Solid

23

Discussion

The traditional linear career path of progressing through prescribed career stages (from apprentice to individual contributor to manager to strategist) within a single company is the exception rather than the rule for today's managers. In the traditional arrangement, large organizations provided security, increasing incremental responsibility, and financial rewards to hardworking and loyal managers. The organization, in turn, received productivity, commitment, and satisfaction from its employees. Reitman and Schneer (2003) estimate that the traditional linear model describes roughly *one-third* of current managerial career paths. While individuals still may work in a particular career stage, it is no longer hierarchical and linear. People may move into different stages depending on their assignment.

The era of downsizing and restructuring that occurred during the 1980s and 1990s is most often cited as the "beginning of the end" for traditional expectations between employees and large employers. During this period, the unwritten agreement of lifetime employment in exchange for hard and loyal work was broken for many people and organizations. There is speculation that that era will never return as the world becomes ever more global.

23

The career path that has taken the place of the traditional model is more self-directed (by the employee) and less organization-driven. It is characterized by voluntary or involuntary job loss, lateral job movements, and path interruptions. This new model is commonly referred to as a "protean" or "boundaryless" career path. It encompasses any career path that deviates from the traditional. Although this model does not necessarily result in increased job security, it does result in more diverse skill and knowledge acquisition and employment flexibility. Some have described the change as moving from "employment security" to "employability security" (Peiperl & Arthur, 2000). Employability security is obtained by workers who leverage their earlier job experiences to enhance personal skill and knowledge sets, thereby making themselves more marketable to future employers. Early career diversity results in more freedom and more choices later.

As organizations move toward more adaptive, flexible, and responsive structures in the increasingly global marketplace, the employee requirements will have to match that level of organizational flexibility. Individuals who wish to succeed in this environment must engage in a continuous learning process, updating and enhancing the skill and knowledge sets that make them marketable to evolving organizations. Individuals also have to take increased responsibility for their personal and professional development, not depending on the corporation to do it for them.

Selected Research

- Surveying MBAs over a 13-year period (1984 through 1997), Reitman and Schneer (2003) found that the boundaryless model currently describes the majority of management careers. Traditional linear career paths are most likely to be found in larger organizations.

- If the boundaryless career includes gaps in employment, negative compensation-based consequences do tend to occur. These gaps are fairly common (more than half of surveyed MBAs report periods of unemployment), and individuals who have had gaps in their employment history earn lower salaries up to 25 years after their period of unemployment. This effect does not differ based on whether gaps are attributable to voluntary or involuntary forces (Reitman & Schneer, 2005).

23

- Eby, Butts, and Lockwood (2003) found that "proactive" individuals (individuals who take initiative) are *most* likely to be successful in a boundaryless career. These individuals are more self-aware, develop more extensive networks of contacts (both inside and outside of their current organization), and engage in more continuous learning exercises. These activities, in turn, lead to greater perceptions of success and marketability.

- King, Burke, and Pemberton (2005) found, for IT professionals, that knowledge, skill, and education were not as important (for being closely considered for a job) as was being "known" by employment agency representatives. This suggests that networking is an important element to obtain employment opportunities for individuals who follow a boundaryless career path. Furthermore, moving around from job to job does not impact the likelihood of being considered for a temporary job, but it does negatively impact the likelihood of being considered for a permanent job.

- Employees who engage in visible career-enhancing practices (i.e., those who take control of their careers in a manner that's observable to others) are more likely to also receive career-management assistance from their organization (through both formal and informal means). Receiving career assistance fulfills the psychological contract for these specific employees, resulting in higher levels of organizational commitment and productivity (Sturges, Conway, Guest, & Liefooghe, 2005).

So what difference do these findings make?

- **From the viewpoint of the individual:** It is increasingly important that individuals take initiative to manage their own careers, rather than relying on their employing organization to manage their careers. Suggestions for self-directed management include joining professional organizations, subscribing to and reading relevant trade publications/ journals, applying for new jobs, and generally engaging in self-examination and continuous learning exercises. Mentoring relationships can be sought both within and outside of the current employing organization. The future will be more self-defined than it has been in the past. Individuals can no longer depend on others to manage their careers. Social networking is important for getting job offers within the protean career path. Although job-jumping is becoming more accepted as a tool for career management, the general perception (by potential employers) is still predominantly negative. Individuals who desire long-term employment but who have short-lived tenures of previous employment should be prepared to confront this general stigma, even in this age of boundaryless careers.

- **From the viewpoint of organizations:** The workforce is becoming splintered. A smaller but still sizeable percent of the workforce will be career stable and work in the same company for many years; an increasing percent may make a few horizontal or lateral moves; and an increasing percent may become free agents who are mobile in their professional affiliations. Overall, the trend is toward more mobile and less organization loyalty. Careering is being taken over by the employees. Lifelong employment is waning. With this increased churn, more rapid orienteering is probably called for. Getting people up to speed more quickly will help productivity and temporary retention. Building cultures that attract travelling talent will become more important. If the predicted baby boom retirement wave does increase job options for the upcoming generations, then mobility will increase. In the extreme sense, organizations will have to adjust to a larger percent of their workforce being temporary or moving into and out of job assignments. Temporary workforce management as a core competency might become the competitive advantage of the future. And because the major source of unwanted turnover is having a "bad" boss, the costs associated with having "bad" (usually interpersonal issues like not listening and not treating people fairly) will increase.

23

Some Key Sources

Arthur, M. B., Khapova, S. N., & Wilderom, C. P. M. (2005). Career success in a boundaryless career world. *Journal of Organizational Behavior, 26,* 177-202.

Eby, L. T., Butts, M., & Lockwood, A. (2003). Predictors of success in the era of the boundaryless career. *Journal of Organizational Behavior, 24,* 689-708.

Hall, D. T., & Moss, J. E. (1998). The new protean career contract: Helping organizations and employees adapt. *Organizational Dynamics, 26*(3), 22-37.

King, Z., Burke, S., & Pemberton, J. (2005). The "bounded" career: An empirical study of human capital, career mobility and employment outcomes in a mediated labor market. *Human Relations, 58,* 981-1007.

Kondratuk, T. B., Hausdorf, P. A., Korabik, K., & Rosin, H. M. (2004). Linking career mobility with corporate loyalty: How does job change relate to organizational commitment? *Journal of Vocational Behavior, 65,* 332-349.

Peiperl, M. A., & Arthur, M. B. (2000). Topics for conversation: Career themes old and new. In M. A. Peiperl, M. B. Arthur, R. Goffee, & T. Morris (Eds.), *Career Frontiers: New Conceptions of Working Lives* (pp. 1-19). New York: Oxford University Press.

Reitman, F., & Schneer, J. A. (2003). The promised path: A longitudinal study of managerial careers. *Journal of Managerial Psychology, 18*(1), 60-75.

Reitman, F., & Schneer, J. A. (2005). The long-term negative impacts of managerial career interruptions: A longitudinal study of men and women MBAs. *Group & Organization Management, 30*, 243-262.

Singh, R., & Greenhaus, J. H. (2004). The relation between career decision-making strategies and person-job fit: A study of job changers. *Journal of Vocational Behavior, 64*, 198-221.

Sturges, J., Conway, N., Guest, D., & Liefooghe, A. (2005). Managing the career deal: The psychological contract as a framework for understanding career management, organizational commitment and work behavior. *Journal of Organizational Behavior, 26*, 821-833.

Sullivan, S. E. (1999). The changing nature of careers: A review and research agenda. *Journal of Management, 25*, 457-484.

24.

Can managers make more accurate hiring decisions using typical (informal, casual, or unstructured) interviewing methods than a decision made using a standardized psychological assessment?

SELECT ONE:

☐ A. No.

☐ B. Yes, if they receive interviewer training.

☐ C. Yes, if they are experienced (more than five years) interviewers.

☐ D. Yes, if they are very familiar with the needs of the position.

☐ E. Yes, if they once held the position to be filled.

24. **Can managers make more accurate hiring decisions using typical (informal, casual, or unstructured) interviewing methods than a decision made using standardized psychological assessment?**

The correct answer is A: No.

HOW SURE ARE WE AT THIS TIME?				
1	2	3	**4**	5
Hint	Suggestive	Trending	**Substantial**	Solid

24

Discussion

Although the typical (casual or informal or unstructured) interview is commonly used for making selection decisions, it suffers from some inherent problems. For example, hiring managers tend to rate candidates more favorably if they are viewed as being similar to themselves, and the amount of applicant information an interviewer is able to cognitively process is limited. Additionally, the applicant characteristics being assessed are frequently not clearly articulated (i.e., social skills, perceived fit with the organization, personality tendencies, etc.). This lack of specification can result in inaccurate hiring decisions and leave an organization (or hiring manager) vulnerable to claims of unfair discrimination.

Many of the above issues are decreased if the interview is *structured,* essentially taking the traditional, unstructured interview and turning it into a standardized assessment by administering the same questions and scoring criteria to each candidate. This *structuring* process reduces the flexibility and interactive components of the traditional, unstructured interview—these elements, unfortunately, are typically what make the unstructured interview appealing to the hiring manager.

While it is possible for one interviewing manager to occasionally outperform the accuracy of a standardized psychological assessment, over the long haul an appropriate standardized psychological assessment will *consistently* yield more accurate predictions than a number of highly experienced managers.

Reviewing 85 years of research on the effectiveness of 19 different employee selection procedures for predicting job performance (of primarily nonmanagerial positions), Schmidt and Hunter (1998) concluded that, not using information regarding previous work in the job, the best predictor of performance is an applicant's general cognitive ability. This is best assessed through standardized psychological assessment. Unstructured interviews in this review fared better than reference checks or personality assessments, but not as good as work samples, cognitive ability, *structured* interviews, job-knowledge tests, or integrity assessments (see Chapter 39, *100 Things You Need to Know*).

24

Selected Research

- Interviews will sometimes assess applicant characteristics similar to those measured by standardized psychological instruments. Salgado and Moscoso (2002) found that an applicant's interview evaluation was closely related to scores on psychological assessments of general cognitive ability, emotional stability, and extraversion. In general, these researchers found that the ability of the interview to accurately predict performance was dependent on (1) the extent to which the interview is structured, and (2) the content of the interview (i.e., what questions are asked).

- Campion, Palmer, and Campion (1997) compared structured and unstructured interviews, concluding that structured approaches are fairly simple to incorporate. The researchers recommend that unstructured interviews be "tweaked" to increase their reliability and validity (important utility and legal requirements).

24

- On average (across a wide variety of primarily nonmanagerial jobs), structured interviews predict 26% of subsequent applicant performance, while unstructured interviews predict 14% (although this average number is likely quite lower for carelessly administered interviews; Schmidt & Hunter, 1998). The combination of a structured interview with a measure of general cognitive ability provides good applicant information. However, an unstructured interview on top of a cognitive ability test does not provide much additional information regarding probable nonmanagerial performance. Most jobs have some amount of tasks and activities that require cognitive ability. The more complex the job and the higher the level it is, the more cognitive ability might be required. General cognitive ability is best evaluated by a standardized test.

- Confirming the results found by Schmidt and Hunter (1998), Cortina et al. (2000) found that unstructured interview information does not contribute to prediction of performance if cognitive ability and conscientiousness (a personality characteristic) have already been assessed. If a structured interview is administered, however, this information does meaningfully contribute to prediction of performance (above and beyond knowledge of cognitive ability and conscientiousness).

- Looking at relative accuracy in predicting good organizational performers, Hermelin and Robertson (2001) found that unstructured interviews were (1) not as good as cognitive ability assessments or structured interviews, (2) roughly as good as integrity assessments and life experience information, and (3) better than most personality information (although the personality dimension of Conscientiousness is generally found to be a good predictor of performance).

- Organizations that do not have *structured* interviews can still increase the likelihood that traditional interviews will find productive workers if they (1) provide training for the interviewers, and (2) ensure that the same interviewer (or panel of interviewers) evaluates each candidate.

So what difference do these findings make?

- Most people are hired today based upon weak assessment methods. Most frequent among them are the typical, casual, informal and unstructured interview and reference checks. There are better methods available, like structured interviews, job samples, and standardized assessment tests and assessment centers. But the more systematic assessment processes are more costly and difficult to implement, although from a cost/benefit standpoint, probably worth the effort. At minimum, multiple interviewers need to meet with candidates and probe a set of structured questions related to the potential hire's job assignment.

- Most managers believe they are better interviewers and assessors of people than they really are. It's rare to hear a manager self-declare he/she is a marginal evaluator of people. This is why it is important to broaden the assessment pool—to mediate bias of any single manager.

- Managers who believe they can "outpredict" standardized psychological assessments are generally wrong. If the appropriate psychological assessment is used (i.e., a measure of general cognitive ability or a job-specific work sample assessment), the assessment scores of candidates will be more strongly related to eventual employee performance than will typical interview assessments.

- Every organization that hires people critical to its success should explore, at the very least, structured interview technology. It is readily available from a number of vendors and consultants.

24

- In addition to structured interviewing, more standardized assessment procedures should be considered.

- Legitimate assessment tests and process publishers have evidence supporting the use of their tests for different characteristics and positions (and industries). Ask the provider for information regarding the usefulness of different tests for the position you wish to fill.

- It is not recommended that typical interviews be used as the sole tool for selection. However, if they are used as the primary basis of candidate decision making, they are more useful if (1) they focus on job-related dimensions, (2) they are applied consistently and in the same manner to every applicant (i.e., there is some standardization of administration), and (3) multiple interviewers provide ratings (cf., Posthuma, Morgeson, & Campion, 2002).

24

Some Key Sources

Campion, M. A., Campion, J. E., & Hudson, J. P. (1994). Structured interviewing: A note on incremental validity and alternative question types. *Journal of Applied Psychology, 79,* 998-1102.

Campion, M. A., Palmer, D. K., & Campion, J. E. (1997). A review of structure in the selection interview. *Personnel Psychology, 50,* 655-702.

Cortina, J. M., Goldstein, N. B., Payne, S. C., Davison, H. K., & Gilliland, S. W. (2000). The incremental validity of interview scores over and above cognitive ability and conscientiousness scores. *Personnel Psychology, 53,* 325-351.

Gehrlein, T. M., Dipboye, R. L., & Shahani, C. (1993). Nontraditional validity calculations and differential interviewer experience: Implications for selection interviews. *Educational and Psychological Measurement, 53,* 457-469.

Hermelin, E., & Robertson, I. T. (2001). A critique and standardization of meta-analytic validity coefficients in personnel selection. *Journal of Occupational and Organizational Psychology, 74,* 253-277.

Huffcutt, A. I., Roth, P. L., & McDaniel, M. A. (1996). A meta-analytic investigation of cognitive ability in employment interview evaluations: Moderating characteristics and implications for incremental validity. *Journal of Applied Psychology, 81,* 459-473.

Huffcutt, A. I., & Woehr, D. J. (1999). Further analysis of employment interview validity: A quantitative evaluation of interviewer-related structuring methods. *Journal of Organizational Behavior, 20,* 549-560.

Posthuma, R. A., Morgeson, F. P., & Campion, M. A. (2002). Beyond employment interview validity: A comprehensive narrative review of recent research and trends over time. *Personnel Psychology, 55,* 1-81.

Salgado, J. F., Anderson, N., Moscoso, S., Bertua, C., de Fruyt, F., & Rolland, J. P. (2003). A meta-analytic study of general mental ability validity for different occupations in the European community. *Journal of Applied Psychology, 88,* 1068-1081.

Salgado, J. F., & Moscoso, S. (2002). Comprehensive meta-analysis of the construct validity of the employment interview. *European Journal of Work and Organizational Psychology, 11,* 299-324.

Schmidt, F. L., & Hunter, J. E. (1998). The validity and utility of selection methods in personnel psychology: Practical and theoretical implications of 85 years of research findings. *Psychological Bulletin, 124,* 262-274.

24

JOB ATTITUDES

25.

What is the most typical employee reaction when a manager uses humor in the workplace?

SELECT ONE:

☐ A. Perceptions of unprofessionalism.

☐ B. Increases in harassment-related litigation.

☐ C. Increases in workgroup productivity.

☐ D. Increases in workgroup playfulness and a decrease in productivity.

☐ E. Increases in workgroup job satisfaction.

25

25. What is the most typical employee reaction when a manager uses humor in the workplace?

The correct answer is E: Increases in workgroup job satisfaction.

HOW SURE ARE WE AT THIS TIME?				
1	2	3	**4**	5
Hint	Suggestive	Trending	**Substantial**	Solid

Discussion

Humor is an element of communication that can *enhance* subordinates' perceptions of a leader's ability to lead effectively and positively affect the general work environment (Decker & Rotondo, 2001). The effective use of humor lets others know that the leader is interpersonally competent (quick on one's feet, effectively persuasive, open to learning, and socially adept, for instance). The most consistent effect of humor on the work environment is an increase in general levels of job satisfaction (Brief, 1998; Decker, 1987).

The potential of humor as a tool for managers/leaders can be channeled into four categories: (1) humor can be used to assist learning (i.e., in training contexts); (2) humor can be used to facilitate behavior change (i.e., in feedback/development contexts); (3) it can be used to enhance creative thinking (i.e., in brainstorming/idea generation contexts); and (4) humor can be used as a tool to alleviate the fear that's inherent in change (i.e., in a redesign or restructuring context; Barbour, 1998).

Managers/leaders who use humor effectively use humor to emphasize critical learning points—analogies are especially helpful in this arena. Whatever the learning point is for the leader, that content must be incorporated into the

25

anecdote/joke in order for humor to facilitate learning or a point to be made.

It is important that humor is used constructively. Humor can also be used inappropriately and for negative reasons. Humor used to hurt others, diminish specific people or groups, or ethnic humor would be examples of humor with a dark side.

Selected Research

- One method to increase general levels of employees' job satisfaction is to introduce humor (Brief, 1998; Decker, 1987).

- Humor in leadership/management positions should be used for a specific purpose. Three common categories where this can be an effective management strategy are (1) to reduce stress, (2) to serve as points for management concerns, or (3) to motivate. It is very important, if humor is used, that it is not used in an inappropriate manner (Davis & Kleiner, 1989).

- Men may use humor to different ends than women, but the use of positive rather than negative humor is generally related to increased perceptions of management effectiveness (rated by subordinates; Decker & Rotondo, 2001).

- The *subject* of the humor can mask organizational dysfunction—joking about (and subsequently trivializing) sexual harassment, for example, has been cited as one reason that the general societal problem (of harassment) has persisted as long as it has (Montemurro, 2003).

- Similarly, the use of subversive humor or satire can subvert management's authority (Taylor & Bain, 2003). Although humor in general tends to be much more frequent in informal settings, the use of *subversive humor* may be used proportionately more frequently in formal work settings

25

(meetings, for example; Holmes & Marra, 2002). This does not serve any positive purpose and should be stopped.

- Workplace humor may or may not be related to physical well-being. Looking at Finnish police chiefs, ratings of a chief's sense of humor were not related to subsequent (three years later) health indices (blood pressure, cholesterol levels, alcohol consumption; Kerkkanen, Kuiper, & Martin, 2004). If workplace humor alleviates stress (cf., Weaver & Wilson, 1997), however, there is a possibility that it also subsequently impacts stress-related physical well-being.

- Employees (in general) who are perceived as having a sense of humor tend to receive more social support from coworkers (Bowling et al., 2004).

25

So what difference do these findings make?
- Engaging in workplace humor is generally helpful in making the workplace a more enjoyable setting, as long as the humor is not personally demeaning or derogatory.

- The presence or absence of humor can help define an organization's culture—the presence of humor is often indicative of more informal or relaxed cultures. Using humor to help through a change effort can ease anxiety associated with the "unknowns" of change.

- Leaders who wish to use humor as a management tool would be wise to consider that *what* and *how* humor is used reflects on power differentials and general social relations. Using the Davis and Kleiner (1989) framework, leaders should think of this tool as an option to (1) reduce stress/ease tension, (2) communicate concerns, and/or (3) motivate employees. On the other hand, humor used to diminish others or to deliver disguised messages probably would not be as well-received. Types of humor to avoid (here called negative humor): puns, hostile/mean-spirited jokes, teasing/humor at the expense of a specific someone (cf., Davis & Kleiner, 1989).

- Managers should not feel compelled to stifle their natural humor in fear of being viewed as unprofessional or inappropriate. Humor, when used properly, can be an effective management tool and can in fact increase perceptions of leader effectiveness.

- There are a number of vendors in the business of teaching positive workplace humor for managers without the natural bent.

Some Key Sources

Barbour, G. (1998). Want to be a successful manager? Now that's a laughing matter! *Public Management, 80,* 6-9.

Bowling, N. A., Beehr, T. A., Johnson, A. L., Semmer, N. K., Hendricks, E. A., & Webster, H. A. (2004). Explaining potential antecedents of workplace social support: Reciprocity or attractiveness? *Journal of Occupational Health Psychology, 9,* 339-350.

Brief, A. P. (1998). *Attitudes in and around organizations.* Thousand Oaks, CA: Sage.

Clouse, R. W., & Spurgeon, K. L. (1995). Corporate analysis of humor. *Psychology: A Journal of Human Behavior, 32,* 1-24.

Davis, A., & Kleiner, B. H. (1989). The value of humour in effective leadership. *Leadership & Organization Development Journal, 10,* 1-3.

Decker, W. H. (1987). Managerial humor and subordinate satisfaction. *Social Behavior and Personality, 15,* 225-232.

Decker, W. H., & Rotondo, D. M. (2001). Relationships among gender, type of humor, and perceived leader effectiveness. *Journal of Managerial Issues, 13,* 450-465.

Holmes, J., & Marra, M. (2002). Over the edge? Subversive humor between colleagues and friends. *Humor: International Journal of Humor Research, 15,* 65-87.

25

Kerkkanen, P., Kuiper, N. A., & Martin, R. A. (2004). Sense of humor, physical health, and well-being at work: A three-year longitudinal study of Finnish police officers. *Humor: International Journal of Humor Research, 17,* 21-35.

Meisiek, S., & Yao, X. (2005). Nonsense makes sense: Humor in social sharing of emotion at the workplace. In C. E. Hartel, W. J. Zerbe, & N. M. Ashkanasy, (Eds.), *Emotions in organizational behavior* (pp. 143-165). Mahway, NJ: Lawrence Erlbaum Associates.

Montemurro, B. (2003). Not a laughing matter: Sexual harassment as "material" on workplace-based situation comedies. *Sex Roles, 48,* 433-445.

Morreall, J. (1991). Humor and work. *Humor: International Journal of Humor Research, 4,* 359-373.

Taylor, P., & Bain, P. (2003). "Subterranean worksick blues": Humour as subversion in two call centers. *Organization Studies, 24,* 1487-1509.

Weaver, S. T., & Wilson, C. N. (1997). Addiction counselors can benefit from appropriate humor in the work setting. *Journal of Employment Counseling, 34,* 108-114.

25

26.

Is the balanced scorecard approach a proven performance management tool?

SELECT ONE:

☐ A. Maybe, if it is actually used and clearly communicated to all organizational constituents.

☐ B. Yes, if it focuses more on financial indicators and less on "soft" measures.

☐ C. Yes, if it is closely tied in the reward system.

26

☐ D. No, it confuses decision makers and diffuses attention and focus.

☐ E. Not yet; few have actually been able to implement it.

26. Is the balanced scorecard approach a proven performance management tool?

The correct answer is A: Maybe, if it is actually used and clearly communicated to all organizational constituents.

HOW SURE ARE WE AT THIS TIME?				
1	2	**3**	4	5
Hint	Suggestive	**Trending**	Substantial	Solid

Discussion

Attempts to assess and drive organizational success have moved beyond just financial indicators. A balanced scorecard management system expands the financial perspective on organizational performance to also consider the customer perspective, the internal business perspective, and the innovation and learning perspective. Focus on the customer, internal business, and innovation/learning perspectives serves to attain financial goals. (Kaplan & Norton, 1992).

The premise of the balanced scorecard approach is that there are multiple stakeholders for any organization. Each stakeholder gets something from contributing to the organization. The balanced scorecard approach identifies goals within each of the four performance dimensions and specific measures to gauge the attainment of those goals. The goals and measures may differ from organization to organization, but the general four-dimension "goal/measure" framework is consistent across most balanced scorecard initiatives. Typically, there are a limited number of measures used—ideally between 15 and 25. To make appropriate business decisions, key decision makers need to consider all four perspectives. The concept of "balance" refers to a mutual focus on long- and short-term goals, lagging/leading, and internal/external performance indicators (cf., Hepworth, 1998). Some of these domains are more likely to be lead indicators and some lag indicators. For example, employee attitude is a lead indicator of customer attitude, and customer attitude is a lead indicator of firm financial performance. The balanced scorecard helps executives serve multiple stakeholders and begin to see cause and effect of managerial practices.

Originally put forth as a performance measurement framework, today the balanced scorecard is used as a strategic management tool—translating an organization's mission into measurable and manageable performance indicators. The approach can be applied at the corporate, division, or project management levels.

The use of some version of the balanced scorecard approach is widespread—as many as 60% of Fortune 500 companies have used a balanced scorecard approach in one or more business units (Silk, 1998). The use of these scorecards varies widely. Some scorecards measure performance from multiple dimensions; others use two or three dimensions. Some measures are more likely to be tracked and acted on than others. Overall, the *effectiveness* of the approach is difficult to quantify, in part because the very nature of the balanced scorecard expands the dimensions of effectiveness that are considered. McWilliams (1996) highlights this conundrum with a case study from Mobil Oil:

26

> When Bob McCool called a meeting of the Mobil North America Marketing and Refining division (NAM&R) to discuss first-quarter 1995 results, it looked to many employees like an invitation to a beheading...everyone knew the quarter had been terrible, thanks in part to the mild winter's subpar natural-gas and heating-oil sales. But...after some remarks about Q1's disappointing financial performance, McCool shifted the conversation abruptly. Market share in key customer segments

191

was up, he said. Refinery operating expenses were down. And results from an employee-satisfaction survey were positive. "In all the areas we could control, we moved the needle in the right direction," McCool concluded (McWilliams, 1996, p. 16).

Unfortunately, there is not a great deal of research looking specifically at the extent to which a balanced scorecard approach actually improves organizational decision making and performance. One of the few studies that has investigated *outcomes* of balanced scorecard implementation (Malina & Selto, 2001) suggests the approach can have either benefits or detriments, depending on communication and implementation.

Selected Research

- As with many other initiatives, if balanced scorecard elements are effectively communicated, managers will be motivated to work toward the organizational goals. Unfortunately, if the balanced scorecard is not communicated or implemented effectively, relations between middle and upper management can be adversely affected (Malina & Selto, 2001).

26

- Investigating the extent to which a balanced scorecard improves managerial decision making, Lipe and Salterio (2000) determined that balanced scorecard effectiveness is limited by information processing limitations of managers. Specifically, upper-level managers may have a tendency to overvalue shared performance dimensions and undervalue unique performance dimensions (i.e., performance indicators that are unique to a business unit). This will lead to a disconnect between levels of management.

- Ahn (2001) describes a case study of the balanced scorecard approach, suggesting that it requires extensive management capacity—the development process lasted four months and consisted of multiple full-day workshops. Additionally, during implementation, the measurement and monitoring of performance indicators "required a great amount of time and energy." Positive aspects of the implementation included linking budget planning with long-term strategic goals and evaluating progress toward goals at quarterly balanced scorecard meetings. This organization utilized a parallel "communication program" to inform employees of the balanced scorecard approach.

- Wisniewski and Ólafsson (2004) suggest a slight alteration of the traditional balanced scorecard if the approach is to be used in public sector (government) applications. For example, the areas of focus for a Scottish municipality were (1) impact (result of a service for the community), (2) service management (how well the service is delivered), (3) resource management (the effective use of people, equipment, or physical resources), and (4) improvement (use of new technology, training programs, or service improvement review). These authors claim that the four performance dimension labels commonly do not fit the needs of public sector organizations.

26

- Lawrie and Cobbold (2004) differentiate between 1st, 2nd, and 3rd (current) generations of balanced scorecards, noting that practitioners have had difficulty in implementing 1st generation balanced scorecards. The current preferred method of balanced scorecard implementation includes a "destination statement" that quantifies the future appearance of the organization. This destination statement is articulated within each of the four balanced scorecard performance dimensions.

So what difference do these findings make?

- The concept and practice of the balanced scorecard is spreading. As with any other "new" tool or way of thinking, it has had a shaky start. Very preliminary findings are beginning to show that if properly designed and implemented, it aids decision making and organizational performance. It also broadens the discussions about organizational performance beyond pure financial outcomes. It may also help translate strategy and vision into tactics and measures.

- Enterprise-wide communication of the balanced scorecard strategy is important for its effectiveness.

- Ultimately, the balanced scorecard approach or any other measurement system for organizations should focus attention and resources on what is important and reward members for accomplishments against those goals. To that end, it is critical that the goals and measures be real and appropriate, that is, they actually, upon successful completion, lead to important measurable organizational outcomes. Nice-to-haves or nice-to-dos that ultimately do not add to important outcomes will decrease the benefits of the balanced scorecard.

- It seems that sometimes there is a disconnect between levels of management. Top management sometimes endorses a one-size-fits-all implementation. Everybody needs to measure against the same elements, structure, or even specific measures. It is looking like the further away from top management you get, the less relevant the one-size-fits-all preference works. Best practice would seem to be adding some lower level flexibility to adjust goals and measures to local needs.

- It appears we have a way to go to get to the best practice level.

Some Key Sources

Ahn, H. (2001). Applying the balanced scorecard concept: An experience report. *Long Range Planning: International Journal of Strategic Management, 34,* 441-461.

Hepworth, P. (1998). Weighing it up—A literature review for the balanced scorecard. *Journal of Management Development, 17,* 559-563.

Kaplan, R. S., & Norton, D. P. (1992). The balanced scorecard—Measures that drive performance. *Harvard Business Review, 70*(1), 71-79.

Lawrie, G., & Cobbold, I. (2004). Third-generation balanced scorecard: Evolution of an effective strategic control tool. *International Journal of Productivity and Performance Management, 53,* 611-623.

Lipe, M. G., & Salterio, S. E. (2000). The balanced scorecard: Judgmental effects of common and unique performance measures. *Accounting Review, 75*(3), 283-298.

Malina, M. A., & Selto, F. H. (2001). Communicating and controlling strategy: An empirical study of the effectiveness of the balanced scorecard. *Journal of Management Accounting Research, 13,* 47-90.

Maltz, A. C., Shenhar, A. J., & Reilly, R. R. (2003). Beyond the balanced scorecard: Refining the search for organizational success measures. *Long Range Planning: International Journal of Strategic Management, 36,* 187-204.

Martinsons, M., Davison, R., & Tse, D. (1999). The balanced scorecard: A foundation for the strategic management of information systems. *Decision Support Systems, 25,* 71-88.

McWilliams, B. (1996). The measure of success. *Across the Board, 33*(2), 16-20.

Silk, S. (1998). Automating the balanced scorecard. *Management Accounting, 79*(11), 38-42.

Wisniewski, M., & Ólafsson, S. (2004). Developing balanced scorecards in local authorities: A comparison of experience. *International Journal of Productivity and Performance Management, 53,* 602-610.

26

ORGANIZATIONAL DOWNSIZING

27.

What is the most common reaction of surviving employees after a "downsizing"?

SELECT ONE:

☐ A. Generally quite positive because they survived, a proof of their value to the organization.

☐ B. Usually positive because downsizing clears out deadwood and people who were not contributing, making the retained employees' work easier.

☐ C. Neutral, waiting to see what comes next.

☐ D. Usually negative.

☐ E. Highly variable, depending upon how fair the employees perceive the cutbacks were implemented.

27. What is the most common reaction of surviving employees after "downsizing"?

The correct answer is D: Usually negative.

HOW SURE ARE WE AT THIS TIME?				
1	2	3	**4**	5
Hint	Suggestive	Trending	**Substantial**	Solid

Discussion

Increased stress is pervasive at the announcement of, during, and after a downsizing effort. The stress can manifest itself in those who survive the downsizing initiative into what has been labeled the "survivor syndrome." This refers to the mix of largely negative emotions held by retained employees after a downsizing initiative has been implemented. These emotions and beliefs include anger, a loss of security, perceptions of unfairness, and reduced levels of motivation and morale. Productivity usually dips for a period of time.

There are a variety of reasons why retained employees may exhibit negative attitudes and behaviors. Those that remain have to "do more" with fewer resources, and they have to do so at a time when many employees are emotionally distraught. Often when people are taken out, the work remains, so those who stay have to fulfill the work obligations of those who left. Survivors may find themselves working "harder, not smarter"—doing more work, but feeling as though they are accomplishing less. Furthermore, it is very likely that the downsizing activity is perceived as violating the psychological contract—the implicit relationship between an employee and his/her employing organization that hard work is rewarded with security and protection, although this is dissipating in most companies. When a violation of the psychological contract occurs, employees exhibit reduced motivation toward completing organizational goals. They may experience a greater sense of cynicism, decreased morale, and anxiety about the future (Marks & De Meuse, 2005). Additionally, the resulting restructuring often results in a lack of clarity regarding the survivors' roles within the new workplace. When downsizing is not tied to employee or organization performance but applied equally to all (e.g., 10% cutback in every department), talented employees may feel mistreated. And, in the absence of a good performance management system that informs employees on how the company is doing, when a company announces a downsizing of 10% six months from now, sometimes up to 40% of employees think they are likely to go, causing enormous disruption in the ensuing six months.

Downsizing necessarily involves management making subjective calls on who stays and who leaves. Since there are no perfect and unassailable ways to make those decisions, second-guessing is always at play. Most surviving employees have a friend or two who was asked to leave. Also, many times employees blame management for the conditions that led to the need for downsizing (loss of market, loss of revenues, insufficient profits, out-of-date products and services, etc.). In most downsizings, the employees take a bigger hit than management. As a result, there is usually a downturn in the trust between management and employees.

27

Although not every downsizing survivor will exhibit these negative reactions, it is important to note that these experiences are more common than not. Downsizing initiatives should be made with a realization that retained employees may exhibit some or all of these negative consequences for some time, and productivity might suffer.

Selected Research

- Armstrong-Stassen (2005) investigated the reactions of executives and middle managers before, during, and after a downsizing initiative. In general, middle managers report less job security, lower levels of performance, and a greater number of physical stress indicators than do executives. However, across the downsizing stages, both executives and middle managers tend to have an increasing sense of powerlessness. Because executives also suffer some of the negative consequences of downsizing, they should not be excluded from stress management programs.

- Amundson, Borgen, Jordan, and Erlebach (2004) interviewed downsizing survivors and noted that the psychological contract changes the moment the intent to downsize has been communicated. This speaks to the need for open lines of communication, because the way in which employees perceive the downsizing takes place (with or without integrity) can "destroy or build new loyalties" (p. 268).

- Armstrong-Stassen, Wagar, and Cattaneo (2004) classified survivors' workgroups as somewhat, moderately, or highly affected (in terms of the number of team members lost to downsizing). Somewhat surprisingly, survivors whose workgroups did not appreciably change during downsizing tended to have more negative reactions. Survivors who had "new" workgroups exhibited increases in satisfaction, performance, and morale two years after the initiative. These "new workgroup" employees may have felt the organization treated their departed coworkers fairly, as most departures were voluntary and included generous incentives.

- Retained employees who were previously affectively committed to the organization (i.e., had an emotional attachment) reported more job satisfaction and less perceptions of insecurity, job alienation, and intentions to

27

leave the organization than did less-committed survivors (Armstrong-Stassen, 2004). Employees who had previous levels of continuance commitment (i.e., were committed because they perceived the costs associated with leaving to be high) did not experience these beneficial post-downsizing boosts. The form of prior attachment to the organization, then, can impact how downsizing will be experienced.

- Repeated downsizing efforts result in more negative consequences for survivors than do single downsizing efforts (Moore, Grunberg, & Greenberg, 2004). That is, downsizing survivors do not become "used to" or resilient to the negative effects of downsizing. These individuals suffer from more job insecurity, depression, and general health problems than do individual survivors who have either no layoff experience or only one layoff wave.

- Noer (1998) contends that "lean and mean" for the organization becomes "sad and angry" for the retained employees. The "survivor syndrome" is best treated by means of progressing through four levels of interventions: (1) overcommunicate, (2) uncover repressed feelings and encourage grieving, (3) facilitate self-empowerment, and (4) embrace the new employment contract—set up systems that are supportive of a mobile workforce.

27

- Clair and Dufresne (2004) investigated the effect of downsizing efforts on those who implement the downsizing—the actual agents of change. The researchers noted that downsizing agents try to cognitively, physically, and emotionally distance themselves from the downsizing event. These individuals face emotionally-draining tasks, such as making uncertain decisions, dealing with others' emotions, and being stigmatized as a "downsizer."

So what difference do these findings make?

- As if downsizing were not bad enough, there are serious problems the survivors will exhibit. Those problems will be mostly negative and may have a negative effect on productivity for some time to come following the downsizing. From a financial standpoint, in addition to allocating a cost to the downsizing effort, additional estimates of losses might need to be assigned to temporary decreased productivity. When forced to do downsizing, it is important to be bold. This means taking action quickly (within legal constraints) and going deep enough into the employee population pool to not have to downsize a second or third time, which is even more demoralizing. If employees have been continually briefed about the business and results, the downsizing should not come as a shock or surprise (De Meuse & Marks, 2003).

- As in all change management research and practice, downsizing requires communication, communication, communication. Employees should be prepared well in advance for the downsizing. These "what to expect" messages should be delivered in person whenever possible—additionally, supervisors should be visible during this period. It is difficult to be truthful (especially if managers do not have all of the answers), but it is important. Overcommunication (more than usual or seemingly necessary) can be a useful strategy both prior to and during the downsizing initiative. There is no such thing as too much information for retained employees—if not given information, employees will create their own (which may or may not be accurate). Sharing customer and financial data helps employees know *why* things are happening as much as *what* is happening. When employees understand the why, they are more likely to accept the what.

27

- Brockner et al. (2004) suggest that negative survivor reactions can be helped after the downsizing effort by increasing survivors' perceptions of self-control. To do this, managers can seek input from surviving subordinates and give survivors tasks at which they are likely to be successful. Influencing important others also provides a sense of increased control—executives and important organizational members should, therefore, be accessible (via email or face-to-face opportunities) following downsizing. In particular, survivors can be informed that the downsizing was done not only for performance reasons but for strategic rationale. Removing more employees from one area of the business versus another sends a strategic signal about what is important.

- Downsizing agents will face certain emotionally-draining experiences, such as confronting employees targeted for termination and being exposed to their emotional reactions. Empathizing with these individuals may provide comfort to the laid-off coworkers, but it also magnifies the negative experiences of the downsizing agent. If you are involved in the downsizing process, it is better to sympathize with the laid-off workers' plight while attempting to maintain some emotional distance (i.e., do not try to view the event from their perspective). Furthermore, training in these issues should be provided to downsizing agents.

27

- Treating the employees who are downsized with dignity and respect also sends a message to remaining employees. While most employees who lose their jobs are distraught, if they are treated with dignity, those employees who remain can expect the same treatment of and for them.

Some Key Sources

Amundson, N. E., Borgen, W. A., Jordan, S., & Erlebach, A. C. (2004). Survivors of downsizing: Helpful and hindering experiences. *Career Development Quarterly, 52*, 256-271.

Armstrong-Stassen, M. (2004). The influence of prior commitment on the reactions of layoff survivors to organizational downsizing. *Journal of Occupational Health Psychology, 9*, 46-60.

Armstrong-Stassen, M. (2005). Coping with downsizing: A comparison of executive-level and middle managers. *International Journal of Stress Management, 12*, 117-141.

Armstrong-Stassen, M. (2006). Determinants of how managers cope with organizational downsizing. *Applied Psychology: An International Review, 55*, 1-26.

Armstrong-Stassen, M., Wagar, T. H., & Cattaneo, R. J. (2004). Work-group membership (in)stability and survivors' reactions to organizational downsizing. *Journal of Applied Social Psychology, 34*, 2023-2044.

Brockner, J., Spreitzer, G., Mishra, A., Hochwarter, W., Pepper, L., & Weinberg, J. (2004). Perceived control as an antidote to the negative effects of layoffs on survivors' organizational commitment and job performance. *Administrative Science Quarterly, 49*, 76-100.

Clair, J. A., & Dufresne, R. L. (2004). Playing the grim reaper: How employees experience carrying out a downsizing. *Human Relations, 57*, 1597-1625.

De Meuse, K. P., & Marks, M. L. (2003). *Resizing the organization: Managing layoffs, divestitures, and closings.* San Francisco: Jossey-Bass.

Kernan, M. C., & Hanges, P. J. (2002). Survivor reactions to reorganization: Antecedents and consequences of procedural, interpersonal, and informational justice. *Journal of Applied Psychology, 87*, 916-928.

27

Marks, M. L., & De Meuse, K. P. (2005). Resizing the organization: Maximizing the gain while minimizing the pain of layoffs, divestitures, and closings. *Organizational Dynamics, 34,* 19-35.

McElroy, J. C., Morrow, P. C., & Rude, S. N. (2001). Turnover and organizational performance: A comparative analysis of the effects of voluntary, involuntary, and reduction-in-force turnover. *Journal of Applied Psychology, 86,* 1294-1299.

Moore, S., Grunberg, L., & Greenberg, E. (2004). Repeated downsizing contact: The effects of similar and dissimilar layoff experiences on work and well-being outcomes. *Journal of Occupational Health Psychology, 9,* 247-257.

Noer, D. (1995). Center for Creative Leadership: Leadership in an age of layoffs. *The Journal of Management Development, 14*(5), 27-38.

Noer, D. (1998). Layoff survivor sickness: What it is and what to do about it. In M. K. Gowing, J. D. Kraft, and J. C. Quick (Eds.), *The new organizational reality: Downsizing, restructuring, and revitalization* (pp. 207-221). Washington, DC: American Psychological Association.

Petzall, B. J., Parker, G. E., & Stoeberl, P. A. (2000). Another side to downsizing: Survivors' behavior and self-affirmation. *Journal of Business and Psychology, 14,* 593-603.

27

28.

How does coffee consumption affect performance at work?

SELECT ONE:

☐ A. It doesn't; it's a myth.

☐ B. It causes increased anxiety and emotionality.

☐ C. It increases mental processing at first, but later depresses it.

☐ D. It helps workers to focus and think faster.

☐ E. It helps workers make more accurate decisions.

28

28. How does coffee consumption affect performance at work?

The correct answer is D: It helps workers to focus and think faster.

HOW SURE ARE WE AT THIS TIME?				
1	2	**3**	4	5
Hint	Suggestive	**Trending**	Substantial	Solid

Discussion

Although excessive coffee consumption can increase anxiety, restlessness, or insomnia, moderate intake can increase alertness, positive mood, information-processing speed, and the ability to focus. These positive "psychostimulant" effects of coffee constitute the benefits of caffeine.

The amount of caffeine necessary to achieve the beneficial psychostimulating effects may be as little as 60 mg (cf., Durlach, 1998). The optimal amount to maximize these effects, however, may be as high as 400 mg (Jarvis, 1993). Freshly ground coffee (as opposed to less-potent instant coffee) is estimated to have anywhere between 80 and 200 mg of caffeine per 8 ounce cup. The concentration depends on the type of beans used and the strength of the brewing (percentage of beans to water). Unfortunately, the variability in the amount of caffeine in a cup of coffee tends to be quite large, even if the same individual brews coffee from the same ground beans (Eisenberg, 1988).

To get 400 mg of caffeine per day, an employee would have to either drink two strong 8 oz. cups of coffee or four relatively weaker cups. Comparatively, according to the National Soft Drink Association, there are 45.6 mg of caffeine in a 12 oz. can of Coca-Cola, and 55 mg in a 12 oz. can of Mountain Dew

28

(using two widely-known American examples). So two to four servings might have the same effect.

The purpose of this chapter is not to encourage employees to start or stop drinking coffee or to render medical advice. In fact, regular coffee drinkers who decrease or stop may experience withdrawal symptoms, such as headaches, fatigue, depressed moods, or increased drowsiness, and non-regular drinkers who start may feel jittery or have upset stomachs (cf., Rogers & Dernoncourt, 1998). The purpose is rather to let the persistent coffee drinkers know that they are not, in all likelihood, drinking away the profits of the organization—there is a fairly suggestive cognitive performance-related boost associated with caffeine intake.

Selected Research

- Jarvis (1993) studied habitual coffee and tea drinking in British adults and found the greatest increase in memory, reasoning, and reaction time at a dose of 400 mg of caffeine per day. This study documented the cognitive processing increases associated with long-term consumption of caffeine (i.e., not a one-time boost).

- Caffeine consumption decreases the likelihood of workplace accidents and increases cognitive functioning. Smith (2005) split workers into high (over 220 mg) and low (under 220 mg) caffeine drinkers and found high consumers to have greater reaction times and fewer cognitive failures (memory or attention lapses) and workplace accidents.

28

- Christopher, Sutherland, and Smith (2005) documented improvements in mood and cognitive performance in experimental participants who were given caffeine. This study documented that the beneficial effects of caffeine were due to the substance itself and not merely attributable to withdrawal-reducing effects of caffeine ingestion.

- A dose of caffeine as low as 60 mg (the amount in an average cup of tea) can provide immediate beneficial effects on cognitive processing. Reaction times (dependent upon alertness and speed) to computerized cognitive tasks were faster for participants who drank a beverage containing 60 mg of caffeine than for non-caffeine presented participants. Accuracy of judgments was not affected by caffeine intake (Durlach, 1998).

- Drinking a lot of caffeine in one sitting is similar to the effect of drinking reasonable doses throughout the day (Brice & Smith, 2001).

- Large doses of caffeine (600 mg) can increase anxiety levels in some individuals (Smith, 2002). Moderate doses increase alertness and vigilance and decrease drowsiness. The general conclusion from this review is that moderate consumption by the majority of individuals has few negative effects, but *excessive* consumption (differentially defined as between 600 and 1500 mg) will generally have negative effects that accompany the positive.

So what difference do these findings make?

- Moderate coffee consumption can aid a worker's level of alertness and speed of cognitive processing, but these beneficial effects need to be weighed against the *potential* harmful effects of excess caffeine. Physical dependency may occur if individuals regularly consume 350 mg or more per day, and regular consumption may be especially harmful to employees prone to hypertension (cf., Nurminen et al., 1999).

- Organization support (access and financial aid) of moderate coffee and caffeine intake seems supported by research.

28

- This chapter is not recommending that employees drink more coffee or other caffeinated beverages—it is simply presenting *performance*-based information regarding caffeine consumption because coffee is such a regular feature in organizational life. The ultimate choice of an appropriate amount of caffeine per employee should, of course, be made in consultation with his or her physician.

Some Key Sources

Brice, C. F., & Smith, A. P. (2001). The effects of caffeine on simulated driving, subjective alertness and sustained attention. *Human Psychopharmacology, 16,* 523-531.

Christopher, G., Sutherland, D., & Smith, A. (2005). Effects of caffeine in non-withdrawn volunteers. *Human Psychopharmacology, 20,* 47-53.

Durlach, P. J. (1998). The effects of low doses of caffeine on cognitive performance. *Psychopharmacology, 140,* 116-119.

Eisenberg, S. (1988). Looking for the perfect brew. *Science News, 133*(16), 252-253.

Friedman, A. S., Granick, S., Utada, A., & Tomko, L. A. (1992). Drug use/abuse and supermarket workers' job performance. *Employee Assistance Quarterly, 7,* 17-34.

Jarvis, M. J. (1993). Does caffeine intake enhance absolute levels of cognitive performance? *Psychopharmacology, 110,* 45-52.

Nurminen, M. L., Niittynen, L., Korpela, R., & Vapaatalo, H. (1999). Coffee, caffeine and blood pressure: A critical review. *European Journal of Clinical Nutrition, 53,* 831-839.

Rogers, P. J., & Dernoncourt, C. (1998). Regular caffeine consumption: A balance of adverse and beneficial effects for mood and psychomotor performance. *Pharmacology, Biochemistry and Behavior, 59,* 1039-1045.

Smith, A. P. (2002). Effects of caffeine on human behaviour. *Food and Chemical Toxicology, 40,* 1243-1255.

28

Smith, A. P. (2005). Caffeine at work. *Human Psychopharmacology: Clinical and Experimental, 20,* 441-445.

Streufert, S., Satish, U., Pogash, R., Gingrich, D., Landis, R., & Roache, J., et al. (1997). Excess coffee consumption in simulated complex work settings: Detriment or facilitation of performance. *Journal of Applied Psychology, 82,* 774-782.

28

29.

What are the health care and lost productivity costs associated with smokers in the workforce?

SELECT ONE:

☐ A. Approximately $400 per smoker per year.

☐ B. Approximately $3,400 per smoker per year.

☐ C. Approximately $6,400 per smoker per year.

☐ D. Approximately $9,400 per smoker per year.

☐ E. Approximately $12,400 per smoker per year.

29

29. What are the health care and lost productivity costs associated with smokers in the workforce?

The correct answer is B: Approximately $3,400 per smoker per year.

HOW SURE ARE WE AT THIS TIME?				
1	2	**3**	4	5
Hint	Suggestive	**Trending**	Substantial	Solid

Discussion

According to the Centers for Disease Control and Prevention, an employee who smokes cigarettes costs roughly $3,400 more per year in lost productivity and health care costs compared to a nonsmoker. Although different sources cite different dollar amounts, all sources agree that there are additional financial costs associated with workers who smoke (compared with nonsmoking employees).

The Conference Board of Canada estimates that the average smoking employee costs an employer roughly $2,400 (Canadian dollars) per year in productivity costs. Looking just at time instead of monetary figures—if 30 minutes a day is spent on cigarette breaks, those 30 minutes a day add up to 18 days per year for smoking breaks.

In response to these financial estimates, and perceptions of differential treatment/unfairness by nonsmokers who do not take "smoke breaks" (cf., Sarna et al., 2005), organizations are increasingly instituting smoke-free workplace initiatives. Smoke-free workplace policies serve two primary functions: (1) they protect nonsmokers from the effects of second-hand smoke, and (2) they establish an environment that encourages smokers to quit.

29

Some organizations are also attempting to minimize health-care costs by implementing policies that encourage a *smoke-free workforce*. For example, Scotts Miracle-Gro Company threatened to fire workers beginning October of 2006, even if they were smoking off-the-job (Brat, 2005). Humana, Inc. provides (or provided) bonuses to nonsmokers, and General Mills, Inc. enforces a monthly health-benefit surcharge for smokers. These measures are largely taken to attempt to reduce employer health-care costs and are not a strictly American phenomenon. The British government asked its National Health Service to be smoke-free by the end of 2006 ("Unions Divided," 2005).

The bigger question is one of a smoke-free *workforce* versus simply a smoke-free workplace. The evidence is clear that instituting a smoke-free workplace policy leads to less smoking and more cessation than not having a smoke-free workplace policy. The unsettled issue concerns an employer's rights to institute *smoke-free employee* policies (considering smoking behavior both on- and off-the-job).

As of early 2006, 30 states in the U.S. have laws protecting smokers—terminating smokers in these states would be considered a form of unfair discrimination (i.e., illegal). Outside of these 30 states, however, organizations can fire at will (there is no federal protection for smokers).

Adding to the health-care cost-related pressures on organizations is research from a public policy perspective that cites the cost-effectiveness and general benefits of using workplace smoking bans (over tax increases or free nicotine therapy programs, for example, to achieve general public smoking cessation; Fichtenberg & Glantz, 2002; Ong & Glantz, 2005).

29

Selected Research

- In 2004, approximately 20.9% of adults in the United States smoked. This number is trending downward (22.5% in 2002, 21.6% in 2003), but 70% of smokers still claim they would like to quit (Centers for Disease Control and Prevention, 2005).

- Smoke-free workplace policies do help employees either reduce their daily cigarette use or quit smoking altogether (Bauer, Hyland, Li, Steger, & Cummings, 2005). Furthermore, the more restrictive the policy, the more likely employees are to quit smoking.

- Employees of smoke-free organizations are 25% more likely to attempt to quit smoking than are employees of organizations that do not have a smoke-free policy. Those who work for a smoke-free workplace employer, but who continue to smoke, consume 2.75 fewer cigarettes per day (on average) than do workers whose employers do not have restrictive smoking policies (Glasgow, Cummings, & Hyland, 1997).

- Fichtenberg and Glantz (2002), in a review of previous public policy research, estimated that instituting smoke-free workplace legislation would reduce smoking, on average, by 3.1 cigarettes per day (per smoker). Similar reductions obtained by increasing taxes on cigarettes would require tax *increases* of 400% in U.S. dollars. If all workplaces instituted a complete smoking ban, total public smoking consumption might decrease 29%. Smoke-free workplaces protect nonsmokers, but also encourage smokers to either quit or significantly reduce their smoking.

- Ong and Glantz (2005) looked at the relative cost and benefits of implementing a smoke-free workplace policy versus a nicotine replacement therapy program as a *general public health program*. These investigators found the enactment of a statewide smoke-free workplace policy to be almost nine times as cost-effective (per quitter) as a nicotine replacement program (i.e., providing a nicotine patch or gum).

So what difference do these findings make?

- Research is simple and clear. Smoking employees cost companies money. And, they cost those who smoke health and well-being. Further, the adverse health effects of second-hand smoke are beginning to be realized. Smoking appears to have many health-related concerns for *all* employees, including the nonsmokers.

- There is research supporting the effectiveness of various responses to smoking cessation.

- Organizations are currently encouraging employees to quit smoking through a number of means. Some of these include:
  - Providing bonuses to nonsmokers.
  - Implementing a surcharge (monthly) on health benefits for smokers.
  - Giving away free "stop smoking" products (i.e., nicotine patches).
  - Providing free "stop smoking" therapy programs.
  - Termination or other administrative penalties for smokers.
  - Applying peer or social pressure to stop smoking.

- Companies need to check state laws prior to instituting smoke-free *workforce* initiatives. Smoke-free workplace policies seem to be legally allowable thus far.

29

- As part of an overall healthy workplace program, policies related to smoking can pay off for individuals (personal health improvement) and organizations. It is likely that research will also point to other unhealthy lifestyle aspects like obesity, lack of sound diet, or lack of exercise to be in line with the findings on smoking.

Some Key Sources

Bauer, J. E., Hyland, A., Li, Q., Steger, C., & Cummings, K. M. (2005). A longitudinal assessment of the impact of smoke-free worksite policies on tobacco use. *American Journal of Public Health, 95,* 1024-1029.

Borland, R., Chapman, S., Owen, N., & Hill, D. (1990). Effects of workplace smoking bans on cigarette consumption. *American Journal of Public Health, 80,* 178-181.

Brat, I. (2005, December 20). A company's threat: Quit smoking or leave: Scotts Miracle-Gro joins ranks of employers trying to cut costs by targeting smokers. *The Wall Street Journal* (Eastern edition), p. D 1.

Centers for Disease Control and Prevention. (2005). Cigarette smoking among adults—United States, 2004. *Morbidity and Mortality Weekly Report, 54,* 1121-1124.

Fichtenberg, C. M., & Glantz, S. A. (2002). Effect of smoke-free workplaces on smoking behavior: Systematic review. *British Medical Journal, 325,* 188-191.

Gerlach, K. K., Shopland, D. R., Hartman, A. M., Gibson, J. T., & Pechacek, T. F. (1997). Workplace smoking policies in the United States: Results from a national survey of more than 100,000 workers. *Tobacco Control, 6,* 199-206.

Glasgow, R. E., Cummings, K. M., & Hyland, A. (1997). Relationship of worksite smoking policy to changes in employee tobacco use: Findings from COMMIT. *Tobacco Control, 6* (Supplement 2), s44-s48.

29

Ong, M. K., & Glantz, S. A. (2005). Free nicotine replacement therapy programs vs. implementing smoke-free workplaces: A cost-effectiveness comparison. *American Journal of Public Health, 95,* 969-975.

Sarna, L., Bialous, S. A., Wewers, M. E., Froelicher, E. S., & Danao, L. (2005). Nurses, smoking, and the workplace. *Research in Nursing & Health, 28,* 79-90.

Unions divided over plans for blanket smoking bans at trusts. (2005) *Nursing Standard, 20*(13), 9.

29

30.

The improvements associated with Sarbanes-Oxley (SOX) compliance:

SELECT ONE:

☐ A. Are well worth the costs and have been amply documented.

☐ B. Are reflected in increased stock prices for those organizations taking the lead.

☐ C. The jury is out; the results are mixed.

☐ D. Are definitely not worth the costs.

☐ E. Have simply improved the financial returns for outside audit firms.

30

30. The improvements associated with Sarbanes-Oxley (SOX) compliance:

The correct answer is C: The jury is out; the results are mixed.

HOW SURE ARE WE AT THIS TIME?				
1	**2**	3	4	5
Hint	**Suggestive**	Trending	Substantial	Solid

Discussion

In response to corporate financial scandals, the U.S. congress passed the Sarbanes-Oxley Act in 2002. Some of the logic behind the legislation was that public trust in corporate accounting practices had been harmed. It was believed that enforced public policy could help reestablish consumer and shareholder trust. This Act set strict guidelines for objective and independent accounting procedures for publicly traded firms and established penalties for not making appropriate financial disclosures. Essentially, the Act required public documentation and scrutiny of management processes. Although privately held and not-for-profit organizations are exempt from some provisions of the Sarbanes-Oxley Act, many organizations now view the provisions as "best practices" and follow the guidelines in company policy (Stephens & Schwartz, 2006). The well-publicized domestic scandals have not only affected corporate America. Many industrialized nations have taken complementary action to improve corporate governance (e.g., the United Kingdom's Higgs Review; see Aguilera, 2005).

The cost associated with implementing information systems technology that allows for Sarbanes-Oxley (or simply, SOX, as it often is referred to) control and reporting can be expensive. Because of the exhaustive internal auditing required by the Act,

30

existing data-management systems are typically not sufficient. Financial Executives International estimates that a $2.5 billion revenue organization will spend $3.14 million on Section 404 compliance alone (Stephens & Schwartz, 2006). And, this figure may not include the cost of personnel time, management attention, and productivity lost on such processes.

Although internal controls are costly, they represent only a portion of the total expenses required for compliance (e.g., independent external auditors also must be hired). Because publicly held organizations are subject to the full impact of SOX, a $5 billion or more revenue organization that goes public can expect to spend around $8 million in first-time compliance costs. The Foley & Lardner law firm estimated that the average cost of *maintaining* public status has doubled since the enactment of the Sarbanes-Oxley Act (although this maintenance cost increase is not exclusively attributable to the Act). It is unclear whether the increased corporate credibility that comes with these increased controls is worth the costs associated with the effort. One of the hidden costs of SOX is that senior managers in board and leadership meetings can spend more time dealing with internal administrative process issues than serving their customers.

Although clearly expensive for client organizations, the Act has impacted auditing vendors as well. Some financial service organizations use auditing services as a "foot in the door" for more lucrative financial consulting. This offering of nonauditing services has been closely monitored by the Securities and Exchange Commission (SEC). The Sarbanes-Oxley Act does place limits on the amount of nonauditing consulting that can be provided by auditing firms.

There are claims on both sides of the fence with regard to the overall value of SOX. Some individuals believe the costs associated with compliance are excessive. Others believe that the net effect of the Act on our economy has been positive. The Wilshire 5000 Index, for example, has climbed almost

30

$6 trillion since the bill was signed (Serwer, 2006). To optimize the utility of compliance, some organizations are incorporating the operational changes necessary for compliance into business performance monitoring and general risk management (Holst, 2005). If your organization has manual controls for new business ventures, the Act further provides an opportunity to consider automation (Levinsohn, 2005). Improved internal controls should be viewed as an opportunity to target and mitigate risk. In this way, you can maximize the benefits of SOX compliance.

An underlying flaw in the assumption of the SOX regulation is that one can legislate and create policy that creates ethical behavior. Generally, corporate malfeasance comes from leaders who lack a moral code and act in their self-interest regardless of ethics (refer also to Chapter 48). Ethics generally cannot be legislated and many of the corporate abuses likely would not have been avoided simply because of the passage of this Act. Ethics or a moral compass should become a part of managerial evaluation and performance review.

Selected Research

- The Sarbanes-Oxley Act may hurt smaller or younger organizations, particularly those considering an initial public offering as a source of revenue generation (Stephens & Schwartz, 2006). Consequently, this Act may have prompted more mergers, acquisitions, and joint ventures as alternative capital sources (instead of going public). If the Act is truly inhibiting access to public markets, it could adversely affect the national economy.

- Moore, Tetlock, Tanlu, and Bazerman (2006) believe that complete independence of auditors and client organizations is not possible. Auditing firms may fear losing a client if their audit is not favorable, and individual auditors may have personal incentives tied to individual accounts. In this sense, the Sarbanes-Oxley Act is insufficient as it does not address

30

conflicts of interest that are intimately built into the auditing process.

- It is unclear whether or not providing other services (other than financial auditing) to clients influences the quality of financial statements. Kinney, Palmrose, and Scholz (2004) only found a relationship between providing tax services and making less auditing mistakes (either intentional or unintentional). This finding provides some evidence that banning all nonauditing services may not be such a good idea.

- Implementing internal auditing controls does help an organization better manage risks (Carcello, Hermanson, & Raghunandan, 2005).

- Even prior to the enactment of SOX guidelines, accusations of corporate fraud resulted in organizational action (Marciukaityte, Szewczyk, Uzun, & Varma, 2006). These organizations (measured from 1978 to 2001) increased internal controls (such as appointing external board members) and were able to mend their reputations in the absence of federal legislation. These authors also report that these organizations were able to reestablish their pre-scandal stock performance.

- Surveying chief audit executives and internal audit managers regarding the advantages of SOX, Rittenberg and Miller (2005) documented many benefits for improved internal controls. For example, they pointed out compliance also can uncover other IT vulnerabilities and define the relationship between controls and risks.

30

So what difference do these findings make?

- Costs associated with SOX compliance (particularly internal IT tracking systems) may chill an organization's plans to go public. Alternatively, some publicly traded organizations that are struggling with compliance may elect to go private.

- For boards of directors and among senior leaders, it is easy to get seduced into talking more about corporate governance and, thus, talking less about how to build products and services that deliver value to customers and investors. When SOX audits and discussions dominate agendas and dialogues, executives are misallocating time.

- When executives find subordinates acting unethically, they should act decisively and boldly. People who cheat in small matters (e.g., travel expenses) are likely to cheat in larger ones. Living a strong moral code should be considered essential to movement into senior management positions. When ethical abuses occur, they should not be covered over or hidden, but candidly and openly dealt with to ensure confidence in the future.

- Documenting financial controls provides organizations with much data. This data should not be used only for compliance to a legislated regulation. Risk management and business improvement should be tied to this data. Think of Section 404 compliance as providing a lens for business improvement—similar to Six Sigma (for example).

- A Risk Council can be formed prior to incorporating Section 404 actions and information into a risk management program. (Some organizations choose to go further and appoint a Chief Risk Officer.) Risk, business strategy, regulatory compliance, and performance management all should be carefully considered.

30

- The likelihood of fraud is *lower* if boards of directors have truly independent directors (i.e., individuals who are not otherwise associated with the organization).

- Regarding external auditing, objective independent review is most likely to occur when the following three conditions are met: (1) the external auditing firm provides *only* auditing services, (2) the firm is engaged only temporarily (such as with a five-year "un-fireable" contract), and (3) the auditors are selected by an independent board of directors rather than executive management.

Some Key Sources

Aguilera, R. V. (2005). Corporate governance and director accountability: An institutional comparative perspective. *British Journal of Management, 16,* s39-s53.

Campbell, D. R., Campbell, M., & Adams, G. W. (2006). Adding significant value with internal controls. *The CPA Journal, 76*(6), 20-25.

Carcello, J. V., Hermanson, D. R., & Raghunandan, K. (2005). Factors associated with U.S. public companies' investment in internal auditing. *Accounting Horizons, 19*(2), 69-84.

Cowan, M. J., & English, T. (2006). Sarbanes-Oxley Section 404 and mandatory e-filing. *The CPA Journal, 76*(7), 38-43.

Davis, R. A. (2006). SOX worthy? *Accounting Technology, 22*(5), 39-43.

Holst, S. (2005). Sarbanes-Oxley, year two: The glass is half full. *Risk Management, 52*(3), 41.

Kinney, W. R., Palmrose, Z., & Scholz, S. (2004). Auditor independence, non-audit services, and restatements: Was the U.S. government right? *Journal of Accounting Research, 42,* 561-588.

Levinsohn, A. (2005). A silver lining of SOX. *Strategic Finance, 86*(9), 57-58.

30

Maniam, B., Subramaniam, G., & Johnson, J. (2006). Perspectives of corporate governance in the U.S. and abroad. *The Business Review, Cambridge, 5*(2), 36-42.

Marciukaityte, D., Szewczyk, S. H., Uzun, H., & Varma, R. (2006). Governance and performance changes after accusations of corporate fraud. *Financial Analysts Journal, 62*(3), 32-41.

Moore, D. A., Tetlock, P. E., Tanlu, L., & Bazerman, M. H. (2006). Conflicts of interest and the case of auditor independence: Moral seduction and strategic issue cycling. *Academy of Management Review, 31,* 10-29.

Roberts, J., McNulty, T., & Stiles, P. (2005). Beyond agency conceptions of the work of the non-executive director: Creating accountability in the boardroom. *British Journal of Management, 16,* s5-s26.

Rittenberg, L. E., & Miller, P. K. (2005). *Sarbanes-Oxley Section 404 work: Looking at the benefits.* Altamonte Springs, FL: The Institute of Internal Auditors Research Foundation.

Serwer, A. (2006). Stop whining about SarbOx! *Fortune, 154*(3), 39.

Stephens, L., & Schwartz, R. G. (2006). The chilling effect of Sarbanes-Oxley: Myth or reality? *The CPA Journal, 76*(6), 14-19.

Verschoor, C. C. (2006). Interactions between compliance and ethics. *Strategic Finance, 87*(12), 23-24.

LEADERSHIP

31.

Leaders are born, not made.

SELECT ONE:

☐ A. 100% true.

☐ B. 70% true.

☐ C. 40% true.

☐ D. 10% true.

☐ E. Not true—good leaders are made, not born.

31

31. Leaders are born, not made.

The correct answer is C: 40% true.

HOW SURE ARE WE AT THIS TIME?				
1	**2**	3	4	5
Hint	**Suggestive**	Trending	Substantial	Solid

Discussion

The question of whether a leader is born or made has been a pervasive issue for management scholars and organizational practitioners. Francis Galton (1869) and William James (1880) were among the first to identify "greatness" in men as being associated with family history and therefore, potentially, genetic makeup. Early theories of leadership assumed that there was a reliable pattern of "traits" or inherent characteristics that separated leaders from nonleaders. These theories, however, frequently did not withstand the scrutiny of research.

The relative emphasis leadership theorists have placed on traits versus situations in the intervening period has somewhat roller-coastered. The best current answer is that there are both situational and dispositional factors that contribute to the emergence, style, and effectiveness of leadership (cf., Johnson et al., 1998; Popper, Amit, Gal, Mishkal-Sinai, & Lisak, 2004). The "40% true" answer to the question in this chapter acknowledges a fairly even split between these dispositional and nondispositional factors.

Early studies tried to differentiate leaders from nonleaders based primarily on personality information. Personality is known to be moderately to largely determined by genetic factors (roughly 40% on average). Several studies have consequently investigated the "heritability" of leadership—the extent to which differences in leadership are attributable to genetic rather than environmental influence. Through this emerging

230

field of research, it is becoming quite clear that leadership is dependent on both genetic and environmental factors. The relative contributions of each of these factors, however, are just starting to be determined.

Selected Research

- Looking at whether or not the likelihood that individuals will *emerge* as leaders is genetically influenced, Ilies, Gerhardt, and Le (2004) found that (1) whether someone will emerge as a leader is largely dependent on his/her personality and intelligence, and (2) at least 17% of leadership emergence is attributable to genetic influences. This estimate is thought to be conservative, as these researchers only investigated the genetic influences of personality and intelligence on leadership emergence. The additional consideration of other factors known to influence leadership emergence (such as attractiveness, for example) would no doubt increase estimates of the heritability of leadership emergence.

- Arvey et al. (2006) estimate that 30% of the determination of simply "being a leader" is accounted for by genetic factors related to an individual's personality. Like the Ilies, Gerhardt, and Le (2004) finding, this estimate is likely to be conservative, as there are likely to be other independent genetic influences (additional to the personality influences).

- Looking at the extent to which leadership style and personality share genetic influence, Johnson et al. (2004) found that *transformational* leadership is positively genetically correlated with conscientiousness, extraversion, and openness to experience. *Transactional* leadership is negatively correlated (genetically) with conscientiousness, extraversion, and agreeableness. This means that the same genes that predispose someone to be conscientious, extraverted, and open to experience also predispose a leader to select a transformational leadership style.

31

- Since 1983, the University of Minnesota has been coordinating a large-scale study of twins raised together and apart. According to these studies, the genetic leadership effect should not be considered surprising, as most behavioral traits have a genetic component. Intelligence is as much as two-thirds genetic (Bouchard et al., 1990), personality is 27% to 53% genetic (Johnson, McGue, & Krueger, 2005), and holding authoritarian or open-minded attitudes is about 50% genetically determined (McCourt et al., 1999).

- Intelligence (necessary but certainly not solely sufficient for leadership) is highly influenced by genetic factors—current estimates range from 60% to 80% genetically determined (Posthuma & de Geus, 2006).

- McGue, Bouchard, Iacono, and Lykken (1993) note that the genetic influence on intelligence becomes more pronounced as individuals age. This important element of leadership therefore has different heritability estimates, depending on the age of the leader.

- Most leadership style dimensions have genetic origins (Johnson et al., 1998), although transformational leadership may have a higher genetic determinability (59%) than does transactional style (48%).

- Organizational context influences the extent to which individual managers engage in transformational leadership behavior (e.g., role modeling, caring for others, improving team spirit; Bommer, Rubin, & Baldwin, 2004). Specifically, if management peers (i.e., same-level coworkers) use transformational leadership behaviors, a manager is more likely to engage in those same behaviors. This study suggests a learned component to _engaging in_ appropriate leadership behaviors.

- Although there is a genetic influence on leadership, it is also true that leadership skills can be learned through experience

(Mumford, Marks, Connelly, Zaccaro, & Reiter-Palmon, 2000). Providing future leaders with basic problem-solving rules and principles and encouraging them to apply the basic concepts help the development of integrative, applied leadership skills necessary for higher positions.

- In addition to the above findings, some researchers have speculated that there may be a "willingness" factor that also has a genetic influence. The extent to which someone has a positive or negative attitude toward the general idea of *being a leader* is highly heritable (accounts for 41% of the difference in positive attitudes toward being a leader; Olsen et al., 2001).

- The nature-nurture (i.e., genetic versus environmental influences) categories have a long-standing presence in psychology, but many researchers and theorists claim that these extreme categories are insufficient for explaining human behavior (e.g., McLafferty, 2006). Simply trying to classify the influences of our behavior into only these two categories does not fully capture all of the variables that make people (or leaders) different from others.

So what difference do these findings make?

- Generally speaking, characteristics that are attributable to genetic influences (i.e., genotypes) may manifest different behaviors (i.e., phenotypes) in response to different environmental cues. The heritability estimates of leadership emergence suggest that, even if "born" a leader, it is important to surround oneself with appropriate experiences before one becomes viewed as a true leader.

- Knowing there's a genetic element, leaders should be aware that they may be required to work against their grain for development. Also, some styles are better suited for different hierarchical levels—successful managers have to shift styles as they are promoted. Personality tends to be

31

fairly stable later in life—this means that developmental activities that were effective early in one's career may not be equally effective at later stages.

- Most complex individual difference variables (such as leadership) are determined by the interaction between what you're born with and what your experiences are (see Chapter 48).

- Putting *any* potential leader in the proper environment will increase the likelihood that that individual will develop (as opposed to being born with) leadership skills. Any assignment that stimulates problem-solving, communication, and system-management skills is a good start. Good leaders take the opportunity to explicitly *learn* from all their job experiences. Great experience opportunities for future leaders include cross-functional assignments, responsibility for "last chance" fix-its, international assignment, or any "new" project.

Some Key Sources

Arvey, R. D., Rotundo, M., Johnson, W., Zhang, Z., & McGue, M. (2006). The determinants of leadership role occupancy: Genetic and personality factors. *Leadership Quarterly, 17,* 1-20.

Bommer, W. H., Rubin, R. S., & Baldwin, T. T. (2004). Setting the stage for effective leadership: Antecedents of transformational leadership behavior. *Leadership Quarterly, 15,* 195-210.

Bouchard, T. J., Lykken, D. T., McGue, M. M., Segal, N., & Tellegen, A. (1990). The sources of human psychological differences: The Minnesota study of twins reared apart. *Science, 250,* 223-228.

Galton, F. (1869). *Hereditary genius.* New York: Appleton.

Harris, J. R. (1995). Where is the child's environment? A group socialization theory of development. *Psychological Review, 102,* 458-489.

Harris, J. R. (1998). *The nurture assumption: Why children turn out the way they do.* New York: Free Press.

Ilies, R., Arvey, R. D., & Bouchard, Jr., T. J. (2006). Darwinism, behavioral genetics, and organizational behavior: A review and agenda for future research. *Journal of Organizational Behavior, 27,* 121-141.

Ilies, R., Gerhardt, M. W., & Le, H. (2004). Individual differences in leadership emergence: Integrating meta-analytic findings and behavioral genetics estimates. *International Journal of Selection and Assessment, 12,* 207-219.

James, W. (1880). Great men, great thoughts, and their environment. *Atlantic Monthly, 46,* 441-459.

Johnson, A. M., Vernon, P. A., Harris, J. A., & Jang, K. L. (2004). A behavioral investigation of the relationship between leadership and personality. *Twin Research, 7,* 27-32.

Johnson, A. M., Vernon, P. A., McCarthy, J. M., Molso, M., Harris, J. A., & Jang, K. J. (1998). Nature vs. nurture: Are leaders born or made? A behavior genetic investigation of leadership style. *Twin Research, 1,* 216-223.

Johnson, W., McGue, M., & Krueger, R. F. (2005). Personality stability in late adulthood: A behavioral genetic analysis. *Journal of Personality, 73,* 523-551.

McCourt, K., Bouchard, T. J., Jr., Lykken, D. T., Tellegen, A., & Keyes, M. (1999). Authoritarianism revisited: Genetic and environmental influences examined in twins reared apart and together. *Personality and Individual Differences, 27,* 985-1014.

McGue, M., Bouchard, T. J., Jr., Iacono, W. G., & Lykken, D. T. (1993). Behavioral genetics of cognitive ability: A life-span perspective. In R. Plomin & G. E. McClearn (Eds.), *Nature, nurture, and psychology* (pp. 59-76). Washington, DC: American Psychological Association.

31

McLafferty, C. L., Jr. (2006). Examining unproven assumptions of Galton's nature-nurture paradigm. _American Psychologist, 61,_ 177-178.

Mumford, M. D., Marks, M. A., Connelly, M. S., Zaccaro, S. J., & Reiter-Palmon, R. (2000). Development of leadership skills: Experience and timing. _Leadership Quarterly, 11,_ 87-114.

Olsen, J. M., Vernon, P. A., Harris, J. A., & Jang, K. L. (2001). The heritability of attitudes: A study of twins. _Journal of Personality and Social Psychology, 80,_ 845-860.

Popper, M., Amit, K., Gal, R., Mishkal-Sinai, M., & Lisak, A. (2004). The capacity to lead: Major psychological differences between leaders and nonleaders. _Military Psychology, 16,_ 245-263.

Posthuma, D., & de Geus, E. J. C. (2006). Progress in the molecular-genetic study of intelligence. _Current Directions in Psychological Science, 15,_ 151-155.

Russell, C. J., & Kuhnert, K. W. (1992). Integrating skill acquisition and perspective taking capacity in the development of leaders. _Leadership Quarterly, 3,_ 335-353.

STRESS/MOTIVATION

32.

A moderate amount of worker stress results in:

SELECT ONE:

☐ A. More exhaustion.

☐ B. Better performance.

☐ C. More satisfaction.

☐ D. Greater commitment.

☐ E. Decreased motivation.

32. A moderate amount of worker stress results in:

The correct answer is A: More exhaustion.

32

HOW SURE ARE WE AT THIS TIME?				
1	2	**3**	4	5
Hint	Suggestive	**Trending**	Substantial	Solid

Discussion

The negative consequences of work-related stress on employee well-being are numerous. Certainly in the extreme, stress can lead to health failings, fatigue, burnout and/or a loss of focus and attention capabilities (cf., van der Linden, Keijsers, Eling, & van Schaijk, 2005). In addition to negative health-related employee reactions to stress, the organizational consequences of stress are quite expensive. In the United Kingdom, for example, it is estimated that stress accounts for 60% of all employee absenteeism, and this translates to an economic loss of £7 billion per year (Cartwright & Boyes, 2000).

Although stress results in negative consequences, some *sources* of stress are more problematic than others. Stressors can be perceived as either hindering the attainment of goals (i.e., viewed as red tape or hassles), or they can be perceived as challenges (i.e., increased workload or job complexity that ultimately will lead to increased knowledge or further rewards/recognition). Employees who perceive their workplace stressors as presenting *challenges* may actually exhibit performance increases; unfortunately, however, even this positive form of stress also leads to feelings of exhaustion (cf., Boswell, Olson-Buchanan, & LePine, 2004).

It is clear that attempts should be made at eliminating the workplace of hindering stressors. The management trick, it seems, is to replace the hindering stressors with the appropriate number of challenging stressors such that the negative fatigue-related consequences associated with increased challenges do not exceed the increased positive consequences associated with the elimination of hindering stressors.

32

Selected Research

- Reviewing several previous studies, LePine, Podsakoff, and LePine (2005) noted a positive relationship between challenge stress and performance and a negative relationship between hindrance stress and performance. These researchers suggest that organizational stressors be identified as either hindrances or challenges, and that hindrances be eliminated if at all possible (these do not have any positive benefits).

- The degree to which *trained* material is learned depends on whether stress is perceived as hindering or challenging. There is better learning performance with challenge stress and worse learning performance with hindering stress (through increasing or decreasing an individual's motivation to learn). There are no differences in learning performance if stress is not differentiated as either hindering or challenging (LePine, LePine, & Jackson, 2004).

- Considering the impact of challenging and hindering stress on a number of outcome variables (other than performance), Boswell, Olson-Buchanan, and LePine (2004) found that both types of stress lead to anxiety and exhaustion, but, otherwise, challenging stress has positive outcomes (such as greater organizational commitment) and hindering stress has negative outcomes (such as a greater intention to quit).

32

- Two separate studies found that more *anxious* salespeople are more effortful and, therefore, make more sales than do less anxious coworkers (trait anxiety—a persistent tendency to exhibit anxiety). These "more anxious" but more productive salespeople also tend to experience more stress (likely because of the additional effort they expend; Mughal, Walsh, & Wilding, 1996).

- Van Yperen and Hagedoorn (2003) investigated job characteristics and their impact on the stress-motivation relationship. These researchers found that, with increasing job demands, a large amount of personal control or autonomy is required to avoid becoming fatigued. Employee motivation under these large-demand circumstances is increased by either social support (from coworkers) or autonomy/personal control.

So what difference do these findings make?

- Of course organizational demands dictate that workers are going to be placed in stressful situations—there is no getting around this fact. The point of this chapter is that managers should not attempt to create and sustain an "ideal" level of stress. Rather, a manager's role can be seen as framing stress in a positive light. Whether something is experienced as a "good" or "bad" stressor is largely dependent on the perception of the worker. Providing hope and meaning can help create positive perceptions (even when presented with the same stressor, such as a demanding work deadline).

- Although "challenging" stress tends to lead to higher levels of motivation and performance, all stress leads to feelings of exhaustion. There is, therefore, a trade-off in the positive and negative effects of challenging stress. In addition to framing, managers should at least make attempts to remove any perceived sources of hindrance stress from the workplace. If challenging stressors are utilized as a management tool, it is important that the employee views the stressors (such as increased workload or job complexity) as instrumental toward the attainment of valued outcomes (such as knowledge or skill acquisition).

32

- Good (challenging) stressors:

  - Complex tasks, a full workload, responsibility, time pressures.

- Bad (hindrance) stressors:

  - Bullying, ambiguity, a lack of clarity, red tape, minor hassles, job security concerns, a lack of resources, interpersonal conflict, politics.

- It is possible that personality, in addition to the environment, leads to feelings of stress (cf., Mughal, Walsh, & Wilding, 1996). This suggests that programs aimed at alleviating stress at work should focus on the individual as well as the job context. Some workers are simply more prone to "stress-out"—these individuals will need more training on coping skills. Job-based interventions should provide more autonomy to employees in demanding positions (cf., Van Yperen & Hagedoorn, 2003) in addition to removing hindrance stressors.

Some Key Sources

Boswell, W. R., Olson-Buchanan, J. B., & LePine, M. A. (2004). Relations between stress and work outcomes: The role of felt challenge, job control, and psychological strain. *Journal of Vocational Behavior, 64,* 165-181.

Cartwright, S., & Boyes, R. F. (2000). Taking the pulse of executive health in the UK. *The Academy of Management Executive, 14*(2), 16-24.

Dollard, M. F., Winefield, H. R., Winefield, A. H., & de Jong, J. (2000). Psychosocial job strain and productivity in human service workers: A test of the demand-control-support model. *Journal of Occupational and Organizational Psychology, 73,* 501-510.

LeFevre, M., Matheny, J., & Kolt, G. S. (2003). Eustress, distress, and interpretation in occupational stress. *Journal of Managerial Psychology, 18,* 726-744.

LePine, J. A., LePine, M. A., & Jackson, C. L. (2004). Challenge and hindrance stress: Relationships with exhaustion, motivation to learn, and learning performance. *Journal of Applied Psychology, 89,* 883-891.

LePine, J. A., Podsakoff, N. P., & LePine, M. A. (2005). A meta-analytic test of the challenge stressor-hindrance stressor framework: An explanation for inconsistent relationships among stressors and performance. *Academy of Management Journal, 48,* 764-775.

Mughal, S., Walsh, J., & Wilding, J. (1996). Stress and work performance: The role of trait anxiety. *Personality and Individual Differences, 20,* 685-691.

Muse, L. A., Harris, S. G., & Field, H. S. (2003). Has the inverted-U theory of stress and job performance had a fair test? *Human Performance, 16,* 349-364.

van der Linden, D., Keijsers, G. P J., Eling, P., & van Schaijk, R. (2005). Work stress and attentional difficulties: An initial study on burnout and cognitive failures. *Work & Stress, 19,* 23-36.

Van Yperen, N. W., & Hagedoorn, M. (2003). Do high job demands increase intrinsic motivation or fatigue or both? The role of job control and job social support. *Academy of Management Journal, 46,* 339-348.

E-LEARNING

33.

Generally speaking, how effective is e-learning compared to traditional face-to-face delivery of training content?

SELECT ONE:

☐ A. Much less is learned.

☐ B. Somewhat less is learned.

☐ C. The same amount is learned.

☐ D. Somewhat more is learned.

☐ E. Much more is learned.

33. Generally speaking, how effective is e-learning compared to traditional face-to-face delivery of training content?

The correct answer is C: The same amount is learned.

33

HOW SURE ARE WE AT THIS TIME?				
1	2	**3**	4	5
Hint	Suggestive	**Trending**	Substantial	Solid

Discussion

The use of delivery technology in training is growing—one estimate has 24% of organizations setting aside targeted budgets for technology-based training (Galvin, 2002). Another estimate has 80% of all Fortune 500 companies either currently utilizing or planning to implement e-learning (Hammond, 2001).

E-learning provides 24/7/365 coverage all hours of the day, every day of the week, everywhere on the planet. The "e" methods of delivery might include video, audio, Internet, or intranet applications. The content of the training can be most anything that would traditionally be taught in a more traditional face-to-face training context. Although e-learning is touted as a new technology, similar approaches to learning have been applied for hundreds of years. The first education-based correspondence courses were established toward the end of the nineteenth century. One of the advantages of current e-learning practices is that technology overcomes some of the disadvantages of early distance-learning practices (i.e., whereas feedback was delayed by postal service in the nineteenth century, it can now be provided immediately via the Internet).

The practical advantages of e-leaning are numerous. There is less travel time and administrative cost if training is presented online rather than face-to-face. Additionally, e-training programs can be personalized to the appropriate pace for employees with different baseline ability levels. Employees are self-paced and can go as fast or as slow as they want. When they are learning facts, skills, or specific actions, they have a quick feedback loop on how they are doing and can readily improve. Furthermore, these initiatives can have global coverage, and they facilitate employee skill tracking.

33

Although it is cost-effective (if there are numerous geographically dispersed learners), it is not necessarily cheap. In fact, up-front costs are one of the most commonly cited drawbacks of e-learning initiatives (Welsh, Wanberg, Brown, & Simmering, 2003). Once the initial up-front costs for infrastructure and development have been made, however, rollout is very cost-effective. Cisco Systems, for example, has saved approximately $1 million per quarter through the use of e-learning programs (Pantazis, 2002).

Welsh, Wanberg, Brown, and Simmering (2003), in a fairly comprehensive review, suggest that e-learning can be more effective than traditional classroom instruction, but this is not necessarily so. Similarly, the training content that is most or least likely to be learned has not been well researched. There is speculation, for instance, that "soft" skills (interpersonal) are less likely to benefit from e-learning. This speculation has not been confirmed or rejected by research, however. E-learning does not allow people to engage in group discussions, dialogues, or debates as much as classroom learning. It is generally better for transfer of knowledge and ideas than for building relationships and shared points of view.

33

Although the research generally supports the notion that e-learning is as effective as traditional face-to-face applications with regard to knowledge acquisition, there are many unanswered questions regarding other e-learning outcomes. Organizations that pursue this technology should be aware, for instance, that e-learning initiatives may result in higher noncompletion rates than face-to-face instructional contexts. E-learning is not as useful for discussions about strategy and in exploring alternatives that might be done through small group settings. E-learning also may isolate the learner from colleagues who are a part of an overall learning experience, so the e-learner may learn the facts but lack the personal sensitivity to use those facts to better manage. In addition, some authors assert that organizations frequently ignore some basic realities about technology and learning in their haste to implement it. Consequently, e-learning programs become much less effective than they can be (Cooper, 2007).

Most surveys of face-to-face training reactions report that participants learn as much from each other as they learn from the instruction or the material. This learning may occur both inside and outside the formal classroom. Increasingly, training programs engage participants so that they interact during the training experience to share knowledge with each other. Also, skill and competency training is enhanced by in-session practice and simulation. E-learning is some distance in technology from live action learning.

Selected Research

- Although more opportunity exists for off-the-job learning with e-learning applications, the majority of learning still occurs during formal work time (88%; Galvin, 2002).

- E-learning is most likely to be cost-effective if there are numerous individuals to be trained, those individuals are geographically dispersed, and if the content is reusable (Welsh, Wanberg, Brown, & Simmering, 2003).

- Navarro and Shoemaker (2000) found that "Cyberlearners learn as well as, or better than, traditional learners, regardless of characteristics such as gender, ethnicity, academic background, computer skills, and academic aptitude. And that they do so with a high degree of satisfaction."

- DeRouin, Fritzsche, and Salas (2005) conclude that with respect to actual learning material, e-learning is no better or worse than traditional face-to-face training. Furthermore, e-delivered material does seem to transfer to job contexts, and there is initial evidence that it may impact organizational effectiveness.

- Welsh, Wanberg, Brown, and Simmering (2003) reviewed researcher and practitioner findings, summarizing that employees do learn from technologically delivered training, but those with limited computer experience do not benefit as much as do technologically savvy employees. Generally, results on effectiveness show that technology-delivered training may result in more learning than is realized in traditional classrooms, although this is not always the case.

- Burgess and Russell (2003) found that most studies of e-learning reported positive cost savings. The authors suggested a mix of traditional and e-learning training initiatives be employed. They caution that individuals must be familiar with the technology for learning to occur.

33

33

- Macpherson, Elliot, Harris, and Homan (2004) claimed that the full advantages of utilizing e-learning programs are not being realized. This is primarily attributed to technological limitations and a lack of strategic priority. The researchers recommended that facilitators need to create a culture of organizational readiness prior to implementing a successful e-learning initiative. Likewise, Cooper (2007) asserted that organizations seldom derive all the benefits from e-learning programs because of their failure to adequately plan. The article reviewed what was called "12 unavoidable truths about e-learning." Most importantly, the author suggested to engage the participant during the program, to keep lessons short, and to customize the content to the user's specific needs.

- Brown (2005) investigated e-learning predictors and outcomes for individuals who had access to computer-skill training modules. Employees who were motivated to learn and also did not have an overwhelming workload spent more time in the e-learning courses. The employees' supervisors provided higher ratings of both performance and computer skill for employees who spent more time in the e-learning courses.

- Employees who learn most from computer-based training are those who complete more of the practice activities and take more time to complete them. Brown (2001) concludes, "...the e-learning experience depended upon the learning orientation of the students."

- Investigating the use of e-learning in the Australian Army, Newton and Ellis (2005) noted three important factors for effective learning. Individual trainees needed (1) change drivers (i.e., superiors who supported the learning initiative), (2) a fit with the organizational culture (i.e., utilizing technology suitable for the organization), and (3) needs met (i.e., addressing any fear of failure or apprehension to use technology).

- Possible disadvantages: E-learning may be viewed as being cold or impersonal (compared to traditional face-to-face training), and some employees may have an apprehension to embrace technology (Nisar, 2004). Additionally, Weaver (2002) estimates that trainees do not complete 50% to 90% of online courses.

So what difference do these findings make?

33

- E-learning is now a useful and permanent tool to deliver content and will probably become more so as the delivery technology (e.g., more interactive video) improves. Learning how to use the tool is critical. Just like not every class should be taught by the Socratic case method, not every class should be done through e-learning. Learning to adapt the tool to the purpose and situation is important. However, e-learning should be a part of any training portfolio.

- E-learning will be more appealing to some over others—it is, therefore, ideal to have e-learning options available within a suite of training delivery alternatives. Some care should be taken to protect the less computer-oriented employees. Unintended bias could creep into an ambitious e-learning initiative.

- In order for an e-learning initiative to be well received and used, it should be aligned with organizational goals, be supported by management, and be linked to other human resources systems (performance appraisal or development, for example).

- E-learning may require more up-front costs in developing and delivering material to make sure that they are tailored and accessible through the e-learning distribution.

- Additionally, the effectiveness and reactions to the e-learning system should be monitored. To be truly effective, reactions should be monitored so that improvements can be made.

- Completion rates can differ from traditional classroom instruction to e-learning applications. To maximize the likelihood that e-learning modules will be completed, explicitly link training to developmental goals, pay, job relevance, or career transition. If courses are optional or perceived to have little consequence to one's job or career, completion rates will be lower (than classroom instruction).

33

- E-learning offers a hybrid option. Since e-learning is as effective as face-to-face instruction for some content, it would seem that mixing pre–e-learning content delivery with less time in the classroom would be justified. This mixed-media presentation has been referred to as a "blended" learning approach. In blended learning applications, routine content is a prerequisite (usually with a test of the content) to attending the face-to-face session, which then concentrates on advanced instruction and live skill practice. Less live classroom time will reduce the costs, and tested pre-knowledge should increase the benefits of the classroom time.

- To simulate the person-to-person learning, e-learning chat rooms for people studying the same content modules might, to some small extent, substitute for the lunch and break conversation people feel are valuable in classroom-based training.

Some Key Sources

Brown, K. G. (2001). Using computers to deliver training: Which employees learn and why? *Personnel Psychology, 54,* 271-296.

Brown, K. G. (2005). A field study of employee e-learning activity and outcomes. *Human Resource Development Quarterly, 16,* 465-480.

Burgess, J. R. D., & Russell, J. E. A. (2003). The effectiveness of distance learning initiatives in organizations. *Journal of Vocational Behavior, 63,* 289-303.

Cooper, K. C. (2007). 12 unavoidable truths about e-learning. *Chief Learning Officer, 6*(1), 42-45.

DeRouin, R. E., Fritzsche, B. A., & Salas, E. (2005). E-learning in organizations. *Journal of Management, 31,* 920-940.

Galvin, T. (2002). 2002 Industry report. *Training, 39*(10), 24-73.

Graeme, M., Massey, J., & Clarke, T. (2003). When absorptive capacity meets institutions and (e)learners: Adopting, diffusing and exploiting e-learning in organizations. *International Journal of Training and Development, 7,* 228-244.

Hammond, D. (2001). Reality bytes. *People Management, 7*(2), 26-31.

Hartley, D. (2000). All aboard the e-learning train. *Training & Development, 54*(7), 37-39.

Macpherson, A., Elliot, M., Harris, I., & Homan, G. (2004). E-learning: Reflections and evaluation of corporate programmes. *Human Resource Development International, 7,* 295-313.

Navarro, P., & Shoemaker, J. (2000). Performance and perceptions of distance learners in cyberspace. In M. G. Moore & G. Cozine (Eds.), *Web-based communications, the Internet and distance education* (pp. 1-15). Pennsylvania State University.

33

Newton, D., & Elliss, A. (2005). Effective implementation of e-learning: A case study of the Australian Army. *Journal of Workplace Learning, 17,* 385-397.

Nisar, T. M. (2004). E-learning in public organizations. *Public Personnel Management, 33,* 79-88.

Pantazis, C. (2002). Maximizing e-learning to train the 21st Century workforce. *Public Personnel Management, 31,* 21-25.

Weaver, P. (2002). Preventing e-learning failure. *Training & Development, 56*(8), 45-50.

Welsh, E. T., Wanberg, C. R., Brown, K. G., & Simmering, M. J. (2003). E-learning: Emerging results and future directions. *International Journal of Training and Development, 7,* 245-258.

34.

What accommodation best addresses the self-stated work preferences of Generation Xers (now 25-45)?

SELECT ONE:

☐ A. Flexible work schedules and advancement opportunities.

☐ B. Environmental amenities (like day care, gym, casual dress, etc.).

☐ C. Work in teams.

☐ D. Competitive salary and benefits.

☐ E. High incentive and bonus opportunities for meritorious work.

34. What accommodation best addresses the self-stated work preferences of Generation Xers (now 25-45)?

The correct answer is A: Flexible work schedules and advancement opportunities.

HOW SURE ARE WE AT THIS TIME?				
1	2	3	**4**	5
Hint	Suggestive	Trending	**Substantial**	Solid

34

They would rather hike in the Himalayas than climb a corporate ladder. They have few heroes, no anthems, and no style to call their own. They crave entertainment, but their attention span is as short as one zap of a TV dial. They hate yuppies, hippies and druggies. They postpone marriage because they dread divorce. They sneer at Range Rovers, Rolexes and red suspenders. What they hold dear are family life, local activism, national parks, penny loafers and mountain bikes. They possess only a hazy sense of their own identity but a monumental preoccupation with all the problems the preceding generation will leave for them to fix (Scott, 1990, p. 56).

Discussion

The above quote, taken from *Time* magazine, fairly well encapsulates popular notions of "Gen Xers" that were held by non–Gen Xers at the start of the 1990s. Gen Xers (who were born between the early- to mid-1960s and 1980) represent the next demographic wave of leaders for American organizations after the baby boomers. These individuals also comprise a numerical minority—being outnumbered by baby boomers roughly 77 million to 46 million.

In 2007, Gen Xers are just now entering their prime working ages of 25 to 45, and employers who want to capitalize on this more limited talent pool need to separate the old stereotypes and popular myths from the truly unique wants and needs of the members of this generation. In order for organizations to attract and retain members of this generational group, they need to understand the true values, career goals, and expectations of these individuals.

Very few of the negative stereotypes of this generation seem to have been confirmed (at least in work contexts; see Giancola, 2006). However, one sweeping generalization that does seem to hold true is that these individuals place a great deal of value on *flexible* work schedules and arrangements (cf., Shields, 2003). Also, they value learning skills that provide them long-term marketability, and view professional growth as or more important than salary (at least in early career stages; Bova & Kroth, 2001; Mayfield & Keating, 2003).

Similar to the baby boomers ahead of them, these individuals place a high value on opportunities for advancement. This is one possible reason why there's a perceived antagonistic tinge to the baby boomer/Gen Xer relationship—baby boomers are currently blocking advancement opportunities for many Gen Xers. Some authors have referred to this career impediment as "the gray ceiling." Consequently, while it is true that Gen Xers may use "job-hopping" as a career strategy more than their previous generational counterparts, this behavior also is consistent with their general orientation toward skill and experience acquisition. If their current employing organization provides career growth opportunities, they likely will be happy to stay.

Unfortunately, many untrue stereotypes of this generation continue to persist. When asked how others likely view them, Gen Xers say "lazy, confused, and unfocused." When asked how they view themselves, the same respondents say "ambitious, determined, and independent."

Of course, characterizing any "generation" with generalizations is dangerous because within any generation are all types and styles. Moreover, as Gen Xers mature, some of their patterns also may evolve.

Selected Research

- Work-related *concerns* tend to be quite similar for baby boomers and Gen Xers, with differences existing along a few preference/style dimensions (Rodriguez, Green, & Ree, 2003). Gen Xers, for example, prefer portable 401K packages, a challenging and fun (rather than secure) job, and working flexible hours. Baby boomers, on the other hand, tend to prefer benefit-laden retirement plans and working on a regular predictable schedule.

- Jurkiewicz (2000) found that Gen Xers' work-related motivations and attitudes are generally very similar to baby boomers. These two generations are essentially the same when it comes to what they want out of a job—opportunity for advancement and growth. Gen Xers do tend to view autonomy as being more important than do baby boomers.

- Gen Xers prefer to view themselves as individual contributors (rather than team members), do not expect lifelong employment, and will not "be swept away by talk of teamwork and corporate vision" (O'Bannon, 2001, p. 100). They are multicultural, tend to be tolerant of differences in others, and aim to find balance between their personal and professional lives.

- Contrary to stereotype, Generation X employees are, generally speaking, highly committed to their jobs and organizations. Eighty-five percent claim to "really care" about their organizations and 83% are willing to exert extra effort to help their firm succeed ("Exploding Generation X Myths," 2005). The majority of Gen Xers claim flexibility of work schedules and arrangements as being important for their job satisfaction.

- Interviewing Gen X engineers, Mayfield and Keating (2003) noted a strong concern regarding the ability to manage one's own time. One engineer stated, "If you are not professional enough to keep track of your time, you shouldn't be working, period" (p. 39). Generally speaking, quality of life issues were found to be more important to these individuals than were salary considerations.

- In a recent article, Giancola (2006) questions the meaningfulness of a generation gap. He contends that policy makers and journalists frequently exaggerate such attitudinal and behavioral differences and asserts the notion those generational differences "may be more popular culture than social science" (p. 33). He concludes that HR professionals should realize that differences *within* generations are far greater than differences *between* generations.

34

So what difference do these findings make?

- Especially early in their careers, Gen Xers look for value, skill, and knowledge development, believing these experiences will "pay off" with later salaries and benefits. One young engineer summed it up as, "I would rather go somewhere where I can get the experience to make myself marketable and worry later about the dollars" (Mayfield & Keating, 2003, p. 39). Employment packages that include bonus incentives, for example, may not be as attractive as opportunities for growth and development for early-career Gen Xers.

- Managers can honor Gen Xers' independence and provide motivation through granting them more autonomy, and should be careful of micromanaging members of this generation who will not respond well to such restrictions. This means giving them an assignment (as individuals or a team) and letting them work on it by themselves, providing high standards and lots of autonomy.

34

- Commonly held stereotypes regarding Gen Xers' general lack of motivation have not been validated (at least in organizational contexts). These individuals consistently cite advancement opportunities and flexible work schedules as important for their careers. The perception of Gen Xers as "job-hoppers" is likely attributable to a perceived lack of opportunities for advancement, skill, and knowledge acquisition. Organizations that want to retain these individuals need to provide challenging, continuous learning environments. And, leaders in these organizations need to engage the employees and find out what they want and how to help them meet their needs.

- Ultimately, nothing much has changed in one aspect. Regardless of the generation, people who are committed to the world of work want an opportunity to use their skills free of chilling micromanagement, want opportunities for advancement, and want the lifelong opportunity to upgrade their skills and experiences. This probably always will be the winning formula for attracting and retaining talent.

Some Key Sources

Bova, B., & Kroth, M. (2001). Workplace learning and Generation X. *Journal of Workplace Learning, 13*(2), 57-65.

Exploding Generation X myths. (2005). *Journal of Accountancy, 200*(2), 38-40.

Giancola, F. (2006). The generation gap: More myth than reality. *Human Resource Planning, 29*(4), 32-37.

Jurkiewicz, C. L. (2000). Generation X and the public employee. *Public Personnel Management, 29*, 55-74.

Mayfield, R. W., & Keating, C. B. (2003). Major factors that influence employment decisions of Generation X consulting engineers. *Engineering Management Journal, 15*(2), 35-43.

O'Bannon, G. (2001). Managing our future: The Generation X factor. *Public Personnel Management, 30*, 95-109.

Rodriguez, R. O., Green, M. T., & Ree, M. J. (2003). Leading Generation X: Do the old rules apply? *Journal of Leadership and Organizational Studies, 9*, 67-75.

Scott, S. (1990). Proceeding with caution. *Time, 136*(3), 56-62.

Shields, M. C. (2003). Working with Generation X physicians. *Physician Executive, 29*(6), 14-18.

Zemke, R., Raines, C., & Filipczak, B. (2000). *Generations at work: Managing the clash of veterans, boomers, Xers, and nexters in your workplace.* New York: AMA Publications.

34

ETHICS

35.

The leader/employee perspective that will result in more ethical work behavior is:

SELECT ONE:

☐ A. Ethics are absolute and black and white; they are a part of being human; formal rules of behavior need to be followed always.

☐ B. Ethics are situational and conditional; what may be ethical in one situation might not be in another; setting and context have to be taken into account for effective guidance of behavior.

☐ C. Ethics are culturally and religiously bound; the best ethical behavior is that which conforms to a set of beliefs and universally held assumptions.

☐ D. It doesn't matter where your definition comes from, what matters is the outcome or results of what you do; bad outcomes come from bad behavior; ethics are best defined by consequences.

☐ E. Ethics result from man-made rules and are social constructions of reality; the quality and adherence to the rules dictate the ethics; whether you follow them or not is the relevant variable; there are just ethical and unethical people.

35. The leader/employee perspective that will result in more ethical work behavior is:

The correct answer is A: Ethics are absolute and black and white; they are a part of being human; formal rules of behavior need to be followed always.

HOW SURE ARE WE AT THIS TIME?				
1	**2**	3	4	5
Hint	**Suggestive**	Trending	Substantial	Solid

I have seen examples of people who would never dream of doing anything that they would view as unethical, but in the heat of battle they can sometimes lose their compass (Treviño, Brown, & Hartman, 2003, p. 20).

35

Discussion

Recently, well-publicized ethical scandals in the workplace have arisen from somewhat innocuous violations of professional behaviors (i.e., accounting standards). In many of these cases, harm to the organization and individual was not recognized until the problems had become public, magnified, and insurmountable. For some people, an ethical violation does not present a moral dilemma until such a point of public harm has been reached. These individuals dangerously measure ethics by outcomes.

Research by Reynolds (2006) suggests that individuals who are utilitarians (focus on the outcome of a decision), rather than formalists (who focus on formal rules of behavior—*how* an outcome is achieved), are more likely to overlook early violations as presenting ethical dilemmas. Individuals who have more formalistic principles are more likely to recognize a situation as requiring moral reasoning and are therefore more likely to address a situation before it becomes a moral crisis.

To a utilitarian, morality is solely determined by the consequences of an action—a good outcome is what matters, independent of how that outcome is achieved. This is a different perspective from someone who believes that good *intentions* or *procedures* are what define a proper (or ethical) decision. Some individuals, then, are more prone to making ethical violations (if they focus on the positive outcome rather than the path taken to achieve that outcome). Obviously, the above is somewhat of a conundrum for the business world, where the emphasis is so heavily weighted on outcomes.

None of this means that a person who possesses a utilitarian orientation is more *likely* to be unethical or that businesses should be wary of individuals who possess a "results first" orientation. Knowingly acting in an unethical manner is not a function of whether someone possesses a utilitarian orientation or not (see Chapters 40 and 22 on counterproductivity for identifying individuals who knowingly act unethically). Rather, someone who has a "results first" orientation may receive more benefit from awareness training (than, for instance, someone who already believes that intentions and procedures are important guiding principles). These individuals (utilitarians) are simply more likely to possess a blind spot—thereby finding themselves in an unintended ethical bind later rather than sooner.

35

Individuals who are more utilitarian in perspective are more likely to focus on the end result and, therefore, less likely to recognize *early indicators of a problem*. A significant component of ethical behavior seems to involve this ability of the worker/leader to simply recognize a situation as requiring ethical thought and decision. This ability is referred to as "moral awareness." All employees, regardless of whether they tend to focus on outcomes or processes, need to be morally aware, so they understand when a situation requires ethical consideration.

Selected Research

- Part of ethical behavior is attributable to the individual himself/herself and how he/she thinks about morality. Reynolds (2006) found that an ethical predisposition toward either utilitarianism (possessing primarily utilitarian ideals) or formalism (possessing primarily formalistic ideals) can affect a manager's level of moral awareness. Two equally reasonable managers may therefore disagree on the need for moral reasoning for a particular issue because of their tendency toward either utilitarianism or formalism.

- Treviño, Brown, and Hartman (2003) identified factors that differentiate ethical from "ethically neutral" leaders, noting that those identified as ethical were perceived to be more people-focused. Additionally, ethical leaders are more honest, trustworthy, and act with consistent integrity. An "ethically neutral" leader is one who is concerned primarily with himself or herself and the overall performance of the organization, while lacking as much ethical awareness. This investigation noted that, especially for executive leaders, employees do not necessarily differentiate between a leader's professional and personal lives when evaluating their ethical behavior.

- Weaver, Treviño, and Agle (2005) found that it is coworkers and direct supervisors, more than distant executives, who most effectively serve as ethical role models in organizations. Frequent personal interaction is important for someone at work to be considered an ethical role model. This proximity allows individuals to determine whether or not role models "walk the talk."

- A leader's moral development can impact an organization's ethical climate as well as the general attitudes of employees

(Schminke, Ambrose, & Neubaum, 2005). This effect, however, is stronger in younger organizations and in organizations whose leaders choose to act on their moral development. Followers whose moral development matches the leader's moral development are more likely to be satisfied and exhibit higher levels of organizational commitment.

• Ethical dilemmas are not uncommon but may be more common in some jobs than others. Miller, Yeager, Hildreth, and Rabin (2005) interviewed financial managers at government finance organizations, finding that these individuals (1) felt pressure from others who asked for special treatment, and (2) believed that they were operating under "undue" political pressure.

• Verschoor (1998) investigated large organizations and their financial performance as a function of stated commitment to ethical standards. As of 1997, roughly 27% of America's 500 largest public organizations articulated and adhered to an ethical commitment. These organizations exhibited better financial performance than did organizations that did not communicate a strong ethical stance.

35

• It is estimated that 90% of business schools currently have training on ethics as part of their curriculum (Fulmer, 2004). One faculty member jokingly responded, when asked whether his curriculum included a course of business ethics, "Which one?" His point was that ethics should not be a separate college course but an integral component of every course. Ethical issues should be raised and discussed in strategy, marketing, finance, information technology, accounting, human resources, and *all* business courses.

So what difference do these findings make?

• Recognizing that a situation requires ethical consideration is more than half the battle. Most organizational decisions are not black or white (good or bad), but shades of gray (and shades of good). Learning to apply a disciplined set of standards to these decisions ensures that they are made in ways that meet society's norms of morality.

- Being morally aware is the key to early recognition. And being morally aware comes from candid and open discussion. This does not always mean agreement, but it does mean facing and talking about issues.

- Ethics at the top sets the tone. Employees will do what they see more than what they hear espoused.

- Ethical tone includes both on- and off-the-job behavior. Especially at the senior levels, executives live in glass houses where their behavior is observed and set the tone for the company. This public scrutiny is one of the prices of executive privileges.

35

- Making ethical decisions involves three steps: (1) recognizing that the situation presents a moral dilemma, (2) objectively evaluating all possible alternatives, and (3) acting in a behavior consistent with the objective evaluation. Not every moral dilemma is going to be recognized as such— thereby leading to possible unethical (but also unintentional) decision making.

- Individuals differ in the manner in which they think about morality. At the least, there is a distinction between formalistic (absolute) and utilitarian (relativist) thinkers. Institutionalizing ethics within an organization may meet resistance if all individuals are viewed similarly. The different tendencies to recognize a situation as requiring moral thought (i.e., having formalist or utilitarian tendencies) need to be included in training and awareness programs.

Some Key Sources

Fulmer, R. M. (2004). The challenge of ethical leadership. *Organizational Dynamics, 33,* 307-317.

May, D. R., Chan, A. Y. L., Hodges, T. D., & Avolio, B. J. (2003). Developing the moral component of authentic leadership. *Organizational Dynamics, 32,* 247-260.

Miller, G. J., Yeager, S. J., Hildreth, W. B., & Rabin, J. (2005). How financial managers deal with ethical stress. *Public Administration Review, 65,* 301-312.

Reynolds, S. J. (2006). Moral awareness and ethical predispositions: Investigating the role of individual differences in the recognition of moral issues. *Journal of Applied Psychology, 91,* 233-243.

Russ-Eft, D. (2004). Ethics in a global world: An oxymoron? *Evaluation and Program Planning, 27,* 349-356.

Schminke, M., Ambrose, M. L., & Neubaum, D. O. (2005). The effect of leader moral development on ethical climate and employee attitudes. *Organizational Behavior and Human Decision Processes, 97,* 135-151.

Treviño, L. K., Brown, M., & Hartman, L. P. (2003). A qualitative investigation of perceived executive ethical leadership: Perceptions from inside and outside the executive suite. *Human Relations, 56,* 5-37.

Verschoor, C. C. (1998). A study of the link between a corporation's financial performance and its commitment of ethics. *Journal of Business Ethics, 17,* 1509-1516.

Weaver, G. R., Treviño, L. K., & Agle, B. (2005). Somebody I look up to: Ethical role models in organizations. *Organizational Dynamics, 34,* 313-330.

35

36.

People's behavior matches their stated opinions when it comes to whether pay motivates them (i.e., pay is typically rated as not very important compared to other things like autonomy and being able to contribute).

SELECT ONE:

☐ A. True. As people generally report, pay is not very motivational; differences in pay do not result in differences in performance.

☐ B. Sort of true. Pay motivates, but about in line where most people report it (usually somewhere between 5th and 7th).

☐ C. False. Pay is a strong motivator, regardless of what people say.

☐ D. False. Pay is a stronger motivator than most people report.

☐ E. False. Pay is actually the strongest motivator.

36

36. **People's behavior matches their stated opinions when it comes to whether pay motivates them (i.e., pay is typically rated as not very important compared to other things like autonomy and being able to contribute).**

   The correct answer is D: False. Pay is a stronger motivator than most people report.

HOW SURE ARE WE AT THIS TIME?				
1	2	**3**	4	5
Hint	Suggestive	**Trending**	Substantial	Solid

Discussion

Typically, pay is not considered to be a strong motivator of performance. Paying people more is not thought to increase performance.

Trade magazines frequently state that employees are increasingly "looking for more" from their jobs—consequently, pay is not an important motivator of employee performance (cf., Bates, 2004). Managers have seemed to buy into this notion, tending to believe that pay is not an important motivator of employee behavior (Rynes, Colbert, & Brown, 2002).

When employees self-report the importance of pay, it is true that pay is not identified as an important factor for their satisfaction or performance compared to other "softer" aspects of work. Surveys have found that pay tends to be ranked somewhere around the fifth most important motivator (behind such considerations as job interest, opportunity for advancement, job security, and appreciation). When direct employee output is measured, however, contingency-based pay is often shown

36

to be *the most effective motivator* (cf., Rynes, Gerhart, & Minette, 2004).

At times it is not the amount of pay that one receives, but how that pay compares to what someone else receives. The issue is not the total pay, but the equity or comparable pay. When someone feels that their efforts are justly rewarded, they feel that pay is a motivator. When they feel that their efforts compared to someone else's are minimized and not rewarded, pay is a demotivator. Also, there is a threshold where pay becomes more important. Lower wage earners require pay for the necessities and basic requirements of living. More senior executives use pay more as a symbol of social status and personal achievement. Thus, pay at the lower end may cause more motivation than pay as a social status symbol.

Researchers speculate that the reason some pay-for-performance programs do not work is because of poor implementation (rather than issues related to the effectiveness of pay as a motivator; cf., Stajkovic & Luthans, 2001). Pay, therefore, can be an effective motivator for employee performance. However, for it to be optimally effective, pay needs to be administered fairly.

36

Selected Research

- Rynes, Gerhart, and Minette (2004) believe that pay is more important for employee motivation than employees tend to self-admit. Employees underestimate the importance of pay to their personal levels of motivation on employee surveys. Altering pay, in fact, may be one of the most effective motivational interventions an HR department can undertake. Sometimes pay may be used to reinforce a behavioral change rather than to cause it.

- Asking applicants to report the most important out of a list of 10 job attributes, Jurgensen (1978) found that individuals tended to identify pay as the 5th to 7th most important attribute for themselves. When asked to rank attributes for someone similar to them in age, education, and gender, these same applicants ranked pay as the number one consideration. This implies that people do not like to admit the importance of pay, because it is not socially appropriate to do so.

- The way in which a job is structured can impact motivation. However, even when a job is specifically designed to motivate, this effect is augmented by satisfaction with pay (Thakor & Joshi, 2005). This research suggests that intrinsic motivators (such as how meaningful a job is perceived to be) can be further enhanced through extrinsic motivators such as pay.

- Igalens and Roussel (1999) investigated pay-motivation linkages for exempt and nonexempt employees. They found that exempt employees will be most highly motivated when (1) pay raises are used instead of bonuses, and (2) the raises are directly tied to performance. Interestingly, this second condition is not true for nonexempt employees (who are traditionally paid for overtime). The authors recommend different compensation packages be constructed to motivate exempt versus nonexempt employee groups.

- Stajkovic and Luthans (2001) examined the relative impact of pay on motivation, also considering social recognition and performance feedback (as additional motivators). For their manufacturing sample, the way in which contingency-based pay was administered was important—routine administration resulted in an 11% performance increase while systematic administration resulted in a 32% performance increase. They also report that *both* pay-based incentive systems had greater effects on performance than did either social recognition or performance feedback.

- Although performance can be enhanced with contingency pay, other less-desirable behaviors also may be increased. Investigating the behaviors of salespeople when competing in a sales contest, Murphy (2004) found that these salespeople engaged in unethical behaviors, including encouraging customers to make purchases ahead of schedule and ignoring other (nonincentive based) responsibilities.

So what difference do these findings make?

- Apparently pay motivates more than people report and more than is generally thought. Few people like to publicly (or even privately) admit that money motivates their behavior, but in the end, it often does. Or, if not money, it is the side benefits that come from increased wealth (flexibility, autonomy, access to a higher lifestyle).

- The return on pay programs might be greater if we put more thought into why and how pay is delivered. Ensuring that there are clear standards that govern who is paid what may be more important than the pay programs themselves.

36

- A well-designed compensation system can effectively motivate a company's "best" employees but should be used in conjunction with other well-known motivators, such as providing interesting and challenging work and offering the ability to participate in decision making. It is crucial that the compensation system directly links pay to performance if it is to effectively motivate higher-talent employees.

Some Key Sources

Bates, S. (2004). Getting engaged. *HR Magazine, 49*(2), 44-51.

Igalens, J., & Roussel, P. (1999). A study of the relationships between compensation package, work motivation and job satisfaction. *Journal of Organizational Behavior, 20,* 1003-1025.

Jurgensen, C. E. (1978). Job preferences (What makes a job good or bad?). *Journal of Applied Psychology, 63,* 267-276.

Murphy, W. H. (2004). In pursuit of short-term goals: Anticipating the unintended consequences of using special incentives to motivate the sales force. *Journal of Business Research, 57,* 1265-1275.

Rynes, S. L., Colbert, A., & Brown, K. G. (2002). HR professionals' beliefs about effective human resource practices: Correspondence between research and practice. *Human Resource Management, 41,* 149-174.

Rynes, S. L., Gerhart, B., & Minette, K. A. (2004). The importance of pay in employee motivation: Discrepancies between what people say and what they do. *Human Resource Management, 43,* 381-394.

Stajkovic, A. D., & Luthans, F. (2001). Differential effects of incentive motivators on work performance. *Academy of Management Journal, 44,* 580-590.

Thakor, M. V., & Joshi, A. W. (2005). Motivating salesperson customer orientation: Insights from the job characteristics model. *Journal of Business Research, 58,* 584-592.

Williams, M. L., McDaniel, M. A., & Nguyen, N. T. (2006). A meta-analysis of the antecedents and consequences of pay level satisfaction. *Journal of Applied Psychology, 91,* 392-413.

36

QUALITY IMPROVEMENT AWARDS

37.

American companies winning the Malcolm Baldrige National Quality Award or Deming Prize:

SELECT ONE:

☐ A. Are financially more successful than their counterparts in business and industry who did not win but did apply.

☐ B. Are financially more successful than their counterparts in business and industry who did not apply.

☐ C. Are financially more successful than their counterparts in business and industry who did not apply but had viable quality programs.

☐ D. Are financially more successful than their counterparts in business and industry who have no formal program.

☐ E. Are not financially more successful than their counterparts.

37

37. American companies winning the Malcolm Baldrige National Quality Award or Deming Prize:

The correct answer is E: Are not financially more successful than their counterparts.

HOW SURE ARE WE AT THIS TIME?				
1	**2**	3	4	5
Hint	**Suggestive**	Trending	Substantial	Solid

Discussion

The Malcolm Baldrige National Quality Award was established by Congress in the late-1980s to help stimulate American companies to improve their level of quality and productivity. The Award was designed to nationally recognize the achievements of those companies that significantly enhanced the quality of their goods and services in the global marketplace. It is named for Malcolm Baldrige, who served as the U.S. Secretary of Commerce during the creation of the Award. Some experts largely credit the Malcolm Baldrige Award for helping turn around American business with regard to quality. During the 1970s and 1980s, American business and industry were being strongly challenged by foreign competition. It was claimed that American products and services were inferior, particularly with regards to quality.

When the Award was initiated in 1988, there were three award categories: (1) manufacturing, (2) service, and (3) small business. During the ensuing 19 years, three additional categories have been added: (4) health care in 1999, (5) education in 1999, and (6) nonprofit and government in 2007. Some of the most well-known companies in the United States have won the Malcolm Baldrige Award, such as AT&T, 3M, Xerox, FedEx, General Motors, Texas Instruments, and IBM. As of 2006, a total of 71

37

awards have been given to American organizations. Several companies, or divisions of companies, have won it more than once (e.g., AT&T, Boeing, Xerox, Motorola).

Another prestigious award that honors company efforts with regard to quality is the internationally renowned Deming Prize. This award has a much longer history than the Malcolm Baldrige Award, beginning in 1951. It was established in Japan and honors the American scholar, W. Edwards Deming, for his pioneering efforts in quality improvement that he brought to Japan following World War II. The award is administered by the Union of Japanese Scientists and Engineers and is given to those companies that have achieved distinctive performance improvement through the application of total quality management (TQM). Any organization can apply for this prize—private or public, large or small, Japanese or non-Japanese. In addition, individuals who have made outstanding contributions to the study and dissemination of TQM or statistical methods used for TQM can apply. As of 2006, 196 companies and 69 individuals have won the Deming Prize. Because the initial purpose of the award was to foster the development of quality control activities in Japan, the Deming Prize was first restricted to Japanese companies. During the past two decades, however, the award has been open to overseas companies as well. Nevertheless, the vast majority of award winners have been Japanese. Only three American companies have won it—Florida Power and Light Company in 1989, AT&T in 1994, and a Texas automotive supplier called Sanden International in 2006. No American individuals have won this honor due to the fact that only Japanese are eligible.

A primary benefit of applying and winning either the Malcolm Baldrige Award or the Deming Prize purportedly is to enhance the overall quality of a company's products or services. As part of the application process for both awards, the applying company receives feedback from an expert panel on various strategic criteria. For example, the Malcolm Baldrige Award

37

provides companies with detailed evaluations on seven criteria, ranging from leadership and process management to business results. The Deming Prize provides companies feedback more focused on measurement and statistical methods as it relates to quality. One would expect those companies who have won either accolade should outperform other companies. Winning companies with a demonstrated commitment to quality, nationally acknowledged for this achievement, should be more financially profitable and provide a higher rate of return in the stock market than nonwinning companies. For example, the former Vice President of Quality at Honeywell asserted, "Applying for the Baldrige Award will help U.S. companies improve their competitive performance. The application and review process for the Award is the best, most cost-effective, and comprehensive business health audit you can get" (NIST, 2003).

Selected Research

- One of the first research studies to examine the effect of winning the Malcolm Baldrige Award was published only a few years after the Award was started. Wilson and Russell contrasted the financial performance of the previous 17 winners of the Award with companies in the S&P 500 (see Shadovitz, 1994). They found that Baldrige winning companies' stock had outperformed the S&P by 2.6 to 1. Further, they reported that the return on investment of these 17 winning companies was 460% as compared to 175% for the SAP companies during this period.

- The Malcolm Baldrige National Quality Award is managed by the National Institute of Standards and Technology (NIST), a part of the U.S. Department of Commerce. From 1993 to 2004, NIST has tracked the stock prices of publicly traded Award winning companies (as a group). The so-called "Baldrige Index," then is compared to the mean stock price of the S&P 500 companies. For the first eight years, the Baldrige Index had consistently outperformed the S&P 500 by as much as 6.5 to 1. However, in 2003 and 2004, the results were reversed. For example, in 2004 Baldrige Award winning companies had a *decrease* of 18.15% in stock price from the previous year; whereas, the S&P 500 showed a 35.58% *increase*. The Baldrige Index was discontinued after that year. NIST officials expressed that it no longer accurately reflected the accomplishments and diversity of Baldrige Award recipients. They claimed that since the addition of the education and health care categories in 1999, there had been a substantial increase in the number of Award recipients that were either nonprofit or privately owned businesses. To support this point, NIST officials pointed out that only four of the 23 recipients were publicly traded and therefore could be included in the stock price study between 2000 and 2004.

- For a different reason, Tai and Przasnyski (1999) also contended that the Baldrige Index misrepresented stock value returns across different sets of companies. These authors asserted that it is inappropriate to compare stock returns without considering (i.e., statistically controlling for) the risk of the stocks, because riskier stocks would be expected to earn higher returns. When they did this procedure, they found that only 53% of the Malcolm Baldrige Award winning companies outperformed the market. These authors found similar results in a follow-up study published in 2002. In another study which exclusively examined manufacturing companies that had won the Award, the researchers concluded that the economic success of recipients "may be exaggerated and that success certainly cannot be guaranteed" (Wilson, Walsh, & Needy, 2003, p. 3). These findings are not a strong endorsement for the market value of winning the Award.

37

- Likewise, Kevin Hendricks and Vinod Singhal (2001a, b) conducted a stream of research investigating the market impact of winning quality awards. Their focus, however, is more directly on the effect of TQM programs on a company's stock price. They use the winning of various quality awards as a proxy for effective TQM implementation. Overall, they have found a clear linkage between winning quality awards and winning companies' stock increases. However, their database consists of approximately 3,000 companies that have won 140 different quality awards (including 30 at the state level). These researchers conclude that the effective implementation of TQM philosophies and principles leads to significant wealth creation. Although this finding is important in its own right, we cannot isolate the impact of the Malcolm Baldrige Award (or Deming Prize) on market value since their research studies include a variety of quality improvement awards.

- Given the very limited number of American companies that have won the Deming Prize (three), it is not possible to systematically evaluate its impact on companies in the United States. Nevertheless, it should be noted that three years after the Florida Power and Light Company won the award, it slashed its quality department staff from 85 employees to three. The group chairman of the company reported that many of the staff had feared that the "quality improvement process had become a tyrannical bureaucracy" (Choi & Behling, 1997, p. 37).

- No studies were located in the published literature that demonstrated product quality or service quality of Deming and/or Malcolm Baldrige winning companies had improved. Certainly, one would expect quality to improve when so many company resources are devoted to it. Executives who have been involved in the application process provide numerous testimonials that performance quality and efficiency were increased. For instance, an executive winning the award

37

in 1996 declared, "Applying for the Baldrige Award also helped us set a pace for quality improvement efforts that we otherwise wouldn't have maintained. It created accountability through the Award cycles that moved us faster and moved us further than we could have done on our own." Another winner stated, "We aimed for the Baldrige Award to drive our business processes to world-class levels." Such glowing remarks do not scientifically validate product quality, however. Research evidence in this area is needed.

So what difference do these findings make?

- The Malcolm Baldrige National Quality Award and Deming Prize are two of the most prestigious honors an American company can attain. Both awards acknowledge the achievement of a high level of quality bestowed by an external body of experts. Organizations that receive either award frequently develop special media campaigns promoting this distinction in the marketplace. Public companies proudly include the announcement in their annual reports to shareholders. However, the research does not clearly demonstrate that profits, stock price, and even product/service quality improves over that of their competitors or that it has had a lasting effect on financial performance.

- One of the tremendous benefits an organization obtains from winning either award is the process it goes through completing the application. Both awards outline specific criteria and detailed instructions to carefully address quality improvement. Moreover, it should be noted that award winning companies had instituted their quality improvement programs many years before applying for and winning it. Seldom do companies earn the award on their initial attempt. In fact, Wilson, Walsh, and Needy (2003) report that Malcolm Baldrige Award winning manufacturers began their quality improvement programs on average

37

nearly seven years prior to winning. In addition, the feedback an organization receives from the on-site visitation team of examiners is extremely helpful. For example, the evaluation process for the 2006 Baldrige Award was approximately 1,000 hours of review.

- The Malcolm Baldrige National Quality Award evaluates companies on the following seven criteria:

    1. Leadership
    2. Strategic planning
    3. Customer and market focus
    4. Measurement, analysis and knowledge management
    5. Workforce focus
    6. Process management
    7. Business results

In contrast, the Deming Prize examines on the following ten viewpoints:

    1. Top management leadership
    2. Total quality management (TQM) frameworks
    3. Quality assurance systems
    4. Management systems for business elements
    5. Human resource development
    6. Effective utilization of information
    7. TQM concepts and values
    8. Scientific methods
    9. Organizational powers (core technology, speed, vitality)
    10. Contribution to realization of corporate objectives

Organizational leaders who desire to improve quality would benefit by focusing their attention on factors in either list.

37

- All this concerted effort on the part of executive management, as well as employees throughout the organization, directed to improving product/service quality should pay off in visible, public results. Award winning companies clearly should outperform other companies. Nevertheless, the research does not support this claim. Either no independent investigations have been conducted demonstrating the organization's products and services have markedly improved, or the evidence that does exist has reported mixed findings. Certainly, all organizations need to be diligent at finding opportunities for quality enhancement. Applying and winning the Baldrige Award or Deming Prize should assist them in this effort. But winning the award does not seem to lead to success. Further research is needed to look at lead and lag effects, at performance of companies who apply for the award (versus those who do not), and at which specific factors the Baldrige Award or Deming Prize have the most impact on company performance.

- Ultimately, you have to bet long-term on quality and following the criteria required by the awards. But at the moment, you have to do so based on faith.

Some Key Sources

37

Choi, T. Y., & Behling, O. C. (1997). Top managers and TQM success: One more look after all these years. *Academy of Management Executive, 11*(1), 37-47.

Helton, B. R. (1995). The Baldie play. *Quality Progress, 28*(2), 43-45.

Hendricks, K. B., & Singhal, V. R. (1997). Does implementing an effective TQM program actually improve operating performance? Empirical evidence from firms that have won quality awards. *Management Science, 44*, 1258-1274.

Hendricks, K. B., & Singhal, V. R. (2001a). Firm characteristics, total quality management, and financial performance. *Journal of Operations Management, 19,* 269-285.

Hendricks, K. B., & Singhal, V. R. (2001b). The long-run stock price performance of firms with effective TQM programs as proxied by quality award winners. *Management Science, 47,* 359-368.

National Institute of Standards and Technology. (2003). *Malcolm Baldrige National Quality Award: Why apply?* Gaithersburg, MD: U.S. Department of Commerce.

National Institutes of Standards and Technology. (2006). *Baldrige stock studies.* Retrieved January 19, 2007, from http://www.quality.nist.gov/Stock_Studies.htm

Pomeroy, A. (2006). Winners and learners. *HRMagazine, 51*(4), 62-67.

Przasnyski, Z. H., & Tai, S. S. (2002). Stock performance of Malcolm Baldrige National Quality Award winning companies. *Total Quality Management, 13,* 475-488.

Tai, L. S., & Przasnyski, Z. H. (1999). Baldrige Award winners beat the S&P 500. *Quality Progress, 32*(4), 45-51.

Shadovitz, D. (1994). Winning combination. *Human Resource Executive,* February, pp. 54-55.

Wilson, J. P., Walsh, M. A. T., & Needy, K. L. (2003). An examination of the economic benefits of ISO 9000 and the Baldrige Award to manufacturing firms. *Engineering Management Journal, 15*(4), 3-10.

37

EXPATRIATION

38.

What competency do expatriates develop most while on international assignments?

SELECT ONE:

☐ A. Strategic knowledge.

☐ B. Problem solving.

☐ C. Teamwork.

☐ D. Awareness and perspective.

☐ E. Conflict resolution.

38

38. What competency do expatriates develop most while on international assignments?

The correct answer is D: Awareness and perspective.

HOW SURE ARE WE AT THIS TIME?				
1	2	**3**	4	5
Hint	Suggestive	**Trending**	Substantial	Solid

Discussion

Global corporations need more globally competent leaders. The expectation is that managers who have international experience will be able to initiate and maintain increasingly global strategies. Some have found that CEOs who had international experience led better-performing multinational corporations than did CEOs without international experience (Carpenter, Sanders, & Gregersen, 2001).

The costs (to both the individual and the organization) associated with expatriate assignments are high. Returning expatriates often express frustration at career prospects upon return to their home location (Stahl & Cerdin, 2004). These frustrations are frequently attributed to the lack of attention organizations pay to the repatriation process (see Chapter 19). This lack of attention to repatriation and retention may result in the repatriates leaving the organization. Although quite a bit of research has investigated the types of characteristics or personality traits that predict success in the expatriate assignment (cf., Shaffer, Harrison, Gregersen, Black, & Ferzandi, 2006), there is a lack of research investigating the specific leadership competencies that are developed or learned most while on expatriate assignment.

38

Expatriates do learn on international assignment, and the process by which they learn is no different from the process that explains domestic managers' learning (McCall & Hollenbeck, 2002a). The differentiating factor between domestic and international learning experiences likely stems from culture shock—to learn cultural adaptability and obtain a multicultural perspective, executives need to be placed in environments in which they will be forced to cope with cultural obstacles. Immersion learning occurs when executives live in a culture rather than pass through it as a tourist.

Kohonen (2005) suggests that expatriation forces individuals to reevaluate their personal identities (to engage in self-exploration to determine what *defines* them). To the extent that these assignments provide a context for reconstruction of one's identity, the expatriate will have experienced increased self-awareness regarding his/her strengths, developmental needs, and personal identity. From this increased self-awareness, successful managers would be expected to develop coping and adapting competencies that aren't necessarily developed by their non-expatriate colleagues.

Experts forecast the future will hold even more global expansion and project a shortage of managers with international experience. Unfortunately, the specific competencies learned on international assignment are, as of yet, not altogether clear. In addition to increases of self-awareness, coping, and general adapting abilities, expatriate assignment theoretically increases an employee's perspective-taking ability, *cultural* adaptability, and international business knowledge (cf., Dalton, Ernst, Leslie, Deal, & Ritter, 2002). Together these skills define a broader perspective-taking ability referred to as a "global mind-set" (McCall & Hollenbeck, 2002a).

38

Selected Research
- Carpenter, Sanders, and Gregersen (2001) found that CEOs who had international experience led better-performing

multinational corporations than did CEOs without international experience. The specific competencies gained from international exposure were not measured in this investigation. Rather, international experience at the CEO position was simply identified as rare, valuable, and inimitable—therefore making it a source of competitive firm advantage.

- Tung (2004) believes that the key valued competency obtained from expatriate experience is a "global mind-set." Because women have been historically underrepresented in expatriate assignments, they tend to lack the opportunity to develop this global mind-set (relative to men). Women do not differ from men in the willingness to take an international assignment, however.

- Caligiuri and Di Santo (2001) measured hypothesized dimensions of expatriate competence before, during, and after international assignment. Expatriates and repatriates self-reported that (1) they possessed more knowledge regarding their organization's worldwide business structure, and (2) they had more extensive social networks than did prepatriates. However, those who had not yet embarked on international assignment reported a better ability to make international business transactions as well as more adaptive leadership abilities. It is possible that expatriates and repatriates are more self-aware regarding their adaptive leadership and international business abilities than are those who have not yet had international experience.

38

- Managers with expatriate experience are more sensitive to cultural differences and are more cross-culturally adventurous than are managers without expatriate experience (Spreitzer, McCall, & Mahoney, 1997). It is impossible from this analysis to know if expatriates learned these competencies while on assignment or not.

- Managers view expatriation as an opportunity to develop skills that will make them more marketable in the future. Surveying German expatriates, Stahl, Miller, and Tung (2002) found personal challenge of the assignment and opportunity for professional advancement to be the most important factors contributing to whether or not an international assignment is accepted. These expatriates believe that they are improving their management, professional, and intercultural skills through reducing intolerance, developing a global mind-set, and being forced to take initiative and assume responsibility.

- McCall and Hollenbeck (2002b) interviewed executives who had been successful expatriates to tap into their expertise regarding why some expatriates fail on assignment. These executives cited a resistance to change (failing to be properly adaptive), unrefined interpersonal skills, and the failure to pick up on cues indicating pending or potential problems as common derailers for expatriates. These derailers suggest that an expatriate who develops adaptiveness, interpersonal skill, and cultural cue responsiveness may be less likely to fail.

- Dalton, Ernst, Leslie, Deal, and Ritter (2002) found that perspective-taking, international business knowledge, and cultural adaptability were all related to performance in globally-complex jobs. These three dimensions define what the researchers refer to as "intercultural effectiveness," and although this construct was not specifically compared against non-expatriate managers (to determine if it can be learned on assignment), it does seem to explain some part of effectiveness in expatriate assignments.

38

- Investigating reasons why some Japanese expatriates do not learn while on international assignment, Wong (2005) identified parent country (and organization) culture and perceived control as strong obstacles to organizational learning. The norms and values of expatriates sustained conformity to the parent organization and home culture, rather than adapting to the host organization and country.

- Adler and Bartholomew (1992) surveyed 50 American organizations, finding that, from the organization's perspective, expatriates are used more to simply get an immediate job done than for purposes of either personal or organizational development. This short-term perspective was prominent in the early 1990s—it is unknown if the same mentality predominates today in an increasingly global business environment.

- Sambharya (1996) found that top management teams with more international experience tended to coordinate organizations that engage in more international diversification. The lack of managerial talent with international experience was noted as one constraint on organizational globalization. The specific international experience competencies that lead to diversification were not identified in this study.

So what difference do these findings make?

- Experience outside one's own home country is valuable on a number of levels. It is certainly perspective building. To be successful in someone else's "land," you have to adapt to ways of acting and thinking that are not natural or possibly not comfortable to you. Watching how business is done across international landscapes will lead to valuable global insights. The essence of the process is adapting. In order to adapt, you have to be aware of adapting from what to what. That necessarily leads to increased self-insight. Who am I and what do I need to be in order to be effective and successful? It also leads to a broader portfolio of thinking

38

and skills as one is required to perform across differing settings and cultures. By watching differences around the world, it offers the opportunity to examine oneself in a richer context. Who am I and why do I think and behave like I do? Who are they and why do they think and behave as they do? What's the difference? Does it matter? Given more and broader choices, who exactly do I want to be?

- Learning on international assignment versus being prepared for international assignment are two very different issues. Some employees will be better candidates for expatriate assignment, but the specific learning and personal development objectives of expatriation should be specified prior to departure. Through explicit articulation of what is valued, individuals can make more informed decisions regarding whether or not to accept the expatriate assignment, and organizations can maximize the likelihood that their objectives for employee development and global competence are met.

- International assignments certainly build perspective-taking (the ability to view issues from others' viewpoints), cultural adaptability (the ability to change one's preferred manner of behavior to fit other contexts), and international business knowledge (awareness of international business policies, procedures, and regulations; Dalton, Ernst, Leslie, Deal, & Ritter, 2002).

- Instead of referring to "global competence" in a general, content-devoid manner, assignments should focus on the specifics of perspective-taking, cultural adaptability, and international business knowledge.

- Successful expatriates cite the importance of *people* in their ability to manage effectively. Much of the learning that occurs on international assignment occurs outside of the normal scope of business. Dining and shopping—simply interacting with host country nationals—is perhaps as

38

important to developing a global mind-set as is managing within the host organization. Expatriates in this sense are truly in a continuous learning environment that does not "shut off" when they leave work. Successful expatriates will take advantage of these life opportunities to fully develop their cross-cultural competencies. When expatriates take a foreign assignment but live in a self-contained community of those from their home country, they forgo much of the learning from the assignment.

• Increased self-awareness, even without self-reconstruction, has been related to increased effectiveness and success as a leader. International assignments are one source, albeit a powerful one, to help aspiring leaders gain more self-knowledge.

Some Key Sources

Adler, N. J., & Bartholomew, S. (1992). Managing globally competent people. *Academy of Management Executive, 6*(3), 52-65.

Caligiuri, P., & Di Santo, V. (2001). Global competence: What is it, and can it be developed through global assignments? *Human Resource Planning, 24*(3), 27-35.

Carpenter, M. A., Sanders, W. G., & Gregersen, H. B. (2001). Bundling human capital with organizational context: The impact of international experience on multinational firm performance and CEO pay. *Academy of Management Journal, 44,* 493-511.

Dalton, M., Ernst, C., Leslie, J., Deal, J., & Ritter, W. (2002). Effective global management: Established constructs and novel contexts. *European Journal of Work and Organizational Psychology, 11,* 443-468.

Harvey, M., & Novicevic, M. M. (2004). The development of political skill and political capital by global leaders through global assignments. *International Journal of Human Resource Management, 15,* 1173-1188.

38

Harvey, M., Novicevic, M. M., & Kiessling, T. (2002). Development of multiple IQ maps for use in the selection of inpatriate managers: A practical theory. *International Journal of Intercultural Relations, 26,* 493-524.

Javidan, M., & House, R. J. (2001). Cultural acumen for the global manager: Lessons from project GLOBE. *Organizational Dynamics, 29,* 289-305.

Kohonen, E. (2005). Developing global leaders through international assignments: An identity construction perspective. *Personnel Review, 34,* 22-36.

McCall, M. W., Jr., & Hollenbeck, G. P. (2002a). *Developing global executives: The lessons of international experience.* Boston, MA: Harvard Business School Press.

McCall, M. W., Jr., & Hollenbeck, G. P. (2002b). Global fatalities: When international executives derail. *Ivey Business Journal, 66*(5), 74-78.

Sambharya, R. B. (1996). Foreign experience of top management teams and international diversification strategies of U.S. multinational corporations. *Strategic Management Journal, 17,* 739-746.

Shaffer, M. A., Harrison, D. A., Gregersen, H., Black, J. S., & Ferzandi, L. A. (2006). You can take it with you: Individual differences and expatriate effectiveness. *Journal of Applied Psychology, 91,* 109-125.

Spreitzer, G. M., McCall, M. W., Jr., & Mahoney, J. D. (1997). Early identification of international executive potential. *Journal of Applied Psychology, 82,* 6-29.

Stahl, G. K., & Cerdin, J. L. (2004). Global careers in French and German multinational corporations. *Journal of Management Development, 23,* 885-902.

Stahl, G. K., Miller, E. L., & Tung, R. L. (2002). Toward the boundaryless career: A closer look at the expatriate career concept and the perceived implications of an international assignment. *Journal of World Business, 37,* 216-227.

38

Suutari, V. (2003). Global managers: Career orientation, career tracks, life-style implications and career commitment. *Journal of Managerial Psychology, 18,* 185-207.

Tung, R. L. (1998). American expatriates abroad: From neophytes to cosmopolitans. *Journal of World Business, 33,* 125-144.

Tung, R. L. (2004). Female expatriates: The model global manager? *Organizational Dynamics, 33,* 243-253.

Wong, M. M. L. (2005). Organizational learning via expatriate managers: Collective myopia as blocking mechanism. *Organization Studies, 26,* 325-350.

38

39.

Conflict inside teams is:

SELECT ONE:

☐ A. Always good because conflict increases accuracy.

☐ B. Always bad because the quality of decision making decreases as conflict increases.

☐ C. Always bad because cohesive teams are more productive.

☐ D. Sometimes good, sometimes bad; it depends upon the type of conflict (conflict of ideas helps, interpersonal conflict hurts).

☐ E. Always bad because conflict causes dissatisfaction in the team which, in turn, decreases team performance.

39

39. Conflict inside teams is:

The correct answer is D: Sometimes good, sometimes bad; it depends upon the type of conflict (conflict of ideas helps, interpersonal conflict hurts).

HOW SURE ARE WE AT THIS TIME?				
1	2	3	**4**	5
Hint	Suggestive	Trending	**Substantial**	Solid

Discussion

Conflict inside teams is currently viewed as a possibly useful (instead of always stressful and disruptive) group characteristic. There is a difference between tension (healthy conflict) and contention (unhealthy conflict). Tension means that differences are expected, discussed, and negotiated. Contention denotes that people take sides, quit listening to alternatives, and try to make conflict into a win/lose situation. It is not healthy to have extreme conflict, but it is likewise inefficient to have false compliance within a team (i.e., if everyone thinks and acts the same). Furthermore, groups who value consensus or "getting along" more than they value constructive criticism have the potential to make worse decisions than individual decision makers—the so-called "groupthink" phenomenon (Janis, 1972). However, the findings regarding conflict and team performance are quite mixed. At present, researchers are attempting to isolate the conditions that define "functional or useful conflict."

One stream of thought is that the *source* of conflict is important when viewing conflict as potentially beneficial. Interpersonal conflict is less good (i.e., team members not "getting along" or disliking one another). Conflict of perspectives, ideas, and opinions, however, is helpful for effective decision making.

39

This latter form of conflict is referred to as "cognitive" conflict. Personalizing differences creates more angst than focusing on the behavioral or conceptual differences that might exist. And, focusing conflict on a particular situation is better than starting a dialogue with "you always...."

Management textbooks make this distinction as well. However, it should be pointed out that identifying precisely when conflict is positive versus negative can be tricky. Interpersonal conflict seems to definitely decrease team-member satisfaction, but it may or may not decrease team performance. Cognitive conflict occasionally has been shown to positively impact team performance and sometimes not. Of course, it is possible that "good" conflict (of perspectives) can quickly degenerate into interpersonal conflict, if harsh language is used or team members have an emotional tie to their position. Trying to elicit the good by-product of conflict may, therefore, inadvertently stimulate the bad side of conflict (the unpleasant side effect of people not getting along). Managers walk a fine line between stimulating multiperspective team contributions and chilling team chemistry. Furthermore, although cognitive conflict can lead to better decisions, if interpersonal conflict is present, team members may not be committed to implementing the decision. "On the one hand, conflict improves decision quality; on the other, it may weaken the ability of the group to work together" (Schweiger, Sandberg, & Ragan, 1986, p. 67).

Teams that are able to manage their cognitive conflict without eliciting interpersonal conflict seem to have the best of both worlds. How exactly to get there is, as of yet, murky. Because interpersonal conflict is largely attributable to misinterpretation of team-member motives (cf., Amason, 1996), rotating devil's advocate roles and cultivating high levels of trust seem to be the most promising options to achieve these effective groups.

39

Selected Research

- Amason (1996) found that conflict of perspectives (cognitive conflict) leads to better strategic decision making, while interpersonal conflict leads to worse strategic decisions. Furthermore, team-member attitude and acceptance of the team decision is enhanced with cognitive conflict but reduced with interpersonal conflict.

- Specifically trying to determine how to maximize the benefits of cognitive conflict while minimizing the likelihood of interpersonal conflict, Amason and Sapienza (1997) noted greater conflict (both types) in larger teams. Openness (in terms of willingness to communicate) led to greater cognitive conflict in all teams and less interpersonal conflict in teams with greater mutuality (perceived sharing of consequences of decisions).

- Team-member diversity can either increase or decrease conflict, and different types of diversity lead to different types of conflict (Pelled, Eisenhardt, & Xin, 1999). Cognitive conflict is largely driven by job-related diversity (different experiential backgrounds) while interpersonal conflict is associated with noncognitive-related factors (interpersonal conflict increases with race and tenure diversity but decreases with age diversity). Cognitive conflict here led to greater team performance, while interpersonal conflict did not help or hinder performance.

- "Programming" conflict into a team can lead to better strategic decisions (Schweiger, Sandberg, & Ragan, 1986). Teams make higher-quality decisions if they are instructed to appoint a devil's advocate or engage in dialectical inquiry (explicitly develop and debate opposing ideas). Being instructed to reach consensus (i.e., *not* introducing conflict) leads to higher team-member satisfaction.

39

- De Dreu and Weingart (2003) concluded that the positive effects of cognitive conflict quickly disappear as conflict intensifies. Regarding team-member satisfaction, interpersonal conflict is more problematic than cognitive conflict. It is possible in this study that interpersonal conflict "spilled over" into cognitive conflict, thereby hiding the potentially positive impact of cognitive conflict.

- The ways in which teams deal with conflicts can lead to a norm of behavior for the team that persists across time (Kuhn & Poole, 2000). Teams tend to eventually deal with the majority of conflicts in a similar manner, but teams that employ an "integrative" conflict management strategy are the most productive teams (an integrative strategy is characterized by cooperation toward a mutually acceptable solution).

So what difference do these findings make?

- Teams tend to be unproductive, dissatisfied, and distracted under conditions of extreme conflict. More time is spent trying to be right and to convince others that you are right than solving problems. However, in the absence of conflict, teams become complacent, redundant, and inefficient. Obviously, there is a fine line between optimal and "too much" conflict. For teams that do not challenge teammates' perspectives, the formal assignment of a devil's advocate role can result in better team decisions. It is important that disagreements are not interpreted as personal attacks. A "rotating" devil's advocate role can minimize the likelihood that any one person will be singled out as hardheaded. One approach is to have the team randomly assign people to take "pro" and "con" positions, then debate to get the alternative views out in the open where they can be discussed. This process can address conflicts and/ or differences in a nonthreatening way. By assigning the role of pro or con, it forces a more thorough review of the alternatives being debated.

39

- Interpersonal conflict is less useful. All team members need to work toward getting along with each other on an interpersonal level. Until team members believe that others care about them personally and emotionally, they are less likely to trust or be open to new ideas. Conflict of perspectives can enable team members to consider points of view they may not have considered themselves. However, conflict of personalities, egos, or political motives lead to lower team performance. It is important that team members learn to not view idea disagreements the same as personal attacks. Building a procedure into team processes that includes a simple pro/con analysis for all important decisions can help. If all team members understand that important discussions made in the team need to include both benefits and drawbacks of a decision, attacks of a position will be less likely to be viewed as personal attacks.

- Trust is an important element within teams. Trust comes as people develop the "abilities"—dependability, predictability, sociability, likeability, flexibility, and credibility. These "abilities" generally come from shared experiences where trust emerges from learning to solve common problems. Cognitive conflict "spills over" to interpersonal conflict in the absence of trust. With higher levels of trust, these two forms of conflict tend to be more independent. If you have higher trust and lower interpersonal conflict, you can have higher cognitive conflict with less harm to the morale of the team.

- Team leaders need to understand that cognitive conflict is *better* and interpersonal conflict is *worse*. Team leaders need to know how to initiate constructive conflict and shut down destructive conflict. Team leaders need to know how to recognize when cognitive conflict is slipping into interpersonal conflict and know how to shut it down quickly. Team leaders need to be willing to coach individual team members on their-less-than constructive interpersonal

39

behavior, as well as running productive conflict at a group level. Team leaders need to be free of ego conflicts with team members as well. Above all, team leaders need to know that avoiding cognitive conflict is not a best practice.

Some Key Sources

Amason, A. C. (1996). Distinguishing the effects of functional and dysfunctional conflict on strategic decision making: Resolving a paradox for top management teams. *Academy of Management Journal, 39,* 123-148.

Amason, A. C., & Mooney, A. C. (1999). The effects of past performance on top management team conflict in strategic decision making. *International Journal of Conflict Management, 10,* 340-359.

Amason, A. C., & Sapienza, H. J. (1997). The effects of top management team size and interaction norms on cognitive and affective conflict. *Journal of Management, 23,* 495-516.

Barsade, S. G., Ward, A. J., Turner, J. D. F., & Sonnenfeld, J. A. (2000). To your heart's content: A model of affective diversity in top management teams. *Administrative Science Quarterly, 45,* 802-836.

De Dreu, C. K. W., & Weingart, L. R. (2003). Cognitive versus relationship conflict, team performance, and team member satisfaction: A meta-analysis. *Journal of Applied Psychology, 88,* 741-749.

Janis, I. L. (1972). *Victims of groupthink.* Boston: Houghton-Mifflin.

Kuhn, T., & Poole, M. S. (2000). Do conflict management styles affect group decision making? Evidence from a longitudinal field study. *Human Communication Research, 26,* 558-590.

Passos, A. M., & Caetano, A. (2005). Exploring the effects of intragroup conflict and past performance feedback on team effectiveness. *Journal of Managerial Psychology, 20,* 231-244.

39

Pelled, L. H., Eisenhardt, K. M., & Xin, K. R. (1999). Exploring the black box: An analysis of work group diversity, conflict, and performance. *Administrative Science Quarterly, 44,* 1-28.

Schweiger, D. M., Sandberg, W. R., & Ragan, J. W. (1986). Group approaches for improving strategic decision making: A comparative analysis of dialectical inquiry, devil's advocacy, and consensus approaches to strategic decision making. *Academy of Management Journal, 29,* 51-71.

Shook, C. L., Payne, G. T., & Voges, K. E. (2005). The "what" in top management group conflict: The effects of organizational issue interpretation on conflict among hospital decision makers. *Journal of Managerial Issues, 17,* 162-177.

Shulz-Hardt, S., Jochims, M., & Frey, D. (2002). Productive conflict in group decision making: Genuine and contrived dissent as strategies to counteract biased information seeking. *Organization Behavior and Human Decision Processes, 88,* 563-586.

39

COUNTERPRODUCTIVE BEHAVIOR

40.

What is the best predictor of an employee's likelihood to engage in deviant or counterproductive behaviors (theft, drug use, sabotage)?

SELECT ONE:

☐ A. A bad boss.

☐ B. A lack of self-control.

☐ C. Perceptions of unfair treatment.

☐ D. Boredom.

☐ E. Stress.

40

40. What is the best predictor of an employee's likelihood to engage in deviant or counterproductive behaviors (theft, drug use, sabotage)?

The correct answer is B: A lack of self-control.

HOW SURE ARE WE AT THIS TIME?				
1	2	**3**	4	5
Hint	Suggestive	**Trending**	Substantial	Solid

Discussion

Although *all* of the answers listed in the question contribute to employee deviance, an employee's level of self-control (the willingness to delay personal gratification) is the *best* predictor of counterproductivity (Marcus & Schuler, 2004). Self-control is the tendency to not engage in behaviors whose likely costs (long-term) are greater than short-term benefits. Individuals with low levels of self-control are more likely to engage in acts (such as stealing, drug use, or sabotage) that have a short-term benefit (i.e., monetary or physiological/arousal-based), even if long-term costs (i.e., termination or prosecution) are likely. The level of self-control is established during childhood, and if an acceptable level is not acquired prior to roughly eight years old, it is difficult to develop (Gottfredson & Hirschi, 1990).

Deviant (counterproductive) employee behaviors include various negative activities such as theft, sabotage, loafing, and drug use. These counterproductive behaviors are generally related to each other (an employee who is using drugs at work is more likely to be stealing or loafing than a non-drug-user). Deviant behaviors violate organizational norms and interests by harming either the organization or coworkers (or both). These actions are volitional and carried out with a harmful intent.

40

There are certain conditions that will increase the likelihood that someone with low self-control will engage in deviant workplace behaviors. Specifically, a low-self-control employee is more likely to be deviant if the work environment is not viewed favorably (Colbert et al., 2004). Specific events (anything that leads to a sense of outrage or frustration/disparity) often trigger a response of counterproductivity for these low-self-control employees. Furthermore, if a specific individual can be identified as responsible for an act of injustice, etc., that person will often be the focus of deviant behaviors, rather than the organization or unspecified coworkers.

Selected Research

- Self-control is the most important predictor of general counterproductive behaviors (Gottfredson & Hirschi, 1990). Other factors are important considerations if an employee's level of self-control is not known, but *if an employee's low level of self-control is known,* the other factors (e.g., perceived violations of trust, dissatisfaction, frustration) do not greatly add to the prediction of deviance (Marcus & Schuler, 2004).

- The specific deviant act of *sabotage* is generally a reaction to (1) a perceived lack of freedom/autonomy, (2) someone or something interfering with a personal goal, (3) difficult work (attempts to facilitate work), (4) boredom, or (5) a perception of unfair treatment. Of these five possible motives, perceptions of unfair treatment by a coworker, customer, or the organization are the best predictor of sabotage (Ambrose, Seabright, & Schminke, 2002).

- Emotional arousal can be a good or bad thing—emotion serves as a physiological energizer, inducing the individual to action. Negative emotions lead to counterproductivity, whereas positive emotions lead to positive citizenship behaviors (helping others, staying late at work, etc.). Using this definition, deviant workplace behaviors are

40

analogous to organizational citizenship behaviors, in that both are voluntary, extra-role behaviors. One is destructive/detrimental, the other is constructive/beneficial (Spector & Fox, 2002).

- Sprouse (1992) collected a series of anecdotes documenting worker frustrations and ways in which they dealt with them. The idea came from his own mailroom experiences, where he and coworkers felt undervalued and discontent. He noticed that the discontent of coworkers (and himself) manifested itself in sabotage or stealing. A common theme across these case studies is distrust of management, perceptions of mistreatment or undervaluing, boredom, or retribution for a perceived injustice. For some, it's the pure thrill of the act. Speaking of sabotaging a restaurant's music system with intermittently loud, annoying sounds, a former restaurant employee said, "I think that the rest of my life has been anticlimactic since then. It was a shining moment."

- Deviance can impact the organization's finances, but it can also have a bad influence on the general psychological health and wellness of employees through affecting the climate or culture of the organization. Organizations that communicate a caring orientation toward individual employees are less likely to have employees gossip, show favoritism, or engage in blaming/sniping behaviors (Peterson, 2002).

- Some employees are unlikely to be deviant, even when provoked. Extremely conscientious or emotionally stable employees are unlikely to "withhold effort"—one form of deviance. Similarly, agreeable individuals are not likely to be deviant *toward others,* even if provoked (Colbert et al., 2004).

40

So what difference do these findings make?

- Deviant or counterproductive workplace behaviors are a combination of a lack of self-control and an instigating event. People with lower levels of self-control tend to be "set off" mostly by the personal perception of unfairness or not being treated properly. The instigator will most of the time be the direct boss.

- Because self-control is believed to be a relatively stable trait or characteristic throughout adolescence and adulthood, organizations should select for acceptable amounts of it. Organizations concerned about employee deviance should select employees with acceptable self-control. These selection-based actions (interviews, assessments, background checks) may be more cost-efficient than post-hire situational interventions (i.e., monitoring employees, enforcing consequences to offenders; Marcus & Schuler, 2004).

- For many employees, the supervisor is the embodiment of the organization—good and bad consequences are frequently delivered through this individual. In order to decrease perceptions that employees are being treated unfairly, supervisors should treat their subordinates respectfully. Managers should be given training on how to supervise with integrity, respect, and sensitivity. Explaining the reasons behind decisions or actions that have negative consequences for employees can further increase feelings of being treated "fairly." Supervisors should be alerted if it is discovered that someone they are going to manage has demonstrated less-than-acceptable levels of self-control.

- If an individual is hired who ends up having less-than-acceptable self-control (but not to the extent of terminating the individual), increased monitoring and more rapid conflict resolution should be applied.

40

Some Key Sources

Ambrose, M. L., Seabright, M. A., & Schminke, M. (2002). Sabotage in the workplace: The role of organizational injustice. *Organizational Behavior and Human Decision Processes, 89,* 947-965.

Colbert, A. E., Mount, M. K., Harter, J. K., Witt, L. A., & Barrick, M. R. (2004). Interactive effects of personality and perceptions of the work situation on workplace deviance. *Journal of Applied Psychology, 89,* 599-609.

Gottfredson, M. R., & Hirschi, T. (1990). *A general theory of crime.* Stanford, CA: Stanford University Press.

Greenberg, J. (1993). Stealing in the name of justice: Informational and interpersonal moderators of theft reactions to underpayment inequity. *Organizational Behavior and Human Decision Processes, 54,* 81-103.

Judge, T. A., Scott, B. A., & Ilies, R. (2006). Hostility, job attitudes, and workplace deviance: Test of a multilevel model. *Journal of Applied Psychology, 91,* 126-138.

Lee, K., & Allen, N. J. (2002). Organizational citizenship behavior and workplace deviance: The role of affect and cognitions. *Journal of Applied Psychology, 87,* 131-142.

Marcus, B., & Schuler, H. (2004). Antecedents of counterproductive behavior at work: A general perspective. *Journal of Applied Psychology, 89,* 647-660.

Peterson, D. K. (2002). Deviant workplace behavior and the organization's ethical climate. *Journal of Business and Psychology, 17,* 47-61.

Robinson, S. L., & Bennett, R. J. (1995). A typology of deviant workplace behaviors: A multidimensional scaling study. *Academy of Management Journal, 38,* 555-572.

Sackett, P. R., & DeVore, C. J. (2001). Counterproductive behaviors at work. In N. Anderson, D. S. Ones, H. K. Sinangil, & C. Viswesvaran (Eds.), *Handbook of industrial, work, and organizational psychology* (pp. 145-164). London: Sage.

40

Spector, P. E., & Fox, S. (2002). An emotion-centered model of voluntary work behavior: Some parallels between counterproductive work behavior and organizational citizenship behavior. *Human Resource Management Review, 12,* 269-292.

Sprouse, M. (1992). *Sabotage in the American workplace: Anecdotes of dissatisfaction, revenge, and mischief.* San Francisco, CA: Pressure Drop Press.

40

41.

Going "green" results in:

SELECT ONE:

☐ A. Mostly positive reactions from all stakeholders.

☐ B. Increased cost to do business with no short-term (five years) ROI.

☐ C. An initial increase in cost, but in the long-term a net wash.

☐ D. For now, at least, a competitive disadvantage until all competitors go green.

☐ E. Positive for employees and regulators, but negative for shareholders and customers.

41

41. Going "green" results in:

The correct answer is A: Mostly positive reactions from all stakeholders.

HOW SURE ARE WE AT THIS TIME?				
1	2	**3**	4	5
Hint	Suggestive	**Trending**	Substantial	Solid

Discussion

Going "green" is not simply a new-age or tree-hugging trend, it can result in significant cost-savings to businesses, including better employee productivity, less absenteeism, and greater attraction and retention (cf., Lockwood, 2006). Environmentally friendly facilities are designed to have less environmental impact and to promote worker health and well-being. They also can be more energy efficient. The use of environmentally friendly approaches to building construction involves using alternative, less-toxic building materials, recycling construction waste, and minimizing ground grading and destruction. Green buildings are past the experimental stage and are now viewed as something of a business advantage. Today, sustainability in regards to the environment has become much more than a fancy slogan and is something investors, customers, and employees all pay attention to.

In addition to creating better working environments, there has been a global movement toward encouraging organizations to adopt more environmentally friendly policies. The 1987 Montreal Protocol on Substances That Deplete the Ozone Layer is overseen by the United Nations and requires stopping the production and use of chemicals known to be harmful to the earth's atmosphere. There are currently 189 countries that conform to the Protocol (most of the world's nations). This Protocol further places limits on trade to nations who are not party to the Protocol. The 1997 Kyoto Protocol extends this ban by encouraging a policy to prevent man-made global climate changes. These treaties limit the abilities of multinational corporations to take advantage of less-restrictive environmental laws in less-restrictive countries.

Industry associations also provide pressure for particular organizations to adopt more environmentally friendly practices. Private business can contribute to environmental protection through acting within or beyond simple compliance to these recommended restrictions.

Possible threats to corporate reputation remain an active concern for 75% of CEOs (Capozzi, 2005). An organization's interface with the natural environment is an area that is gaining increasing importance to stakeholders. Engaging in environmentally conscious actions such as reducing toxic emissions, building "green," and limiting the use of hazardous materials are fairly visible actions that can help build and sustain an organization's environmental reputation.

Selected Research

- Building "green" can be both environmentally friendly and provide cost-savings (Lockwood, 2006). Initial construction costs average only 0.8% more than traditional construction costs, but productivity increases, utility savings, and employee morale boosts can quickly make up for this additional up-front cost.

- Kassinis and Vafeas (2006) documented a positive relationship between stakeholder pressures (from governments and local community members) and organizational environmental performance (in terms of pollution emissions). Although more stakeholder pressure is related to less toxic emissions, local community pressure tends to have more impact than legislative action (as measured by House of Representative voting records).

41

- High-growth industries show a stronger association between environmental consciousness and organizational performance than do slower-growth industries (Russo & Fouts, 1997). The authors concluded that the benefits of enacting environmentally friendly policies outweigh the associated costs. Furthermore, viewing current environmental standards as "minimum requirements" positions organizations well for future restrictions (if they enact policies that go beyond the current minimum requirements).

- Hart (1995) argued that creating a positive reputation regarding an organization's interaction with the natural environment can be a source of competitive advantage. Such a reputation can be developed through integrating environmental concerns into strategic decision making. Taking environmental concerns into consideration while developing strategic plans leads to better financial performance (Judge & Douglas, 1998).

- However, it appears that engaging in environmentally friendly practices will not lead to cost savings for all organizations (Christmann, 2000). In order to reduce costs while simultaneously considering the natural environment, firms need to possess "complementary assets" such as a capability for process innovation and implementation. Organizations that possess these capabilities more effectively update and implement new technologies and equipment.

- Capacity for change—the extent to which an organization is capable and willing to adapt—is related to better environmental performance (Judge & Elenkov, 2005). However, if executives and front-line workers differ in terms of personal capacity for change, the organization likely will be less environmentally friendly. The authors suggested that organizations should view environmental restrictions as an opportunity for innovation and positive change, rather than an obstacle to overcome.

So what difference do these findings make?

- Incorporating environmental concerns into strategic decision making can help build an organization's reputation as environmentally friendly. This approach means designating someone in the company to serve as a spokesperson for the environmental impact of a particular decision or choice of activity.

- Aside from the obvious environmental benefits, going green can lead to more green (results). It actually can be used as a strategic tool to enhance an organization's reputation with various stakeholders, including customers. Going green can lead to more cost-effective recruiting for tough-to-get talent by signaling that the organization cares about the environment.

- Green renovations can be made to existing facilities.

- Engaging in reuse and recycling activities and reducing hazardous substance use are fairly low-cost options to start an organization toward "greenness."

Some Key Sources

Aragon-Correa, J. A., & Sharma, S. (2003). A contingent resource-based view of proactive corporate environmental strategy. *Academy of Management Review, 28,* 71-88.

Capozzi, L. (2005). Corporate reputation: Our role in sustaining and building a valuable asset. *Journal of Advertising Research, 45,* 290-293.

Christmann, P. (2000). Effects of "best practices" of environmental management on cost advantage: The role of complementary assets. *Academy of Management Journal, 43,* 663-680.

Christmann, P. (2004). Multinational companies and the natural environment: Determinants of global environmental policy standardization. *Academy of Management Journal, 47,* 747-760.

41

Dasgupta, S., Laplante, B., & Mamingi, N. (2001). Pollution and capital markets in developing countries. _Journal of Environmental Economics and Management, 42,_ 310-335.

Hart, S. (1995). A natural resource-based view of the firm. _Academy of Management Review, 20,_ 986-1014.

Judge, W. Q., & Douglas, T. (1998). Performance implications of incorporating natural environmental issues into the strategic planning process: An empirical assessment. _Journal of Management Studies, 35,_ 241-262.

Judge, W. Q., & Elenkov, D. (2005). Organizational capacity for change and environmental performance: An empirical assessment of Bulgarian firms. _Journal of Business Research, 58,_ 893-901.

Kassinis, G., & Vafeas, N. (2006). Stakeholder pressures and environmental performance. _Academy of Management Journal, 49,_ 145-159.

Lockwood, C. (2006). Building the green way. _Harvard Business Review, 84_(6), 129-137.

Russo, M., & Fouts, P. (1997). A resource-based perspective on corporate environmental performance and profitability. _Academy of Management Journal, 40,_ 534-559.

RECRUITMENT

42.

***Which practice best* attracts minority applicants?**

SELECT ONE:

☐ A. A very public Affirmative Action policy.

☐ B. Being one of the 100 Best Companies to Work For.

☐ C. Offering minority hiring bonuses.

☐ D. Contributing money to minority causes.

☐ E. Including minorities in organizational literature and recruiting efforts.

42. Which practice best attracts minority applicants?

The correct answer is E: Including minorities in organizational literature and recruiting efforts.

42

HOW SURE ARE WE AT THIS TIME?				
1	**2**	3	4	5
Hint	**Suggestive**	Trending	Substantial	Solid

Discussion

Many organizations are making special efforts to attract racial minority candidates, resulting in heightened competition for these workers. The impetus for this war for minority talent is shifting demography and governmental laws and regulations (see Chapter 5). For example, in the United Kingdom it is estimated that by 2010, only 20% of workers will be Caucasian males younger than 45 (Pearn Kandola, 2000).

In addition to changing workforce demographics, there is a positive business case for employing a diverse workforce. Diversity helps organizations gain new markets and intellectual capital—in short, it is good business practice. In 1999, for example, the S&P 500 underperformed *Fortune* magazine's "50 Best Companies for Asians, Blacks, and Hispanics" (Digh, 1999).

However, one of the challenges of diversity is that without unity first, diversity does not work. Unity should not be construed as workforce homogeneity. Unity is not a demographic concept. Rather, unity focuses on a shared commitment to meeting investor and customer expectations. Unless and until employees have unity around organization goals and priorities, the diversity will not matter. With unity, diversity helps raise alternatives, see new approaches, and experiment with new ideas. Lacking unity, diversity may simply be chaos and lack of control. One organization under the rubric of "valuing differences" allowed people throughout the organization to do their own thing and not be focused on common goals. This organization failed miserably in the long-term because there was not a shared purpose.

42

As a group, racial minorities place different emphases on certain organizational attributes than do Caucasian males. Although some of the attraction strategies offered in response to this chapter's question are good ideas for promoting diversity (e.g., an Affirmative Action policy), they are not efficient strategies for *recruiting* minorities while at the same time avoiding majority group marginalization (e.g., selective hiring bonus allocation might be viewed as unfair by majority group members).

The literature does report a minority applicant increase when an organization uses diverse recruiting literature (cf., Avery, 2003; Avery, Hernandez, & Hebl, 2004) and/or organizational representatives (such as attending a college career fair). Furthermore, those strategies do not appear to negatively impact majority-member applications.

Selected Research
- Minority applicants (in this case African American and Hispanic) are more attracted to companies that have the most pictures of racial minorities in advertisements, even if those minorities depicted represent demographic groups other than the applicants' (Avery, Hernandez, & Hebl, 2004). Caucasians are unaffected by the presence or absence of diversity in advertisements. Evidence reveals they are equally attracted to organizations that have a Caucasian, Hispanic, or African American representative in such ads.

42

- Considering organizational level as well as racial status in ads, Avery (2003) found African Americans to be more attracted to organizations that depicted African Americans in managerial positions (more than subordinate positions). Caucasians had similar attractiveness ratings, but did not change their views whether African Americans were depicted in management or not.

- Avery and McKay (2006) suggest that companies should communicate a valuing of diversity through, for example, placing advertisements in targeted (minority readership) magazines and television stations and including a diverse group of individuals in the advertisements.

- Research also indicates that companies that engage in socially responsible practices (including considerations such as diversity and environmental policies) are viewed as more attractive by all job seekers (Backhaus, Stone, & Heiner, 2002). Although consideration of a company's social performance is important at all stages of the job search, they are most important in determining whether or not the candidate will accept the job offer or not. Racial minorities are more interested in an organization's diversity record than are nonminorities.

- African American engineers report greater attraction to a potential employer if that employer conveys an identity-conscious (as opposed to an identity-blind) staffing procedure (Highhouse, Stierwalt, Bachiochi, Elder, & Fisher, 1999). Furthermore, African American engineering students are more attracted to team-based work than individual-based work. There is no documented preference difference for currently employed African American engineers.

So what difference do these findings make?

- The inclusion of racial minorities in company advertisements and literature increases minority applicant flow. Likewise, stressing equal opportunity employment policy increases the probability that an applicant sample will be more demographically diverse. Recruiting at universities with significant racial minority student bodies also will help. When possible, send minority incumbents as recruiters. It signals to potential job candidates that (1) the organization values diversity, (2) potential role models and mentors exist in the organization, and (3) minorities are more likely to succeed.

- An organization's track record regarding diversity is important for recruitment strategies. Efforts should be aimed at current policies as well as outreach efforts. Outreach programs such as internship programs with local high schools or universities with high minority enrollments can help.

- There are conferences, workshops, and publications devoted to the recruitment and retention of historically underrepresented worker groups. Although these events tend to be industry-specific, the strategies advocated cross industry boundaries. For example, the Minnesota Minority Recruitment Conference is held each fall (targeting the law profession), while the National Institute of General Medical Sciences maintains a Web site dedicated to minority recruitment and retention for medical fields. Digh (1999) has compiled a list of minority-affiliated professional groups. This list is a good resource for organizations wishing to partner with professional or student associations.

42

Some Key Sources

Avery, D. R. (2003). Reactions to diversity in recruitment advertising—Are differences black and white? *Journal of Applied Psychology, 88,* 672-679.

Avery, D. R., Hernandez, M., & Hebl, M. R. (2004). Who's watching the race? Racial salience in recruitment advertising. *Journal of Applied Social Psychology, 34,* 146-161.

Avery, D. R., & McKay, P. F. (2006). Target practice: An organizational impression management approach to attracting minority and female job applicants. *Personnel Psychology, 59,* 157-187.

Backhaus, K. B., Stone, B. A., & Heiner, K. (2002). Exploring the relationship between corporate social performance and employer attractiveness. *Business and Society, 41,* 292-318.

Charles, R. O., & McCleary, K. W. (1997). Recruitment and retention of African-American managers. *Cornell Hotel and Restaurant Administration Quarterly, 38,* 24-29.

Dass, P., & Parker, B. (1999). Strategies for managing human resource diversity: From resistance to learning. *Academy of Management Executive, 13,* 68-80.

Digh, P. (1999). Getting people in the pool: Diversity recruitment that works. *HR Magazine, 44,* 94-98.

Doverspike, D., Taylor, M. A., Shultz, K. S., & McKay, P. F. (2000). Responding to the challenge of a changing workforce: Recruiting nontraditional demographic groups. *Public Personnel Management, 29,* 445-457.

Freeman, C. (2003). Recruiting for diversity. *Women in Management Review, 18,* 68-76.

Greening, D. W., & Turban, D. B. (2000). Corporate social performance as a competitive advantage in attracting a quality workforce. *Business and Society, 39,* 254-280.

Highhouse, S., Stierwalt, S. L., Bachiochi, P., Elder, A. E., & Fisher, G. (1999). Effects of advertised human resource management practices on attraction of African American applicants. *Personnel Psychology, 52,* 425-442.

McKay, P. F., & Avery, D. R. (2006). What has race got to do with it? Unraveling the role of racioethnicity in job seekers' reactions to site visits. *Personnel Psychology, 59,* 395-429.

Pearn Kandola (2000). *Cross-Government Statistics.* London.

Thomas, K. M., & Wise, P. G. (1999). Organizational attractiveness and individual differences: Are diverse applicants attracted by different factors? *Journal of Business and Psychology, 13,* 375-390.

42

360-DEGREE FEEDBACK – INTERNATIONAL

43.

In what type of culture might multisource or 360-degree feedback be the least effective?

SELECT ONE:

☐ A. Individualist (focus on the person) cultures with a low (less) power distance between bosses and employees.

☐ B. Individualist cultures with a high (more) power distance.

☐ C. Collectivistic (focus on the group) cultures with a high power distance.

☐ D. Both individualist and collectivistic cultures, when they have a low power distance.

☐ E. Both individualist and collectivistic cultures, when they have a high power distance.

43. In what type of culture might multisource or 360-degree feedback be the least effective?

The correct answer is C: Collectivistic cultures with a high power distance.

43

HOW SURE ARE WE AT THIS TIME?				
1	2	**3**	4	5
Hint	Suggestive	**Trending**	Substantial	Solid

Discussion

Local culture is an important factor that must be considered in organizational life. A local culture is like a microclimate—the average temperature for an area may differ based on terrain and other conditions. Most large firms have subcultures where teams, divisions, or operations have unique ways of doing things. Different cultures bring with them different values, and this can have an influence on performance expectations and the role that feedback plays in organizations (Bretz, Milkovich, & Read, 1992). These subcultures also exist across national boundaries. Different countries have different cultures.

Despite this acknowledgement in the literature, relatively few studies have examined the appraisal and feedback process cross-culturally (Vance, McClaine, Boje, & Stage, 1992). Although few studies have specifically examined the cultural differences in performance appraisal, there is extensive research and theory on cross-cultural differences in two dimensions that have implications for performance appraisal and feedback: power distance and individualism/collectivism (see Hofstede [1980] for one of the most frequently cited works in this area). While cultures certainly differ on additional dimensions, there is theoretical and empirical evidence for the influence of individualism/collectivism and power distance on the performance appraisal and feedback process.

When there is greater power distance, employees tend to be more dependent on their managers, and employees consider themselves less qualified to evaluate people and themselves compared to their bosses. As a result, subordinates tend to refrain from voicing disagreements with their bosses, and bosses tend to be more paternalistic. In addition, it is likely less appropriate to ask subordinates (who have less power) to formally evaluate their bosses (who have more power), maybe for fear of retribution. At the other end of the spectrum, in a smaller power distance culture, employees are less dependent on their managers and managers tend to display more of a consultative or participatory style of management. In such cases, 360-degree feedback tends to be relatively well-received, as it is viewed as more acceptable for direct reports to evaluate their managers.

In individualistic cultures, the interests of the individual tend to take precedence over that of the group, and the employer-employee relationship is viewed as a business relationship. As a result, feedback in individualistic societies tends to focus on the person and be fairly blunt and direct. Given such conditions, 360-degree feedback is more readily accepted and embraced. Collectivistic cultures are often more hierarchical and employees tend to expect and prefer feedback from supervisors, as opposed to peers or direct reports. Also, feedback tends to focus more on the group rather than individuals, so conducting a 360-degree feedback process on an individual might not be well-received.

In addition to Hofstede's, there are other frameworks for understanding the dimensions that differentiate between cultures. One that has received considerable support in the literature can be found in Fons Trompenaars, *Riding the Waves of Culture* (1994). Trompenaars' framework posits seven dimensions (universalistic vs. particularistic; individualistic vs. collectivistic; neutral vs. affective; specific vs. diffuse; ascriptive vs. achievement; internal control vs. external control; past, present, and future cultures) upon which cultures differ.

Selected Research

- Gregersen, Hite, and Black (1996) report that supervisors' requests for feedback from subordinates has a tendency to undermine supervisors' authority in Latin American countries, which tend to be characterized by higher power distance. In such countries, 360-degree feedback is problematic, as subordinates may lose respect for their boss's authority.

43

- Huo and Von Glinow (1995) report that peer evaluation is extremely rare and even nonexistent in China, a relatively high power distance and collectivistic culture. The authors suggest that coworkers may be reluctant to evaluate peers for fear of damaging the harmony of the group and the relationships with coworkers. In such cultures, only leaders tend to be viewed as qualified to evaluate subordinates.

- Lepsinger and Lucia (1997) report that 360-degree feedback is more effective in participative (i.e., individualistic) as opposed to authoritative (i.e., collectivistic) environments.

- Triandis (1989) asserts that employees in high power distance cultures are generally more satisfied with a directive and more persuasive supervisor, while participative supervisors are more desirable in low power distance cultures. Accordingly, in high power distance societies, employees expect feedback to come from supervisors, and they may not give as much consideration to the views of those other than their boss.

So what difference do these findings make?

- National and cultural predispositions matter. It not only applies to this 360-degree issue but probably many other people practices as well. There is always a trade-off between shared practices globally and adapted practices locally. Local cultures and predispositions affect how HR and other management actions should be managed. For an obvious example, religious holidays will vary depending on the religious practices of the dominant employee group. But the other dimensions of national culture will also vary and affect how companies need to adapt global trends to local conditions. Headquarters needs to be sensitive when it implements common "best" practices across the globe. Very few common people practices would work in the same way across all continents and cultures. International perspective and sensitivity needs to be applied.

- Executives need to build a learning mentality where ideas that are developed in one geography can be shared with those in another geography. When ideas are shared, they should be adapted, not adopted. Adaptation means that the principles are modified according to local customs and practices. The generalization of ideas across borders comes by moving people, having best practice forums, doing site visits, sharing video vignettes, and other forms for sharing ideas.

43

Some Key Sources

Ashkenas, R. N., Ulrich, D., Jick, T., & Kerr, S. (1995). *Boundaryless organization: Breaking the chains of organizational structure.* San Francisco: Jossey-Bass.

Bretz, R. D., Milkovich, G. T., & Read, W. (1992). The current state of performance appraisal research and practice: Concerns, direction, and implications. *Journal of Management, 18*, 321-352.

Gregersen, H. B., Hite, J. M., & Black, J. S. (1996). Expatriate performance appraisal in U.S. multinational firms. *Journal of International Business Studies, 27*, 711-738.

Hofstede, G. (1980). *Culture's consequences: International differences in work-related values.* Beverly Hills, CA: Sage.

Huo, Y. P., & Von Glinow, M. A. (1995). On transplanting human resource practices in China: A culture-driven approach. *International Journal of Manpower, 16*, 3-15.

Lepsinger, R., & Lucia, A. D. (1997). 360° feedback and performance appraisal. *Training, 34*, 62-70.

Triandis, H. C. (1989). Cross-cultural industrial and organizational psychology. In H. C. Triandis, M. D. Dunnette, & L. M. Hough (Eds.), *Handbook of industrial and organizational psychology* (2nd ed., pp. 103-172). Palo Alto, CA: Consulting Psychologists Press.

Trompenaars, F. (1994). *Riding the waves of culture.* Burr Ridge, IL: Irwin Professional Publishing.

Vance, C. M., McClaine, S. R., Boje, D. M., & Stage, H. D. (1992). An examination of the transferability of traditional performance appraisal principles across cultural boundaries. *Management International Review, 32*, 313-326.

43

COUNTERPRODUCTIVE BEHAVIOR

44.

Intentional "bullying" in the workplace is:

SELECT ONE:

☐ A. Rare (less than 1% reporting an incident to management per year).

☐ B. A massive problem reported by over 50% of lower-level workers and over 15% for managerial-level employees.

☐ C. Almost always occurs between coworkers as a method of gaining personal advantage.

☐ D. More prevalent in larger, bureaucratic organizations than other types.

☐ E. Experienced and reported by more than 5% of the workforce across all organizational levels.

44

44. Intentional "bullying" in the workplace is:

The correct answer is E: Experienced and reported by more than 5% of the workforce across all organizational levels.

HOW SURE ARE WE AT THIS TIME?				
1	2	3	4	**5**
Hint	Suggestive	Trending	Substantial	**Solid**

44

Discussion

Workplace "bullying" involves acting with hostility toward a coworker or subordinate over a protracted period of time. These acts may involve socially isolating someone, interfering with his/her work tasks, ridiculing, threatening, yelling, or even being physically abusive. The victim of bullying is typically not in a position to defend himself/herself or otherwise avoid the unwanted aggression. The bullying usually takes a verbal form but also can involve physical violence. These behaviors result in a great deal of stress for the victims of bullying. Although this subject may seem more appropriate for a grade-school primer than a management book, workplace bullying has been estimated to be as common as both sexual harassment and school bullying (Einarsen, 1999) and may be as traumatic as physical assaults (Leymann & Gustafsson, 1996; Mayhew et al., 2004).

Typically, the bullying evolves over time. At first, it may involve subtle and indirect forms of sniping, but eventually it grows into more overt acts of abuse and/or isolation. When a supervisor engages in bullying behavior, there is an added level of stress, as a power differential already exists in the supervisor-subordinate relationship. Originating from a supervisor, bullying usually involves public berating, delivering feedback in a threatening or sarcastic manner, or intentional attempts to undermine the subordinate. These actions not only result in direct victim consequences, they tend to "bring down" others in the work environment as well (Jennifer, Cowie, & Ananiadou, 2003).

Targeted victims of bullying tend to differ from their coworkers in terms of personality—they may be viewed as annoying, having extremely low (or high) self-esteem, or simply shy. If a lack of experience or competence is added to this mix, an impatient or perfection-oriented manager can quite easily be drawn into the escalating pattern of bullying.

Research suggests employees who believe that their supervisors engage in bullying are less satisfied, less committed, do not trust coworkers, experience more stress, and are less likely to go "above and beyond" their formal job requirements to help the organization (cf., Tepper, Duffy, Henle, & Lambert, 2006). A quarter of individuals who experience bullying or witness it happening choose to leave their jobs because of these behaviors (Rayner, 1998).

44

In Europe (cf., Liefooghe & Davey, 2001; Salin, 2001), annual cross-industry estimates of bullying have risen to as high as 40% (McAvoy & Murtagh, 2003). However, a wide range of different baseline estimates is given across different studies, making it difficult to assess the true prevalence of bullying. Estimates typically range from 3.5% to the high 40% (cf., Hoel, Cooper, & Faragher, 2001). These different estimates are largely attributable to whether people indicate having experienced bullying in the past six months, the past year, or *ever.*

Selected Research

- Approximately 9% of business professionals directly recall being "bullied" at work, but fully 24% admit to experiencing at least one harassing act per week when further prompted (Salin, 2001). For this white-collar professional sample, work-related bullying (i.e., being ordered to do menial work or being given impossible deadlines) is more common than nonwork-related bullying (i.e., spreading rumors, teasing, or insulting one's private life).

- Research indicated that the more bullying experienced, the more counterproductive behaviors victims engage in (Ayoko, Callan, & Härtel, 2003). Types of bullying recorded in this study included verbal abuse, public humiliation, intimidation, chronic criticism, yelling, and micromanaging. These behaviors result in victim stress that can lead to the intentional waste of company materials, sabotage, and/or intentionally doing incorrect work.

44

- Victims of intense workplace bullying can be traumatized to the point of exhibiting symptoms of post-traumatic stress disorder (Leymann & Gustafsson, 1996). Of 64 bullying victims who voluntarily entered treatment, 59 were diagnosed as suffering from post-traumatic stress disorder; the remaining five were classified as suffering from psychological burnout. The majority of these individuals were subjected to workplace bullying for a period of five to eight years.

- Mayhew et al. (2004) noted the majority of bullying behaviors tend to be "top-down," coming from supervisors and being directed toward subordinates. Furthermore, victims do not become resilient or resistant to repeated bullying. Rather, they reported those employees tend to suffer more as the bullying persists.

- Front-line workers, their supervisors, middle- and senior-level managers tend to experience the same baseline level of bullying (Hoel, Cooper, & Faragher, 2001). If gender of these individuals is considered, however, women in senior- or mid-level management positions are more likely to be bullied than are men in these positions. Seventy-five percent of victims in this study cited a supervisor as perpetrating the abuse, and 67% reported a duration of at least one year.

- Supervisors who are viewed as abusive tend to have higher turnover among subordinates (Tepper, 2000). The victims who do not quit experience lowered levels of satisfaction (with their job and life in general), more work-family conflict, and increased amounts of stress. These effects are particularly pronounced if the subordinates do not have much job mobility (i.e., if they have few or no alternative job options).

- Tepper, Duffy, Henle, and Lambert (2006) found a complicated mix of factors contributing to supervisor bullying. These behaviors are more likely when subordinates have pervasively negative attitudes and emotions, when supervisors experience depression, and/or when supervisors believe that they themselves have not been treated fairly by the organization.

44

- Engaging in organizational citizenship behaviors (helping when that help is not formally required or compensated) can be viewed by coworkers as being either altruistic or self-serving. Working under an abusive supervisor leads to increased cynicism, which tends to taint victims' views of coworkers' organizational citizenship behaviors (viewing them as self-serving, ingratiating, or political; Tepper, Duffy, Hoobler, & Ensley, 2004). Consequently, the way in which subordinates are treated can affect how they view what others do around them.

So what difference do these findings make?

- Bullying in the workplace is real and is a problem. Bullying causes a multitude of workplace problems, ranging from stress to turnover.

- Bullying should be a topic in every supervisory training and orientation process. When bullying is tolerated, either by inattention or indecisiveness, it is encouraged. Bullies often act out of "emotional holes" where their self-esteem is enhanced by attempting to control others. These individuals need to be identified, confronted, and helped to make sure that their bullying behavior does not become a long-term detriment to employee morale.

- There are more people involved in bullying than just the bully and the victim. Workgroups view and recognize bullying, and failing to correct such behavior when it first occurs can actually reinforce it.

- In addition to contributing to a hostile work environment, these behaviors can potentially lead to litigation. Under current U.S. law, bullying can be considered a form of unfair discrimination if the victim claims he/she was singled out because of race, gender, ethnicity, national origin, religion, age (over 40), disability, or other legislated protected-class categories. Several European countries have legislation specifically targeting workplace bullying (regardless of protected-class status). It would be prudent for organizations to create a policy on bullying behavior and ensure that it is understood by all employees.

- Acting quickly is important with bullying behaviors—it does not take long for a norm to develop (i.e., everyone in this group "picks on" Sally). There is an important line between persistent teasing and chronic bullying. If you sense the target is uncomfortable, put a stop to the behavior before it becomes more difficult to handle (after a norm has developed). When bullies are confronted, they may initially resist, but inevitably, they must change to be contributors to their organizations. If bullying persists, perpetrators need to be disciplined.

- Organizational citizenship behaviors are contagious and can contribute to a more positive work environment. Similarly, the perception of being treated unfairly can infect others (i.e., someone who is bullied may mistreat others, who mistreat even others). Training can help supervisors deal effectively with perceptions of injustice (instead of taking their frustrations out on a convenient subordinate).

Some Key Sources

Ayoko, D. B., Callan, V. J., & Härtel, C. E. J. (2003). Workplace conflict, bullying and counterproductive behaviors. *International Journal of Organizational Analysis, 11,* 283-301.

Einarsen, S. (1999). The nature and causes of bullying at work. *International Journal of Manpower, 20,* 16-27.

Hoel, H., Cooper, C. L., & Faragher, B. (2001). The experience of bullying in Great Britain: The impact of organizational status. *European Journal of Work and Organizational Psychology, 10,* 443-466.

Jennifer, D., Cowie, H., & Ananiadou, K. (2003). Perceptions and experience of workplace bullying in five different working populations. *Aggressive Behavior, 29,* 489-496.

Leymann, H., & Gustafsson, A. (1996). Mobbing and the development of post-traumatic stress disorders. *European Journal of Work and Organizational Psychology, 5,* 251-276.

Liefooghe, A. P. D., & MacKenzie Davey, K. (2001). Accounts of workplace bullying: The role of the organization. *European Journal of Work and Organizational Psychology, 10,* 375-393.

Mayhew, C., McCarthy, P., Chappell, D., Quinlan, M., Barker, M., & Sheehan, M. (2004). Measuring the extent of impact from occupational violence and bullying on traumatized workers. *Employee Responsibilities and Rights Journal, 16*(3), 117-134.

McAvoy, B. R., & Murtagh, J. (2003). Workplace bullying: The silent epidemic. *British Medical Journal, 326,* 776-777.

Rayner, C. (1998). Workplace bullying: Do something! *Journal of Occupational Health and Safety Australia and New Zealand, 14,* 581-585.

44

Salin, D. (2001). Prevalence and forms of bullying among business professionals: A comparison of two different strategies for measuring bullying. *European Journal of Work and Organizational Psychology, 10,* 425-442.

Tepper, B. J. (2000). Consequences of abusive supervision. *Academy of Management Journal, 43,* 178-190.

Tepper, B. J., Duffy, M. K., Henle, C. A., & Lambert, L. S. (2006). Procedural injustice, victim precipitation, and abusive supervision. *Personnel Psychology, 59,* 101-123.

Tepper, B. J., Duffy, M. K., Hoobler, J., & Ensley, M. D. (2004). Moderators of the relationships between coworkers' organizational citizenship behavior and fellow employees' attitudes. *Journal of Applied Psychology, 89,* 455-465.

Tepper, B. J., Duffy, M. K., & Shaw, J. D. (2001). Personality moderators of the relationship between abusive supervision and subordinates' resistance. *Journal of Applied Psychology, 86,* 974-983

Zellars, K. L., Tepper, B. J., & Duffy, M. K. (2002). Abusive supervision and subordinates' organizational citizenship behavior. *Journal of Applied Psychology, 87,* 1068-1076.

44

COMMUNICATION

45.

Email as a communication method, at this point in time, is:

SELECT ONE:

☐ A. Virtually equivalent to telephone communication in effectiveness.

☐ B. Equivalent to telephone contact when just facts and information are being conveyed.

☐ C. Okay for the majority of communication for those younger than the mid-30s.

☐ D. Actually preferred over telephone contact by everyone other than baby boomers (born 1946–1964).

☐ E. Very dependent upon what you are trying to accomplish.

45

45. Email as a communication method, at this point in time, is:

The correct answer is E: Very dependent upon what you are trying to accomplish.

HOW SURE ARE WE AT THIS TIME?				
1	2	**3**	4	5
Hint	Suggestive	**Trending**	Substantial	Solid

Discussion

In only a decade, email has dramatically changed the way people communicate in both work and social settings. Email (and text messaging) can be used to reach multiple people with one message. Moreover, that message can be delivered to any part of the world at any time of day or night. Email also provides a convenient "out" for individuals who are not comfortable with cold calls, direct contact, afraid of conflict or disappointment, or simply conversation averse. Email is a very nonthreatening form of communication which is appealing to many people. It is also an easy form of communication to ignore or misinterpret, resulting in an unfavorable response (or no response at all). Using email as a communications crutch can be a real problem.

Email changes communications as much as the telephone once did. The telephone allowed people to communicate when they were in different locations, but they had to be in a similar time zone. Emails allow distance of space, time, and intensity. With email, people can communicate across global boundaries seamlessly (space), at times that are convenient for both the sender and receiver (time), and the same email may be immediately shared with innumerable people (intensity).

Misinterpretation of email is a particularly troublesome land mine. It is natural for email recipients to infer personality, tone, feelings, emotion, or attitude from email, although their inferences are many times wrong (Epley & Kruger, 2005; Gill, Oberlander, & Austin, 2006; Kruger, Epley, Parker, & Ng, 2005). The sender must be careful, therefore, because a short but informative message may be taken as a snub by a misinterpreting receiver. On the other hand, a long narrative similarly might be viewed as wasteful (i.e., not a good use of time). Email that is intended to be context free can be given all sorts of context elements by the receiver.

Direct face-to-face or even telephone communication is interactive, enabling the communicators to gauge each other's interest, intentions, and attitude. Adjustive actions can be taken if the communication starts off wrong. For example, a telephone call to a busy colleague can quickly turn into a short to-the-point conversation; whereas, a long email to the same busy colleague is harder to correct once sent. Email also prevents nonverbal cues that are present in telephone calls (hesitation, pacing, intonation; cf., Epley & Kruger, 2005) and does not allow for rapport-building.

45

Overall, email is convenient and easy. It connects people to work when they are outside the work setting—notice those using their BlackBerrys and doing emails in nonwork settings. While this expands the boundaries of work, it also makes for a difficult work-life balance. Not being "available" 24/7 enables employees to renew and reenergize themselves. Some interpersonal contact is better suited for the telephone or direct communications. Emails may be best for sharing concrete information or simply communicating plans as opposed to making difficult decisions.

Selected Research
- It has been found that individuals with low self-esteem prefer email more than individuals with high self-esteem

(Joinson, 2004). High self-esteem individuals are more likely to be comfortable with face-to-face conversation. However, if rejection or conflict is considered to be likely, most individuals tend to prefer email.

- Men and women do not appear to differ in their use of email to maintain organizational relationships (Harper, 2005).

- Email lacks the nonverbal cues that are present in voice interactions (i.e., *how* something is said). This makes email more susceptible to ambiguous interpretation, as well as less likely to uncover incorrect first impressions or stereotypes (Epley & Kruger, 2005). Email lends itself to misinterpretation; telephone conversations allow for more corrections to be made.

45

- Surveying business-to-business sellers and buyers, Cano, Boles, and Bean (2005) found that the relative preference for telephone, email, or face-to-face contact varied across the purchasing process. In general, however, both buyers and sellers tended to prefer either face-to-face or telephone contact over email.

- Investigating whether or not email will eventually "take-over" telephone conversations, Dimmick, Kline, & Stafford (2000) concluded that the two forms of media serve different purposes. Telephone conversations facilitate social interaction and mutual understanding—email much less so.

So what difference do these findings make?

- Email is not yet, nor may ever be, the complete equivalent of telephone or face-to-face communication. Nor should it be.

- Email is attractive because you are able to process the consequences of what you write (and edit yourself) before you send it. However, it's also a cold transmission method and subject to all kinds of misinterpretation of attitude, intention, and tone.

- The use of email to cover fear of direct communication is probably not a good idea. It will probably cause more problems than it avoids. One company that emailed firing notices to employees found that it created enormously negative publicity—both outside the firm and among employees. Managers should not hide behind the email technology.

- Disputes always should be handled through face-to-face or telephone conversations. Such conflicts can quickly spin out of control when resolution is attempted through the cold medium of email. Simply sharing information or doing routine tasks may be coordinated through email.

- Email might be preferable if the recipient speaks a different native language (but is less than proficient). Email enables them to process and respond at a comfortable pace. Certain occasions and people from cultures that highly value interpersonal conversation need a telephone call. Before using an email message, it's important to gauge the situation as well as the person you're contacting.

- Younger clients/associates are more likely to willingly work through email instead of a personal phone call; whereas, older recipients may be more comfortable with a traditional telephone call. And, text messaging has become a popular form of communication among younger generations. If

45

343

one is uncertain whether an individual accesses email regularly, a simple telephone call prior to the email can ensure communication occurs. Furthermore, a telephone call prior to an email message can help build rapport with the recipient.

Some Key Sources

Bryen, D. N. (2006). Job-related social networks and communication technology. *AAC: Augmentative and Alternative Communication, 22,* 1-9.

Cano, C. R., Boles, J. S., & Bean, C. J. (2005). Communication media preferences in business-to-business transactions: An examination of the purchase process. *Journal of Personal Selling & Sales Management, 25,* 283-294.

Dimmick, J., Kline, S., & Stafford, L. (2000). The gratification niches of personal email and the telephone: Competition, displacement, and complementarity. *Communication Research, 27,* 227-248.

Epley, N., & Kruger, J. (2005). When what you type isn't what they read: The perseverance of stereotypes and expectancies over email. *Journal of Experimental Social Psychology, 41,* 414-422.

Friedman, R. A., & Currall, S. C. (2003). Conflict escalation: Dispute exacerbating elements of email communication. *Human Relations, 56,* 1325-1347.

Gill, A. J., Oberlander, J., & Austin, E. (2006). Rating email personality at zero acquaintance. *Personality and Individual Differences, 40,* 497-507.

Harper, V. B., Jr. (2005). Maintaining interpersonal and organizational relations through electronic mail by men and women. *Psychological Reports, 97,* 903-906.

Joinson, A. N. (2004). Self-esteem, interpersonal risk, and preference for email to face-to-face communication. *CyberPsychology & Behavior, 7,* 472-478.

45

Kruger, J., Epley, N., Parker, J., & Ng, Z. (2005). Egocentrism over email: Can we communicate as well as we think? *Journal of Personality and Social Psychology, 89,* 925-936.

Morris, M., Nadler, J., Kurtzberg, T., & Thompson, L. (2002). Schmooze or lose: Social friction and lubrication in email negotiations. *Group Dynamics: Theory, Research, and Practice, 6,* 89-100.

45

ORGANIZATIONAL DOWNSIZING

46.

How can organizations best reduce the negative impact of downsizings on laid-off employees?

SELECT ONE:

☐ A. Because of the recent high number of downsizings, layoffs no longer have the negative impact they used to.

☐ B. Demonstrate special appreciation for laid-off employees' past contributions.

☐ C. Stagger the layoffs (do them in waves instead of all at once).

☐ D. Use a lottery system to determine who gets laid off.

☐ E. Quickly downsize so employees won't have time to get upset.

46

46. **How can organizations best reduce the negative impact of downsizings on laid-off employees?**

The correct answer is B: Demonstrate special appreciation for laid-off employees' past contributions.

HOW SURE ARE WE AT THIS TIME?				
1	**2**	3	4	5
Hint	**Suggestive**	Trending	Substantial	Solid

Discussion

Organizational downsizing is usually undertaken to improve a firm's financial performance. The action is fairly common, even though the psychological impact on laid-off "victims" as well as retained "survivors" is largely negative. Contributing to the grim view of downsizing, there is evidence that the strategy may not have any direct immediate positive impact on organizational financial performance (Cascio, 1998). Things may have gotten too bad for downsizing to have much immediate impact. Basically, organizations wait too long to act on head count and productivity issues.

Regardless of its utility as a tool for corporate performance (i.e., whether or not it should be used), downsizing is being used as a way to reduce overall costs and increase productivity.

For the laid-off employees, there are long-term negative consequences of unemployment (Reitman & Schneer, 2005). For instance, career interruptions can have a detrimental impact on an employee's future salary and satisfaction with their career. Laid-off employees can also experience long-term scarring from the event, resulting in a decreased sense of job security at their next employing organization; in addition, their self-confidence

46

may be eroded. These individuals may blame themselves for "not seeing it coming," and certainly perceptions and expectations of fairness in employment can be harmed.

Organizations suffer from downsizing as well. In addition to the lack of evidence documenting downsizing's relationship to financial performance, there can be a loss of corporate memory or heritage when large numbers of employees are terminated. And, trust between employees and management may be seriously eroded.

Although being laid off is going to result in stress and uncertainty, there are steps organizations can take to lessen the negative consequences of the downsizing event. Communication of the process helps to counter rumors that accompany such strategies—additionally, showing public appreciation for the workers' past contributions can help minimize a carryover effect of the negative consequences from past to future employment contexts.

Selected Research

46

- De Meuse, Bergmann, Vanderheiden, and Roraff (2004) tracked the financial indicators of Fortune 100 companies over a 12-year period, noting that firms with larger layoffs (operationalized as 10% or more employees) underperformed organizations that had relatively fewer layoffs. Additionally, repeated waves of layoffs (three or more) were associated with worse financial performance. The financial performance of organizations implementing downsizing strategies did tend to eventually recover, however.

- Noer (1994) has noted that the downsizing event may be worse for survivors rather than victims (see Chapter 27). Following one survivor and one victim, the downsized employee was provided psychological and career opportunity counseling. This resulted in better work-life balance, more excitement, and career growth at her next employer. The "survivor," in contrast, was provided no counseling support and was described as guilt-ridden, anxious, fearful, and devoid of influence within the organization.

• Mishra and Spreitzer (1998) documented the disempowering nature of downsizing for victims—when an employee learns that he or she is not required in the new organization, it is disappointing and undermines the employee's sense of control and influence.

• Victims of downsizing report a lack of personal control and a great deal of uncertainty during the downsizing initiative (Paulsen et al., 2005). This is not a good thing, as some of these individuals may remain employed until their contracts expire, and these factors negatively impact the victims' abilities to adjust to the needs of the work situation.

• Downsizing can negatively impact a firm's reputation (as viewed by industry executives, directors, financial analysts, and future employees; Flanagan & O'Shaughnessy, 2005). Furthermore, newer organizations that downsize suffer from a worse reputation "hit" than do older, better-established organizations.

• Perceptions of *distributive* (rather than procedural) fairness can be important for salvaging the organizational commitment of past victims of downsizing (Clay-Warner, Hegtvedt, & Roman, 2005). Victims who perceive the outcome of downsizing to be fair are more likely to exhibit commitment to subsequent organizations—these individuals tend to place more importance on the fairness of job outcomes than procedures.

46

So what difference do these findings make?

- One important consideration is how you treat those being laid off. For the most part, they are not responsible for the managerial decisions and bad times that led up to the downsizing. Usually that blame goes to management, economic conditions, and better competitors. So rather than blaming them, it is important to empathize and understand their plight.

- An inexpensive way to help take some of the sting and negativeness out of the process is to encourage managers to spend time talking with employees about why they are being let go. In addition, managers can show concern and compassion, helping employees through the transition period (cf., De Meuse & Marks, 2003).

- Legally, the Worker Adjustment and Retraining Notification (WARN) Act of 1988 requires that U.S. organizations warn potential large-scale layoff candidates two months prior to the downsizing event. Check with this Act prior to layoffs to determine whether or not your organization is required to give prior notice (i.e., whether or not your layoffs constitute large-scale).

46

- If a buyout strategy is undertaken, showing appreciation for highly tenured individuals who accept the buyout can decrease negative feelings of the downsizing. Coordinating a retirement ceremony, providing mementos for service, and/or noting outgoing employees' contributions can contribute to a one-time expenditure that results in long-term cost savings (cf., Cangemi & Miller, 2004).

- By allowing the workforce to have input into the downsizing solution, it can help ease the pain of the downsizing initiative. There may be cost savings that can be achieved without a significant workforce reduction. For example, an organization's payroll can be decreased by implementing a shorter workweek, instituting a hiring freeze, reducing employee benefits, executing a temporary pay cut, or improving productivity. Sharing the problem with employees and engaging them in the solution to high labor costs might uncover innovative ideas and build commitment to those ideas.

Some Key Sources

Cangemi, J. P., & Miller, R. L. (2004). Exit strategies. *Journal of Management Development, 23*(10), 982-987.

Cascio, W. F. (1998). Learning from outcomes: Financial experiences of 311 firms that have downsized. In M. K. Gowing, J. D. Kraft, & J. C. Quick (Eds.), *The new organizational reality: Downsizing, restructuring, and revitalization* (pp. 55-70). Washington, DC: American Psychological Association.

Clarke, M. (2005). The voluntary redundancy option: Carrot or stick? *British Journal of Management, 16,* 245-251.

Clay-Warner, J., Hegtvedt, K. A., & Roman, P. (2005). Procedural justice, distributive justice: How experiences with downsizing condition their impact on organizational commitment. *Social Psychology Quarterly, 68,* 89-102.

De Meuse, K. P., Bergmann, T. J., Vanderheiden, P. A., & Roraff, C. E. (2004). New evidence regarding organizational downsizing and a firm's financial performance: A long-term analysis. *Journal of Managerial Issues, 16,* 155-177.

De Meuse, K. P., & Marks, M. L. (2003). *Resizing the organization: Managing layoffs, divestitures, and closings.* San Francisco: Jossey-Bass.

Flanagan, D. J., & O'Shaughnessy, K. C. (2005). The effect of layoffs on firm reputation. *Journal of Management, 31,* 445-463.

Mishra, A. K., & Spreitzer, G. M. (1998). Explaining how survivors respond to downsizing: The roles of trust, empowerment, justice, and work redesign. *Academy of Management Review, 23,* 567-588.

46

Moore, S., Grunberg, L., & Greenberg, E. (2004). Repeated downsizing contact: The effects of similar and dissimilar layoff experiences on work and well-being outcomes. *Journal of Occupational Health Psychology, 9,* 247-257.

Noer, D. M. (1994). *Healing the wounds: Overcoming the trauma of layoffs and revitalizing downsized organizations.* San Francisco: Jossey-Bass.

Paulsen, N., Callan, V. J., Grice, T. A., Rooney, D., Gallois, C., Jones, E., Jimmieson, N. L., & Bordia, P. (2005). Job uncertainty and personal control during downsizing: A comparison of survivors and victims. *Human Relations, 58,* 463-496.

Reitman, F., & Schneer, J. A. (2005). The long-term negative impacts of managerial career interruptions: A longitudinal study of men and women MBAs. *Group & Organization Management, 30,* 243-262.

Zyglidopoulos, S. C. (2005). The impact of downsizing on corporate reputation. *British Journal of Management, 16,* 253-259.

46

MOTIVATION

47.

How many employees are procrastinators?

SELECT ONE:

- ☐ A. 5%.
- ☐ B. 20%.
- ☐ C. 50%.
- ☐ D. 75%.
- ☐ E. 100%.

47

47. How many employees are procrastinators?

The correct answer is B: 20%.

HOW SURE ARE WE AT THIS TIME?				
1	2	**3**	4	5
Hint	Suggestive	**Trending**	Substantial	Solid

Discussion

Procrastination is not a desirable worker attribute, although it does tend to be fairly common. Data suggests that approximately 20% of adults are "chronic procrastinators" (at or away from work; Ferrari, O'Callaghan, & Newbegin, 2005). Younger people tend to be more prone to procrastination—as many as 70% of college students "put off" timely completion of *academic* tasks.

Employees often procrastinate by engaging in distracting behaviors (e.g., surfing the Internet) to take their minds off of more daunting work tasks. Research has found the tendency to procrastinate has been associated with a number of factors. For example, various personality dimensions such as conscientiousness (more conscientious people tend to procrastinate less) and task-related concerns (such as fear of failure) influence procrastination. Likewise, employee boredom and characteristics of the work environment affect it. Individuals may procrastinate when they are faced with beginning larger tasks, tasks with no clear process or outcome, or tasks/ projects which inevitably will lead to conflict. They also may avoid tasks which are risky, exposing them to criticism if they fail. Evidence suggests that men and women have the same probability of procrastinating, although "white collar" workers tend to engage in more procrastination than do "blue collar" employees (Hammer & Ferrari, 2002). It is likely that the more

47

structured and time-bound blue collar job requirements prevent as much procrastination to occur.

There is general agreement among researchers that procrastination is a dysfunctional obstacle to job performance. So why do workers procrastinate? Employees who experience little challenge in their jobs may engage in procrastination to alleviate boredom or routine. Additionally, it is possible for procrastination to relieve stress, at least temporarily (Tice & Baumeister, 1997). Unfortunately, these procrastinating individuals sacrifice long-term performance for short-term alleviation of stress, boredom, or fear.

Selected Research

- Procrastinators have different motives for putting off work (Ferrari, O'Callaghan, & Newbegin, 2005). Some individuals enjoy the arousal (being pressure prompted) that comes with a flurry of deadline-daring action. Others procrastinate to offer a face-saving excuse in case they fail at a task (i.e., it's not that I'm not able, it is the time constraints and lack of effort that contributed to failure).

- One explanation that has been forwarded for delaying work is that procrastinators simply prefer to work later in the afternoon and evening than do non-procrastinators (Ferrari et al., 1997). Although it has been found that procrastinators differ from non-procrastinators in time-of-the-day preference for "doing important things," if these activities are social or recreational, procrastinators and non-procrastinators do not differ in morning versus evening preference.

47

- An employee's view of his/her job can affect the extent to which he/she procrastinates (Lonergan & Maher, 2000). An enriched job provides an excellent context for "not putting tasks off." Among other things, job enrichment involves receiving feedback about performance and perceiving that one's job is very important.

- Van Eerde (2003) noted decreases in procrastination and time spent worrying for employees who underwent 1.5 days of time-management training. The training content included task prioritization, how to cope with interruptions, how to "say no," and self-exploration (i.e., identification of when concentration is at its peak for each individual).

- The Myers-Briggs Type Indicator® (MBTI®) contains an "early starting/pressure prompted" scale within the broader context of the "judging/perceiving" dimension. People who are early starters prefer to give themselves enough time to complete a project and experience considerable stress when they have to complete work near the deadline. In contrast, people who are pressure prompted produce their best work when they have little time to complete it (Quenk, Hammer, & Majors, 2001). According to the authors of the MBTI, these pressure-prompted individuals are not actually procrastinating, rather they are working on the task mentally—allowing pressure to build until it stimulates them to successfully complete it.

47

So what difference do these findings make?

- Procrastination by itself does not predict overall job performance. The question about an employee who is a procrastinator should be: Does he/she eventually get the job done (within reasonable time limits and with proscribed resources). The answer to that question will send you down two different paths. If the answer is yes, he/she gets the job done, but it always is just in time and at the last minute, then asking if he/she would like some help would be appropriate. Doing things at the last minute may lead to errors and does not allow others to participate in the discussions that improve performance. It is important to remember that some people are just naturally pressure prompted. On the other hand, if they don't get the job done, then some action is probably legitimate.

- Consequently, what appears to be procrastination actually may not be problematic. That is, if a worker is "pressure prompted," he or she may be able to work more effectively and efficiently under time constraints. The anxiety that comes with working close to a deadline for these individuals is a preferred working style. A worker who falls closer to the MBTI label of early starting, on the other hand, will find the stress associated with nearing deadlines to be debilitating.

- Because different motives drive procrastination, interventions should optimally be tailored to each individual. If an employee (or you) procrastinates, try to determine whether the behavior (1) is something he/she always has done (if so, time-management training might be appropriate), (2) is caused by a fear of failure (if so, increasing the employee's self-confidence might be appropriate), or (3) is attributable to boredom (if so, job enrichment may be needed).

- Time management strategies such as prioritizing tasks and setting short- and long-term goals can help all employees deal with tendencies to procrastinate. Simply being aware of *how much estimated time is required* to successfully complete a project, as well as removing distracting elements from one's workspace can help. It also is helpful to recognize that not all tasks are worth doing equally well. Some tasks are simply worth getting done and don't require the same high level of employee focus.

47

- Some procrastinators prefer to get more productive as the day wears on. These individuals may benefit from a flexible work schedule that allows them to arrive and leave at later hours. An appropriate intervention for dealing with procrastinators who are more comfortable working at later hours is to have the employee identify his or her most productive time, and then try to organize his/her work around that time as much as possible. A common form of flextime involves every employee needing to be present during a core time period (e.g., 10:00 a.m. to 3:00 p.m.). The remaining three hours of an eight-hour work day can be determined by the individual workers.

• Procrastinators may work on both their space (how they organize their work) and their time (how much time and when they spend it on work assignments). Space management allows them to be able to work and produce in the right setting. Time management allows them to create a high return on time invested.

Some Key Sources

Chu, A. H. C., & Choi, J. N. (2005). Rethinking procrastination: Positive effects of "active" procrastination behavior on attitudes and performance. *Journal of Social Psychology, 145,* 245-264.

Ferrari, J. R., Harriott, J. S., Evans, L., Lecik-Michna, D. M., & Wenger, J. M. (1997). Exploring the time preferences of procrastinators: Night or day, which is the one? *European Journal of Personality, 11,* 187-196.

Ferrari, J. R., O'Callaghan, J., & Newbegin, I. (2005). Prevalence of procrastination in the United States, United Kingdom, and Australia: Arousal and avoidance delays among adults. *North American Journal of Psychology, 7,* 1-6.

Hammer, C. A., & Ferrari, J. R. (2002). Differential incidence of procrastination between blue- and white-collar workers. *Current Psychology: Developmental, Learning, Personality, Social, 21,* 333-338.

Lavoie, J. A. A., & Pychyl, T. A. (2001). Cyberslacking and the procrastination superhighway: A Web-based survey of online procrastination, attitudes, and emotion. *Social Science Computer Review, 19,* 431-444.

47

Lonergan, J. M., & Maher, K. J. (2000). The relationship between job characteristics and workplace procrastination as moderated by locus of control. *Journal of Social Behavior & Personality, 15,* 213-224.

Quenk, N. L., Hammer, A. L., & Majors, M. S. (2001). *MBTI Step II Manual: Exploring the next level of type with the Myers-Briggs Type Indicator Form Q.* Palo Alto, CA: Consulting Psychologists Press, Inc.

Robb, H. (1998). Reducing procrastination in the workplace. In S. Klarreich (Ed.), *Handbook of organizational health psychology: Programs to make the workplace healthier* (pp. 55-77). Madison, CT: Psychosocial Press.

Tice, D. M., & Baumeister, R. F. (1997). Longitudinal study of procrastination, performance, stress, and health: The costs and benefits of dawdling. *Psychological Science, 8,* 454-458.

Van Eerde, W. (2000). Procrastination: Self-regulation in initiating aversive goals. *Applied Psychology: An International Review, 49,* 372-389.

Van Eerde, W. (2003). Procrastination at work and time management training. *Journal of Psychology, 137,* 421-434.

47

LEADERSHIP

48.

A leader's character (integrity, ethics, values) is:

SELECT ONE:

☐ A. Directly related to the bottom line; higher character leads to higher results.

☐ B. Directly related to the Best Companies to Work For list but not to the bottom line.

☐ C. Actually negatively related to results; higher character gets in the way at times.

☐ D. Intuitively related to organizational results but very hard to demonstrate.

☐ E. Character is too hard to define or measure, so we will never know for sure.

48

48. A leader's character (integrity, ethics, values) is:

The correct answer is D: Intuitively related to organizational results but very hard to demonstrate.

HOW SURE ARE WE AT THIS TIME?				
1	**2**	3	4	5
Hint	**Suggestive**	Trending	Substantial	Solid

Discussion

Certainly, achieving results is of prime importance. Organizational leaders are measured in terms of shareholder value just as NFL quarterbacks are measured in terms of wins and losses. However, there is much more to organizational success than monetary shareholder value (Lawler, 2003; Pfeffer, 1998). The management of employees, the satisfaction of customers, and being a good corporate citizen all come into play. Moreover, what if an organization achieves success at the expense of ethics or even laws?

Kenneth Lay, Bernie Ebbers, Dennis Kozlowski, Richard Grasso, and Martha Stewart are contemporary CEOs who come quickly to mind when discussing corporate scandals. Companies such as Enron, WorldCom, Health South, and Arthur Andersen collapsed under accusations of mismanagement, corporate fraud, and tax evasion. During the Civil War in this country, a popular saying among military officers was "Feed your horses, feed your men, then feed yourself." The implication was that real leadership is about self-sacrifice and self-discipline. Real leadership is about values, ethics, trust, and honor. Real leadership is about doing the right thing rather than simply doing things right (Bennis, 1989). Real leadership is as much

48

about character as results. The achievement of results with integrity is the winning combination.

Character is the moral and ethical fiber to ensure that organizational decisions are carried out in a fair, objective manner. According to Lisoski (2003, p. 19), character is "the guide rails you place on your day-to-day decisions." During the past 10 years or so, there has been a growing interest in the nature of character. It is generally believed that positive character traits (e.g., honesty, integrity, trustworthiness, ethics, compassion, humility) are critical to a leader's effectiveness. For example, in a book entitled *The Soul's Code: In Search of Character and Calling,* James Hillman describes the "invisible source of personal consistency" (1996; p. 260). In another book entitled *On Becoming a Leader,* Warren Bennis identifies "vision, inspiration, empathy, and trustworthiness" as important characteristics of successful leaders. In a journal article on leadership, it was declared that "More than knowledge, leaders need character. Values and ethics are vitally important" (Doh, 2003, p. 54).

Consequently, an important question may be: Can character be taught? The concept of leadership training or leadership development began centuries ago. Much of the focus, however, has been on the development of specific leadership skills or competencies (e.g., delegation, listening, decision making). Traditionally, this approach to leadership development consisted of three steps: (1) Assess leadership competencies based on observable indicators of success to identify specific strengths and performance gaps. (2) Provide developmental challenges to close those gaps. And, (3) Offer ongoing support to nurture leader growth and development (McCall, Lombardo, & Morrison, 1988; McCall, 1998). A number and variety of leadership development activities can be employed to foster leader growth (e.g., special assignments, job rotation, executive coaching, mentoring). Obviously, there also are numerous vendors who offer seminars and workshops in hopes of

48

enhancing a leader's skills (Yukl, 2002). On the other hand, the ability to teach "leadership traits," such as character, is much more uncertain.

Selected Research

* The Harvard Business School was the first university to offer a course on "social factors in business enterprise." The year was 1915. However, the modern movement on business ethics began during the widespread distrust of government following the Watergate scandal. The alleged cover-up by Ford of the Pinto's exploding gas tank and the illegal payments made by overseas government contractors added to this movement. In 1976, the Center for Business Ethics at Bentley College first applied to the National Endowment for the Humanities for a grant to fund the Center. It was rejected; the agency had never heard of business ethics. When the *Wall Street Journal* wrote about this Center for Business Ethics, they claimed that business ethics was an oxymoron.

* Robert Greenleaf coined the term "servant-leadership" in 1970. He contended that traditional autocratic and hierarchical models of leadership were obsolete. He viewed servant-leadership as a means of involving others in decision making and cultivating an ethical, caring relationship with one's followers. Today, many well-known authors endorse a servant-leadership approach (e.g., Warren Bennis, Peter Block, Max DePree, Peter Senge, Margaret Wheatley, Danah Zohar). According to Greenleaf, the following set of 10 characteristics are required to be a servant-leader: (1) listening, (2) empathy, (3) healing, (4) awareness, (5) persuasion, (6) conceptualization, (7) foresight, (8) stewardship, (9) commitment to the growth of people, and (10) building community.

- During the 1980s, the importance of business ethics became readily apparent with the crisis of the junk bond market, accusations of insider trading schemes, and stories of $600 hammers and $800 toilet seats purchased by the U.S. Department of Defense. More recently, the passage of the Federal Sentencing Guidelines for Organizations and the Sarbanes-Oxley Act attempted to legislate effective business ethics (see Chapter 30). Today, many organizations have created ethics officer positions, installed ethics hotlines, and crafted codes of business conduct. A 2000 study conducted by the Society of Financial Service Professionals discovered that nearly 90% of respondents revealed that their companies had formal codes of ethics and conduct. Given these practices, the Enrons of the world were not supposed to happen.

- In a recent journal article entitled "Can We Teach Character? An Aristotelian Answer," Edwin Hartman (2006) asserts that the question of whether we can actually teach character is as old as Socrates. He contends that business schools can and must help college students develop good character. He recommends the use of case studies and business simulations to assist students in learning to make ethical decisions in complex situations. Current estimates are that 90% of colleges and schools of business teach ethics in their curriculum (Fulmer, 2004).

- The search for specific leadership traits began as far back as the 1930s. After reviewing approximately 300 studies, Stogdill (1974) concluded that eight traits show a strong relationship to effective leadership. The "character" of a leader in the form of integrity, honesty, and ethics was one of those traits. This finding has been supported by more recent research (Dubrin, 2004; Kirkpatrick & Locke, 1991).

48

- If a leader's character is deemed a "trait" of his or her personality, it may be difficult to modify. Developmental psychologies have contended that one's personality is (at least, in part) genetic, or if it is learned, it most likely is learned early in life (Briggs Myers & Myers, 1980). Consequently, one might question whether character is teachable. The issue really is whether a leader's character is subject to change through experience—in the classroom or workplace? Since 1983, the University of Minnesota has been conducting a longitudinal study of twins raised together and apart. The researchers have found a genetic effect of leadership (Bouchard, et al., 1990; Johnson, McGue, & Krueger, 2005). With regard to personality, they report that 27% to 53% of it is genetic. Hence, character appears to have a facet of it that comes standard with the body.

- Studies in social work and criminal justice have tracked recidivism rates of prisoners in an attempt to examine the effect of hereditary and environmental factors. In general, recidivism rates are extraordinarily high in the U.S., with the majority of inmates returning to prison within three to five years of their release (Marbley & Ferguson, 2005). One study found 30% of released inmates were rearrested within the first six months and nearly 60% within the first year (Langan & Levin, 2002). Although it is difficult to discern the precise role genetics plays in criminal behavior, it is clear that once individuals break the law, they are very likely to break it again. Perhaps, the "character" of the criminal influences the behavior. If this is so, perhaps, the character of a leader likewise will be consistent over time—whether due to enduring personality traits or selecting organizational cultures compatible with his or her ethical preferences.

48

So what difference do these findings make?

- Obviously, the recent scandals widely publicized in the media strongly indicate the character of organizational leaders is critical. At least, it is critical to staying off the front page of the *Wall Street Journal*. The reputation, financial success, and ultimate survivability of companies are affected by the decisions executives make. An executive's ability to achieve financial success is important for shareholders as well as employees. The values, integrity, ethics, and honor exhibited in the process are crucial to that success. The magic combination would seem to be making effective and successful decisions within the boundaries of acceptable ethics. (See also Chapters 40 and 35.)

- Research evidence with regard to whether leadership character is teachable is less clear. Certainly, leadership skills and competencies can be developed over time. Numerous courses, programs, activities, and exercises have been marketed over the years to do just that. Special assignments, mentoring, and executive coaching have been widely used to groom tomorrow's leaders. Character, on the other hand, is a bit different. If one's character is mostly established during childhood, how can simply attending a college course on leadership or working on a special job assignment improve character? Character may be a trait that largely is established *before* the leader is hired. If this is the case, employment selection would be a much more critical endeavor than training. Character enhancement may be learned best by modeling significant others along the way to the top. Lessons of character are learned from people (both positive and negative—what to do and what not to do) and by living through tough situations.

48

- Although there doesn't appear to be any scientific research directly correlating organizational results with character, it is intuitive that there has to be some relationship. Maybe the emphasis on leadership character is more in terms of preventing bad things from happening to the organization than on causing good things to happen.

- Leaders throughout the organization—from the CEO to first-line supervisors—need to be diligent about their behaviors and decisions. The perception of impropriety will send strong signals inside and outside the company. If a manager is unsure of the ethical ramifications of a given action, it is critical to solicit the input from another individual. Character, like trust, once broken is difficult to reestablish.

Some Key Sources

Bennis, W. (1989). *On becoming a leader.* Reading, MA: Addison-Wesley Publishing.

Bouchard, T. J., Lykken, D. T., McGue, M. M., Segal, N., & Tellegen, A. (1990). The sources of human psychological differences: The Minnesota study of twins reared apart. *Science, 250,* 223-228.

Briggs Myers, I., & Myers, P. B. (1980). *Gifts differing.* Palo Alto, CA: Consulting Psychologists Press.

Doh, J. P. (2003). Can leadership be taught? Perspectives from management educators. *Academy of Management Learning and Education, 2*(1), 54-67.

Dubrin, A. J. (2004). *Leadership: Research findings, practice, and skills* (4th ed.). New York: Houghton Mifflin.

Fulmer, R. M. (2004). The challenge of ethical leadership. *Organizational Dynamics, 33,* 307-317.

Greenleaf, R. K. (1977). *Servant-Leadership: A journey into the nature of legitimate power and greatness.* Mahwah, NJ: Paulist Press.

48

Hartman, E. M. (2006). Can we teach character? An Aristotelian answer. *Academy of Management Learning & Education, 5*(1), 68-81.

Hillman, J. (1996). *The soul's code: In search of character and calling.* New York: Random House.

Johnson, W., McGue, M., & Krueger, R. F. (2005). Personality stability in late adulthood: A behavioral genetic analysis. *Journal of Personality, 73,* 523-551.

Kirkpatrick, S. A., & Locke, E. A. (1991). Leadership: Do traits matter? *Academy of Management Executive, 5*(3), 48-60.

Langan, P. A., & Levin, D. J. (2002). Recidivism of prisoners released in 1994. *Federal Sentences Reporter, 1*(1), 58-64.

Lawler, E. E., III. (2003). *Treat people right! How organizations and individuals can propel each other into a virtuous spiral of success.* San Francisco: Jossey-Bass.

Lisoski, E. (2003). Courage, character and conviction—The three "c's" of outstanding supervision. *Supervision, 64*(3), 19-21.

Marbley, A. R., & Ferguson, R. (2005). Responding to prisoner reentry, recidivism, and incarceration of inmates of color: A call to the communities. *Journal of Black Studies, 35,* 633-649.

McCall, M. W., Jr. (1998). *High flyers: Developing the next generation of leaders.* Boston: Harvard Business School Press.

McCall, M. W., Jr., Lombardo, M. M., & Morrison, A. M. (1988). *The lessons of experience: How successful executives develop on the job.* New York: Free Press.

McCauley, C., & Van Velsor, E. (2003). *The Center for Creative Leadership handbook of leadership development.* San Francisco: Jossey-Bass.

Pfeffer, J. (1998). *The human equation: Building profits by putting people first.* Boston: Harvard Business School Press.

48

Stogdill, R. M. (1974). *Handbook of leadership: A survey of the literature.* New York: Free Press.

Yukl, G. (2002). *Leadership in organizations* (5th ed). Upper Saddle River, NJ: Prentice Hall.

48

INTANGIBLES

49.

Which type of organizational culture leads to the greatest financial performance over the long-term?

SELECT ONE:

☐ A. Strong consistent-legacy cultures.

☐ B. Adaptive and flexible cultures.

☐ C. A group of diverse, decentralized cultures.

☐ D. Integrated, but diverse cultures.

☐ E. Absence of a defined culture.

49

49. Which type of organizational culture leads to the greatest financial performance over the long-term?

The correct answer is B: Adaptive and flexible cultures.

HOW SURE ARE WE AT THIS TIME?				
1	**2**	3	4	5
Hint	**Suggestive**	Trending	Substantial	Solid

Discussion

Culture makes a difference when defined and managed correctly. Culture is frequently defined as "how and why things are done around here." Just like an individual has a personality which reflects the unique traits of his or her "personhood" to others, so too does a company have a culture which reflects its unique qualities and characteristics to the outside world. Although a company's culture often is construed only in terms of how it impacts employees (e.g., norms and expectations regarding how employees dress, whether meetings start on time, if employees work weekends), it likewise can have a direct impact on customers. In many ways, culture becomes the identity of the firm in the eyes of customers. When you think of Wal-Mart, what comes to mind (low prices)? When you think of Starbucks, what comes to mind (premium coffee)? When you think of Mercedes-Benz, what comes to mind (luxury cars)? Culture can add value to customers because they become loyal to a company brand.

The shift is to think about culture as a company's brand (Ulrich & Smallwood, 2003). Culture enables a company to charge a premium price for its products or services. The advantage of a well-defined and articulated culture is that it helps priority setting and decision making. When employees see a direct line

49

of sight from their actions inside the company to the customer's buying criteria, they are more likely to sustain those actions. Many studies have shown that a shared mind-set enhances organizational performance.

In this time of rough water and rapid change, an internal culture that reflects this change will be more stable and successful. This generally means a flexible and adaptive culture works best. Adapting to current conditions and anticipating change are critical. Giving up the legacy of the past, if that's what's necessary, is essential.

Selected Research

- Kotter and Heskett (1992) studied 207 companies over an 11-year period and found that financial performance was highest among companies that had adaptive and flexible cultures. The assumption was that these cultural styles help organizations anticipate and adapt to changes more effectively than other types of organizational cultures. It was also noted that a strong culture was not necessarily always the best; the nature of the culture's central values is more important than its strength. The authors assert that "...strong cultures can easily become somewhat arrogant, inwardly focused, politicized, and bureaucratic... that kind of culture unquestionably undermines economic performance."

- Research conducted at MIT (Sorensen, 2002) found that firms with strong cultures performed better and more reliably over a six-year period than those with weak cultures. However, during times of volatility, the advantage of strong cultures decreased and often became nonexistent. Based on advanced modeling techniques, Sorensen concluded that strong cultures perform best when the business environment is stable. However, when new capabilities are required due to changes in the environment, strong cultures are often slow to adapt. Thus, strong cultures can provide

49

organizations with significant advantages, but when success and survival rests on an organization's ability to change and adapt, a strong culture can be a liability.

- After studying 1,000 organizations over 15 years, Denison and Mishra (1995) found that the most successful cultures are those that are adaptable, involve employees, have a clear mission, and are consistent in beliefs and values. The authors report that while strong cultures often enhance short-term success, they may inhibit long-term performance by preventing it from adapting to changing conditions.

- Gagliardi (1986) suggested that firms with strong cultures are capable of only limited change due to its members adhering so strictly to existing core values. Members are only willing to change within the limits of those existing core values, rather than adopting new or significantly different values.

- Wilkins and Ouchi (1983) report that strong cultures are capable of adapting, but cannot withstand radical changes that challenge basic values and assumptions. When change is required, adaptive and flexible cultures win over established, strong cultures.

- Ulrich and Yeung (1989) found that when businesses had more cognitive consensuality, or shared mind-set and culture, their performance was higher.

So what difference do these findings make?

- Don't begin culture by focusing on values of the leader or the leadership team. These internal values statements often lack staying power and reflect the predispositions of the current leaders. Begin a focus on culture with the identity the organization wants to be known for by key customers. This identity they can translate into employee behavior, management practices, and HR systems. When a company's

49

internal actions reflect customers' desired brand, the culture is more likely to be sustained and successful.

- Culture is a catch-22. While the stronger the culture the better in some ways, the looser the better in other ways. A strong culture that is focused internally is in danger because it does not adapt to external trends. This is the culture that continually looks forward by anchoring current and future activities in what has always been. This is dangerous because a culture should evolve as customer expectations evolve (think Kentucky Fried Chicken becoming KFC or the Pillsbury Dough Boy losing weight). There is a fine line between having a strong legacy culture that has served the organization well for many years or even decades versus a need to change rapidly to adjust to some new element of the competitive landscape (strong foreign competitor enters the market—Ikea, change in consumer behavior—Internet shopping, or alternative economic model—outsourcing and offshoring) in your industry.
- The best cultures are those that start with executives answering the question: What do we want to be known for by our best customers in the future? When executives have a unity around this question and when that unity is consistent with what target customers want the firm to be known for, culture becomes a competitive weapon.
- Being respectful of the past, but being opportunistic about the future is the magic combination.

COPYRIGHT © 2013 LOMINGER INTERNATIONAL: A KORN/FERRY COMPANY.

Some Key Sources

Denison, D. R., & Mishra, A. K. (1995). Toward a theory of organizational culture and effectiveness. *Organizational Science, 6,* 204-223.

Gagliardi, P. (1986). The creation and change of organizational cultures: A conceptual framework. *Organizational Studies, 7*(2), 117-134.

Kotter, J. P., & Heskett, J. L. (1992). *Corporate culture and performance.* New York: Free Press.

Sorensen, J. B. (2002). The strength of corporate culture and the reliability of firm performance. *Administrative Science Quarterly, 47,* 70-91.

Ulrich, D., & Smallwood, N. (2003). *Why the bottom line isn't: How to build value through people and organization.* Hoboken, NJ: John Wiley.

Ulrich, D., & Yeung, A. (1989). A shared mind-set. *Personnel Administrator, 34*(3), 38-45.

Wilkins, A. L., & Ouchi, W. G. (1983). Efficient cultures: Exploring the relationship between culture and organizational performance. *Administrative Science Quarterly, 28,* 468-481.

49

DECISION MAKING

50.

What role does intuition play in the quality of managerial decision making?

SELECT ONE:

☐ A. Intuition is a necessary component of managerial decision making.

☐ B. Since intuition is emotionally based, it decreases long-term accuracy.

☐ C. Intuition speeds up decision making but decreases accuracy.

☐ D. Waiting for more data is always better than using intuition.

☐ E. Intuition helps with people decisions but not business decisions.

50

50. What role does intuition play in the quality of managerial decision making?

The correct answer is A: Intuition is a necessary component of managerial decision making.

HOW SURE ARE WE AT THIS TIME?				
1	2	**3**	4	5
Hint	Suggestive	**Trending**	Substantial	Solid

In a volatile world, we must have more sensors, processing information faster and leading to faster (and by definition more informal) action taking (Peters, 1988, p. 109).

Discussion

Managers do not always have the luxury of having all of the data to use rational analysis of information and systematic deduction of a solution or answer. Especially in rapidly changing environments, shifts occur with such frequency that adequate decision-making information may not be available if a decision is to be made in a timely manner. Managers in these environments need to use more intuitive routes to decision making (cf., Simon, 1987).

All managers struggle to find enough data for comfortable decision making. Often there is too little information to provide appropriate guidance. Intuition can help guide decisions when information is lacking—it also can help identify "what's important" in an information-saturated (too much) situation.

Intuition draws on subconscious (below awareness) processes—these are more flexible and generate more (and more varied) alternatives than do linear, conscious-thought processes. The intuitive process involves an internal scanning for concepts and information that may seem (on a conscious level) to be

50

unrelated. This process can result in innovative decisions and answers. Really, intuition is an automatic application of past knowledge and experience which can help increase the speed as well as the quality of decision making.

Intuition is also the culmination of many years of experience. An executive manager we were coaching had a significant personnel decision ahead of him: Should he fire or keep a senior leader in the company? This executive manager had many years of making similar difficult people decisions. We probed his intuition and instinct. What did he sense? What did he feel? And he acted on that intuition. Another senior leader new to leadership positions had a similar dilemma. But, he did not have years of facing similar decisions. We advised him strongly to not act on intuition, but to collect data from the problem employee's supervisors, peers, and subordinates. Quality of decision making through intuition increases with experience and should be trusted less with less experience.

Gladwell (2005) frames intuition as a process that individuals experience when new, confusing, and/or multiple pieces of information are presented. He claims that our brains engage in two separate processes in these situations: one conscious and logical, the other essentially intuitive. The conscious and logical path is a *slower* information-processing route. The intuitive path is faster. The conscious path has the advantage of providing individuals with awareness of how they arrived at a decision. The intuitive path has the disadvantage of masking awareness, at least initially. With intuition, brains are sent signals, but the person does not consciously understand why those signals have been sent. This may result in a reluctance to rely on decisions made from intuition. Because the route to decision making often cannot be fully explained, an individual may not feel completely comfortable "going public" with it.

The science of management tends to receive more attention than does the art of management. However, no matter how well a manager knows business formulas and logical decision trees,

50

there will always be an "art" side of management. Because management as a discipline straddles this art/science divide, effective managers need to be able to use both the "analytical" and "intuitive" aspects of their brains. Some may view intuition as a soft skill and resist developing intuitive capabilities. It should be noted, however, that analytical individuals such as Albert Einstein and Carl Jung frequently cited intuition as critical to their success (cf., Johnson & Daumer, 1993).

The preferred styles (also called psychological "types") of action specified by Carl Jung and popularized in management applications by the Myers-Briggs Type Indicator (MBTI) most often have been investigated with regard to intuition and decision quality. Top executives, for example, tend to rate higher in intuition than do middle- or lower-level managers (Agor, 1986).

Selected Research

- Intuition and rational analysis are complementary—not contradictory—processes for managers (Simon, 1987). The difference in the application of intuition can be best understood by looking at expert versus novice managers. Expert managers diagnose and solve problems more quickly, without an ability to describe *how* they solved the problem. Novices take more conscious, deliberate, and explicitly analytical approaches. Experts are able to rely on their experience to consider analytical information but process it intuitively—leading to quicker decisions.

- The more experience CEOs have with problems and solutions, the more knowledge they will informally acquire (called tacit knowledge; Brockmann & Simmonds, 1997). Furthermore, the more intuitive the CEOs are, the more likely they will be able to tap into their tacit knowledge to solve problems or otherwise make decisions. This point is illustrated in the above case of an executive manager making a difficult people decision.

50

- Harper (1998) suggests that it is precisely intuition that separates a few extraordinary executives from many merely effective managers. In contexts in which data does not indicate a clear path, sensing an appropriate direction and having the wherewithal to follow through on the decision are important executive characteristics.

- "Cognitive style," as measured by the Myers-Briggs Type Indicator, can impact the quality and speed of decision making (Hough & Ogilvie, 2005). For both decision speed and quality, those scoring as **NTs** (intuiting/thinking) were the best managerial decision makers, outperforming **NFs** (intuiting/feeling), **STs** (sensing/thinking), and **SFs** (sensing/feeling). These NTs use a combination of intuition and rational analysis to come to a timely and effective decision.

- Sternberg (2004) argues that intelligence, memory, and analytical skills are important, but not necessarily sufficient for success. Leadership effectiveness is dependent on intelligence, but also on "tacit" knowledge and practicality— sometimes referred to as professional intuition (Hedlund et al., 2003). This form of intuition stems from *experience* (the learning from past successes and failures and then applying that knowledge to future situations).

- When confronted with uncertain or changing conditions, managers who are more cognitively complex seem to have an advantage (Streufert, Pogash, & Piasecki, 1988). These individuals are better at differentiating and integrating multiple pieces of information—they think and act with flexibility. Intuition considered through this lens is a very systematic (but still not conscious) activity.

So what difference do these findings make?

- Intuition, whatever it really is, is a legitimate tool for decision making. The best way to build intuition is to practice and use it. Any skill is enhanced through practice. So newly minted

50

managers might test their intuition decisions with the more rational and logically derived decisions—they may examine rigorously which decisions worked and which did not to find out how to hone their intuition. At times managers who act wisely on intuition may be pushed and asked "why" they took a particular action. If there is a logical, rational explanation for their decision, the intuition is grounded.

- Managers should be urged to allow intuition to play a bigger part in their decision making. However, this intuitive ability should develop just like a manager's ability to set strategy, execute decisions, and manage talent. Intuition is a skill that can grow and develop with practice.

- Sometimes more information does not lead to a more effective decision. Rather, a wise manager needs to be able to sift through the information and make an appropriate decision based on a subset of important, deciding factors. Part of intuition is the ability to separate the wheat from the chaff and get to the essence of the problem to be solved.

- It is permissible to rely on your intuition if you find yourself emotionally invested in an outcome. Remember: Intelligent people who *want* something to happen can use logic to rationalize benefits to nearly any decision, even the wrong ones.

- By its very nature, intuition is difficult to communicate. Managers may not be able to fully articulate their intuitive position as well as they would a data-driven decision. This means that these intuitive individuals may have more difficulty gaining buy-in from others regarding their decisions. Furthermore, the use of intuition is most closely associated with situations in which information is sparse— this makes intuitive decisions, by definition, *risky.*

50

- Using intuition does not mean that a decision maker goes by pure gut feelings or emotion. The effective use of intuition is accomplished by realizing when information is scarce, incomplete, saturated, or incorrect, knowing that a decision must be made, and acting on that decision based upon the net guidance of the individual's past experience. Managers can tap into their intuition to assess a problem and devise possible solutions when hard data are either not available or overwhelming. Therefore, intuition side-steps the potential decision-making land mine of "paralysis by analysis."

• Intuition is best acquired through variety and diversity of experience. Certain activities can increase the likelihood that intuitive processes will be invoked to solve a problem or make a decision. One common technique is to gather as many facts as possible and then let the issue incubate, allowing the mind to work on the issue while not directly focusing.

Some Key Sources

Agor, W. H. (1986). The logic of intuition: How top executives make important decisions. *Organizational Dynamics, 14*(3), 5-29.

Behling, O., & Eckel, N. L. (1991). Making sense out of intuition. *Academy of Management Executive, 5,* 46-54.

Brockmann, E. N., & Simmonds, P. G. (1997). Strategic decision making: The influence of CEO experience and use of tacit knowledge. *Journal of Managerial Issues, 9,* 454-467.

Gladwell, M. (2005). *Blink: The power of thinking without thinking.* New York: Little, Brown and Company.

Harper, S. C. (1988). Intuition: What separates executives from managers? *Business Horizons, 31*(5), 13-20.

Hedlund, J., Forsythe, G. B., Horvath, J. A., Williams, W. M., Snook, S., & Sternberg, R. J. (2003). Identifying and assessing tacit knowledge: Understanding the practical intelligence of military leaders. *Leadership Quarterly, 14,* 117-140.

50

Hough, J. R., & Ogilvie, D. (2005). An empirical test of cognitive style and strategic decision outcomes. *Journal of Management Studies, 42,* 417-448.

Johnson, P. R., & Daumer, C. R. (1993). Intuitive development: Communication in the nineties. *Public Personnel Management, 22,* 257-268.

Perlow, L. A., Okhuysen, G. A., & Repenning, N. P. (2002). The speed trap: Exploring the relationship between decision making and temporal context. *Academy of Management Journal, 45,* 931-955.

Peters, T. (1988). Restoring American competitiveness: Looking for new models of organizations. *Academy of Management Executive, 2*(2), 103-109.

Simon, H. A. (1987). Making management decisions: The role of intuition and emotion. *Academy of Management Executive, 1,* 57-64.

Sinclair, M., & Ashkanasy, N. M. (2005). Intuition: Myth or a decision-making tool? *Management Learning, 36,* 353-370.

Sternberg, R. J. (2004). What is wisdom and how can we develop it? *The Annals of the American Academy of Political and Social Science, 591,* 164-174.

Streufert, S., Pogash, R., & Piasecki, M. (1988). Simulation-based assessment for managerial competence: Reliability and validity. *Personnel Psychology, 41,* 537-557.

50

Author Index
Chapter Number Referenced

AUTHOR INDEX

Key Word Index

Chapter Number Referenced

Subject Matter Index
Chapter Number Referenced

Subject matter covered in both *100 Things You Need to Know* – Volume One (2004) and *50 More Things You Need to Know* – Volume Two (2007).

360-Degree Feedback

Brain Development

Business Strategy

Career Advancement and Development

Career Advancement and Development (continued)

Change Management

100 Things You Need to Know

Communication

50 More Things You Need to Know

Corporate Culture

50 More Things You Need to Know

Corporate Governance

50 More Things You Need to Know

Counterproductive Behavior

50 More Things You Need to Know

100 Things You Need to Know

Generation X Employees

50 More Things You Need to Know

Goal Setting

100 Things You Need to Know

HR Effectiveness

100 Things You Need to Know

Intangibles

50 More Things You Need to Know

Interviewing

100 Things You Need to Know

Job Attitudes

50 More Things You Need to Know

SUBJECT MATTER INDEX

Success Prediction

100 Things You Need to Know

Succession Planning

100 Things You Need to Know

Talent Management

100 Things You Need to Know

Teams

50 More Things You Need to Know

100 Things You Need to Know

Training and Development

50 More Things You Need to Know

Training and Development (continued)

100 Things You Need to Know